THE
COUNTDOWN
CONSPIRACY

KATIE SLIVENSKY

HARPER
An Imprint of HarperCollinsPublishers

Library of Congress Control Number: 2016950337
ISBN 978-0-06-246255-8

Typography by Jenna Stempel
17 18 19 20 21   CG/LSCH   10 9 8 7 6 5 4 3 2 1

First Edition

For Mom and Dad:

You've given me the strength to pursue my dreams and the work ethic to achieve them, all while cheering me on every step of the way.

"Thank you" just isn't enough. Here, have a book.

DESTINED FOR MARS: FIRST ROUND APPLICATION

Legal Name: _____

Date of Birth: _____

Country of Birth: _____

For the following, please answer **YES** or **NO**:

1. This mission will require an intensive nine-year training schedule, during most of which you will live away from your family at a remote location. Visits will typically consist of two-week vacations, four to six times per year. Do you agree to these terms?

2. Can you currently lift/carry over twenty-five kilograms? Can you currently run five kilometers in under twenty-five minutes?

3. Do you have 20/20 vision? If not, do you have corrective lenses that bring you to 20/20 vision? Would you agree to have laser eye surgery at age eighteen to permanently bring you to 20/20 vision?

4. Can you speak conversational-level English and/or Russian? If only one of the two, would you be capable of learning the other within the next ten months, before your country's National Finals?

5. Would you agree to travel to a space center of our choosing for specialized tests, including, but not limited to, tests of intelligence, strength, wit, dexterity, teamwork skills, and the ability to withstand nausea?

6. Finally, should you be selected, would you be willing to commit to the full duration of a Mars mission, including nine months of travel to the planet, a year-long mission on Mars itself, and the nine-month journey home?

Please include with your application a three-to-five-page personal essay, and a resume listing any relevant awards, scholastic reports, or extracurricular activities.

You will be contacted within four to six weeks if you are chosen to move on in the application process. Up to one thousand candidates from every country will be selected for each nation's Quarterfinals. From there, seventy-five candidates will be chosen to move on to their National Semifinals, and out of those, five will be chosen for their National Finals. The winner of the National Finals will then move on to the International Finals, where six candidates will be ultimately chosen for the Destined for Mars program.

Do not let these odds deter you from applying. Mars belongs to us all.

Sincerely,

Robert E. Schuber, Director of the International Space Exploration Coordination Group

Your signature: _____

Date: _____

Signature of legal guardian: _____

Date: _____

CHAPTER ONE

Nearly every single person in this auditorium is wearing a T-shirt with my name emblazoned across the front. This might be the most nauseating thing that's ever happened to me, and I rode the Vomit Comet three months ago, so that's really saying something.

"You look a little ill, kiddo." My dad nudges me from the seat next to mine in the front row.

I stare at him. "Not helping, Dad."

"Oh, come on." He grins as my sister tugs at his shirt from the next seat over. "At least *try* to enjoy this. A smile isn't going to jinx things, you know."

The corners of my mouth turn up a little, but I can't push them much more. Part of me wishes I was back on the Vomit Comet right now. Free-falling in a specialized plane from the edge of Earth's atmosphere? Yes, please. Waiting to find out if I get to live my biggest dream? If I'm one of six kids chosen out of 197 for the first-ever Mars mission?

I honestly don't know if my nerves are going to survive.

There are cameras flashing nonstop. I feel like we're caught in the pulsing light of a rotating neutron star—except that out in space it'd be silent, and in here it's anything but.

"HEY, MIRANDA!"

I turn to see some high schooler I barely recognize. He's beaming at me like we've been friends forever. "You *got* this!"

Before I can even begin to respond, he stands up and turns to face the crowd like some sort of band conductor.

"MIR-AN-DA! MIR-AN-DA!"

It takes less than four seconds before the entire auditorium is in on the chant. News cameras begin to pan around, and I'm sure at least one of them is zoomed in on me for a reaction shot. I shrink back in my seat, hoping my face isn't too red.

In order for kids across America to watch and "relate" to me better, a bunch of government officials put me in our high school auditorium for the big broadcast. I technically graduated high school last year already—and I'm only thirteen anyway—so I don't actually know most of these students. The few I do know, I don't particularly care to remember, which makes all this chanting super awkward.

My mom smiles as someone tosses an inflatable Mars past our heads. "Noisy, aren't they?"

"Yeah," I say, taking a steadying breath.

"Imagine what they'll do when you win!" My little sister

leans over my dad's lap to poke me in the side.

I laugh, letting out some of the tension. It's not "when" I win, it's "if," but Emmaline's been convinced since day one that I've got this in the bag. She's the one who designed the "MIRANDA FOR MARS!" T-shirts everyone's wearing, after all. Featuring the cute block lettering of a five-year-old, they caught on like wildfire. In fact, there's a total of 886 of the shirts in here at this exact moment. I know because I've counted. I can't help it.

The auditorium lights dim. I grab the little flashcard hanging on a chain around my neck. "I wish Ruby was here," I say without thinking.

My mom raises a knowing eyebrow. "I told you taking her apart last night wasn't the best idea."

"Well, it will give me the edge if I lose today," I defend my decision. "I can start revamping her for the next robotics competition right away." I hold Ruby's flashcard and imagine her with new nanowiring to fire her processors faster than ever, maybe even helping me in astronaut training. . . .

I shake my head. *Don't get ahead of yourself, now.*

"Oh, look, they're lowering the SmartScreen!" my mom says.

I hazard one more glance at my dad and notice with alarm that he's actually welling up. Next to him, my sister rocks back and forth in her oversized T-shirt, looking ready to burst, as if she's the one who could be going to Mars. I'm struck by the differences in their expressions. Is my dad crying because he's nervous? Proud? Or because he's thinking about how if I win, I have to move away?

I refocus on the screen. I can't think too hard about leaving my family, or I'll risk crying myself.

The principal flickers the lights a few times onstage, getting everyone to quiet down as the SmartScreen switches to a livestream of Dr. Robert Schuber, head of the International Space Exploration Coordination Group. According to the news ticker below, he's being broadcast from an island off the coast of Antarctica. Neutral ground. Makes sense.

"What do you think Sasha's doing right now?" I ask my mom.

"Probably the same thing as you—freaking out," my mom replies. "Have you heard from him at all?"

"Not since yesterday." I glance at my wrist to check my droidlet. The motion triggers the screen to flash the time: 9:53. Seven minutes to go. *Seven. Prime.*

"It's an absolute pleasure to be here this morning." I look up to see our state governor standing behind the podium onstage, beaming at what feels like each of us in turn.

Seven, eleven, thirteen, seventeen, nineteen, twenty-three . . . There are no blinking dots on my droidlet to tell me I have any sort of text message. If Sasha was half as nervous as I am right now he'd be sure to deal with it by harassing me, so I guess he must be handling this way better than I am.

"What we're about to witness is history in the making," our governor continues, cameras flashing around him. "Judging by the cheering, I believe you all realize that."

Of course, the moment he says that, everyone starts cheering even louder.

"Today, we celebrate a true Ohioan treasure," Governor Hull goes on to say. "Miranda Regent—the nominee for the entire United States, and our hometown hero!"

The cheering continues, and my face grows pinker by the minute. I check my droidlet again, tapping it back to display the time. Five minutes to go, and still no text from Sasha. *Five, twenty-five, six hundred twenty-five, three hundred ninety thousand six-hundred twenty-five* . . .

"Without further ado, let's listen in as the decision is made. And as the shirts say . . ." Governor Hull opens up his sport jacket to reveal his own "MIRANDA FOR MARS!" shirt, then gestures for the audience to shout that very phrase back.

Everyone more than obliges, and I struggle not to let my imagination run wild at the thought that any moment now, I actually *could* be picked to go to Mars. Instead, I revise my T-shirt tally: *887.*

On the SmartScreen, Dr. Schuber's 3D image begins talking. "Hello and welcome to the Destined for Mars International Finals," he says, spreading his arms wide. He's dressed in a suit and looks way fancier than he did when I interviewed with the ISECG three months ago. Back then he was in jeans. "Today marks a monumental day for the World Peace Treaty.

"Fifteen years ago, a team of astronauts returned to Earth from the first and only Asteroid Exploratory Mission, bringing with them riches beyond imagining." His face takes on a somber expression. "And although it was an international effort to produce this mission, AEM was American in design and execution—thus the majority of the mined minerals remained with the United States. We are not here today to comment on whether or not that was the appropriate decision."

One of the high school boys shouts something he *really* shouldn't in response, and a teacher drags him out by his T-shirt. I do my best not to react to the commotion, remembering what my PR team told me about how to behave when that subject comes up.

"What we are here to do is to celebrate the fulfillment of the peace treaty signed last August, which ended the AEM War that plagued our world for over a decade," Dr. Schuber continues. "Something few remember, given the events that followed its return, is that AEM had a significant purpose beyond asteroid exploration—namely, testing human limits in preparation for the first manned mission to Mars. Needless to say, that Mars mission never came to pass. Until now."

Dr. Schuber pauses to take a drink of water, and Emmaline nearly bounces out of her seat. "When are they going to get to it?!" she blurts out. Mom has to lean across me and Dad to remind Emmaline to control herself while we're all on camera.

"Today, the ISECG will choose six cadets from around the globe to train as the world's first Martian astronauts. These young people will become a uniting force—our world's first ambassadors to another planet. They will be the brightest and bravest that Earth has to offer." With that, Dr. Schuber smiles. "It was a nearly impossible task to narrow the field down to six, but doing the impossible is what space programs are all about. Now, before we announce the cadets—"

My entire body is jittering, so I grab Ruby's flashcard to steady myself. *It's happening!*

"—I would like to review the selection process."

What? Really?! I don't know how much more of this I can take.

"To be nominated for the Destined for Mars program, candidates had to meet the following qualifications: first, they had to pass a series of rigorous examinations, both academic and physical."

"Remember when you thought you'd flunked those?" my mom whispers.

"And now here you are!" my dad whispers on my other side. I wave my hands at them to shush them.

"Second," Dr. Schuber continues, "all candidates must have birth dates after the start of the AEM War, in order to completely remove them from the generation at fault. Third, all candidates are required to speak—at the bare minimum—conversational English and Russian. Fourth . . ."

I grip Ruby's flashcard even tighter. Dr. Schuber's voice drones on, and I can barely listen anymore. The broadcast shifts to take up only the top half of the SmartScreen. The bottom half of the screen is split into six slots. An image of Mars rotating on its axis fills each slot for the time being, but I know what will go there soon: faces of the chosen candidates.

Next to my dad, Emmaline squeals. "This is it! This is it, right?!"

I can't even bring myself to answer her.

"And now, what you have been waiting for," Dr. Schuber finally says. "The first chosen cadet is—"

The entire auditorium sucks in an audible breath, and my mom grabs for my hand. Mentally, I recite each possible candidate who matches my skillset of robotics, engineering, and programming, even though I know the only one who comes close as a whole package is Sasha. We've traded titles back and forth all our lives.

I bore my gaze into the first slot on the SmartScreen. *Come on . . .*

Dr. Schuber looks into the camera. "—fourteen-year-old Matsuo Tomoki of Japan!"

My heart drops as a picture of Matsuo Tomoki fills up slot number one. Around me, everyone roars their disappointment.

"It's not Sasha." My dad exhales, reassuring himself as much as he's reassuring me. "Just because Tomoki has an engineering background doesn't mean they won't need you. Solar car racing is very different from robotics."

"Tomoki's a celebrity, of course he got picked," I reply. My face and brain go a little numb as I stare at the headshot in the first slot. *Of course.* People continue to yell around me, but my ears feel like they've been filled with insulator foam.

"WE'RE PRACTICING GOOD SPORTSMANSHIP!" a teacher shouts, attempting to reel in the students' reactions. Her voice sounds muffled to me, but when Dr. Schuber speaks again, my ears clear up immediately.

"The second chosen cadet—"

I don't think I could tear my eyes away from the SmartScreen if I tried. *They're calling three girls, three boys. As of now, my odds are still—*

"—twelve-year-old Najma Odero of Kenya!"

And there it is. My odds really have dropped. An African girl's face shows up in the second slot, and I almost find myself joining in the disappointed cries this time, but remind myself over and over that I'm on camera. *Still two more chances for you. Two more.*

My mom squeezes my hand. "It's fine, it's fine . . ."

My mouth feels dry. It's *not* fine. Part of my portfolio was my programming abilities, and Najma Odero is the best in the business as far as that goes. She cracked the Kenyan government's entire computer network in a matter of minutes.

"The third chosen cadet—"

Massive amounts of shushing noises overtake the auditorium, and I struggle to hear Dr. Schuber as he says:

"—thirteen-year-old Esteban Castillo of Peru!"

A smiling boy's face fills up the third slot. The noise in the auditorium is completely out of hand now. Our principal toggles the microphone switch on the wall.

"QUIET OUT THERE!"

Several students are startled into silence, while the rest don't take much notice and keep up their shouts.

"Come on, Miranda! You're not out of this yet!"

"Hah, no way, she's totally doomed!"

My mom grips my hand nearly as hard as I squeeze Ruby's flashcard. "You're fine, you're fine, you're fine—" she says on repeat. I can feel her shaking. Or maybe that's me shaking. It's hard to tell. Esteban Castillo is a computer engineer. They're rapidly chipping away at each of my skills. If they call someone with a robotics background next, then whoever shouted about me being doomed is going to be completely correct. I'm ashamed to admit I'd almost assumed all along either Sasha or I would get in for sure, but now . . .

"The fourth chosen cadet—"

I hold my breath, staring at Dr. Schuber and the three remaining slots. *Please. Please.*

"—thirteen-year-old Miranda Regent of the United States of America!"

The auditorium explodes. My face shows up in slot four.

They picked me.

I'm paralyzed.

They picked me!

The screams are deafening. It's like a giant waterfall has been released over our heads at the same time a hundred rockets launch around us. Cheers roar through the entire auditorium. A group of kids chanting, "*USA! USA!*" get escorted out almost immediately.

And then, I'm in the air. Someone's hoisting me up onto the stage. My parents' faces disappear among the crowd of 887 T-shirts. Somehow, I can still pick out Emmaline's shrieks of joy. Part of me remembers that there were two more cadets yet to be chosen, and I crane my neck back up to the SmartScreen. The final two slots have been filled, but before I can sort out the faces, a surge of camera flashes all but blind me. And with those flashes, my brain finally manages to shake off the shock and begins to process what just happened.

I'm a Mars cadet. I'm going to go to *Mars*.

A huge grin breaks over my face, and I actually laugh out loud as I stumble to get back to my family, who've managed to fight their way out of the crowd and onto the stage with the help of some security officers. None of this feels real, even as my parents both scoop me into a giant bear hug in front of all the cameras, and my sister jumps on my back, squealing.

"We knew you could do it, kiddo!" my dad says, ruffling my hair.

"We're so proud of you!" my mom exclaims.

"As am I!" a voice says. I look up at the SmartScreen, expecting to see the rest of the cadets listed. Instead, the face of the president of the United States stares back at me.

"Madam President!" I gasp. I step backward, and my sister has to quickly clasp her hands around my neck so she doesn't slide off me.

"Hello, Miranda," President Nelson says. "It's good to see you again."

The auditorium screams behind me, and I struggle to find words to respond. Talking to the president isn't any easier now than it was two weeks ago when she called to congratulate me on my nomination to the International Finals.

"It's . . . it's good to see you again, too, Madam President," I stammer.

"Come on, Emmaline." My mom pulls my sister off my back. "Let's give Miranda her moment."

My family retreats back a ways on the stage, and I consciously have to close my mouth so I stop gaping at the SmartScreen.

"Congratulations, Mars cadet," the president continues. "You're a national hero."

Governor Hull hands me a huge plaque, thwapping me proudly on the back. I stumble a bit, but that doesn't shake the giddiness that's bubbling inside me.

"Your dedicated spirit has helped you achieve so much at such a young age," President Nelson says. "Multiple prizes at international science competitions, completing your first triathlon last year at the age of twelve, and of course, inventing your famous mechbot, Ruby."

The president knows about Ruby?! I nearly drop the giant plaque I'm holding.

"You truly are the embodiment of the strong American character we all strive to exemplify." The president smiles down at me from the screen. "But beyond representing America, you now represent the world. You are one of six citizens of planet Earth who will reach out to touch the stars."

I have to bite down on my lip to keep from replying that touching the stars would be a death sentence and no astronaut would ever attempt such a thing.

The president continues to talk. "It might have been a Cold

War that got us to the moon, but it's going to be peace that gets us to Mars!"

There's a standing ovation at that and a million buzzing droidlets, each probably messaging that out in video clips.

"So congratulations, Miranda," President Nelson concludes. "Your future, and the future of our peaceful planet, is bright." She gives me one last smile, and then the SmartScreen flickers back to a generic shot of the ISECG meeting, with various scientists and political figures wandering around.

"That was the president of the United States, personally calling to congratulate young Miranda Regent, who, if you're just joining us, has been chosen as one of six cadets to train for the very first mission to Mars, scheduled to launch nine years from now."

Reporters all around the stage are talking into their cameras, each babbling some equivalent of what the one nearest me is saying. I take the opportunity to slip offstage with my family before any of them can snatch me up. It's impossible to keep a grin off my face as I reach for the flashcard around my neck. *We're going to Mars, Ruby! We did it!*

"Miranda, there are a bunch of reporters who have questions for you," my dad says from behind me, offering to take my plaque. "You should probably talk to them for at least a little bit. Remember, you don't have to answer anything you don't feel comfortable answering."

I hand my plaque to him and then grab and hug him, squealing. "Mars, Dad! Mars!"

"I know, sweetie." He smiles.

"Hold on, hold on, hold on!" A short woman in a brown suit pushes her way through the crowds toward me. A heavier-set man in a blue suit follows her.

"Oh, look, Mary and Michael, your favorite people." My dad winks at me.

My PR team nearly trips over one another trying to get to us. "Wait! We need to have a conversation with your daughter before she speaks to the media!"

I'm in too much of a gleeful daze to care as Mary and Michael escort me toward a cordoned-off room just outside the auditorium. My dad follows. I try to glance back at my mom, who I think is shrugging at me, but I can't be sure because my view of the auditorium gets blocked as the door shuts.

"Miranda, we have a situation," Mary says.

"Well, first of all, congratulations," Michael says.

"Yes, yes, that." Mary waves a hand at Michael. "But more importantly, we need to ensure we head off any international crises."

"International crises?" my dad asks.

My droidlet pings at me, drawing my attention down. Sasha's finally texted me.

You got me this time, Regent. Congratulations. Best of luck to you and Ruby.

And there it is: the first puncture to my giddy high—Sasha didn't get in.

I stare at the text, conflicting emotions circling in me like quarks in a particle accelerator. This isn't like the other times. This isn't a competition that repeats next year. I actually beat Sasha, and he's never going to have another chance at this title.

"What are you looking at?" Mary asks, pinching her nails into one of my shoulders. "That isn't Wirldwindo, or whatever social platform you kids use nowadays, is it?"

"No," I reply, holding my droidlet back somewhat protectively. I can't help but get the feeling that she wants to snatch it from my wrist.

"Good. Don't use that anytime soon," she says. "We need to run damage control on the international reaction. Out of all the major players in the AEM War, guess which was the only one to actually have a cadet chosen?"

Is this a trick question? "Uh . . . us?"

"Exactly," Mary says. "And do you know what that means?"

"That means Russia *didn't*," Michael answers for me. He looks me square in the face. "The biggest thing to happen since the first moon landing, and Russia doesn't have a cadet in the program."

"Yeah, I just heard." I glance up at my dad, showing him my droidlet. "Sasha didn't get in, Dad."

"Oh, kiddo," my dad says. "We knew that would be the case if you won, didn't we?"

"Yeah. Yeah, we did." I turn back to my PR team, burying my disappointment. "Don't worry. I'll be careful about what I say, especially on social media."

"That's our girl." Michael gives me a thumbs-up.

The adults begin to talk as if I'm not in the room, so I glance back at my wrist, trying to decide how to respond to Sasha's text. But then I notice I actually *do* have a Wirldwindo message. I tap the edge of my droidlet quickly, so no one notices. A little giddiness trickles back into me, anticipating the flood of congratulations messages I'll be getting soon. I flick my thumb so the message surfaces, and my eyes go as wide as gas giants.

The message isn't a congratulation at all.

YOU'RE IN DANGER. TRUST NO ONE.

CHAPTER 2

"Okay, now they're just grandstanding," my dad says the next day, as he peers out our kitchen window at a new team of agents joining the police perimeter around our house. "How much security do they think we need?"

"At least they're keeping the paparazzi back," I say, glancing up the staircase to my bedroom, where I can hear some suspicious thumps.

"There weren't this many yesterday." He frowns.

"Yeah, well, yesterday I wasn't a Mars cadet," I reply. I don't particularly mind the added security, but the fact that it's freaking my dad out makes me glad that I decided *not* to tell my parents about the anonymous Wirldwindo messenger. It was probably just a troll, and I'm not going to let a troll frighten my parents right before they send their daughter away for basically ever. Besides,

I'm used to negative messages online—especially since becoming the US Mars nominee. They're usually just a string of misspelled insults, but I guess people are getting creative now that I've won. "How many more interviews today?" I ask, changing the subject.

"Four."

I hold back a groan. I've barely put a dent in packing. Mom's had to do it all day for me, and I haven't even gotten a chance to see if she's doing it right. Judging by the noises upstairs, I somehow doubt it. "Call up whenever the next people get here, okay?"

"No vidchatting!" my dad shouts after me as I dash upstairs. "We don't have time for that today!"

"I know!" I shout back. *Like I'm running off to vidchat. Honestly.* I turn the corner to my room. "Mom, please don't touch—"

"Ruby's circuits, I know," my mom says as I enter. My shoulders relax when I see that my desk hasn't been disturbed. All of my robotic components are right where I'd left them. The rest of my room, however . . .

Several suitcases are sprawled out on the floor. All of my dresser drawers are open to varying degrees. A bottle of shampoo is knocked over on my nightstand, slowly oozing out next to the lamp. Hangers litter the carpet, and my closet door is wide open.

This isn't my room anymore. It's a disaster zone.

"Wow, Mom. You're, uh, really going for it, huh?" I sidle over to my nightstand to grab the shampoo bottle and start sopping up the mess.

"You have a lot of stuff," she replies, standing up and wiping her forehead. She's got her rocket-ship bandana tied around her curly hair, keeping at least some of it out of her face. "And we haven't even begun to tackle that." She gestures in the vague direction of my desk.

"I'll take care of those things," I say quickly, putting the shampoo bottle down and scooting around the suitcases to stand protectively in front of Ruby. My mechbot isn't something just anyone can pack up in boxes. She's broken up into 473 pieces right now, and that's not even counting the screws.

I pick up my wire cutters and twirl them around my fingers. My mom shakes her head slowly at me. "Miranda, you know we aren't going to have time to pack your way."

My way. She means *carefully*. "I'll make time." We stare at each other for several moments, and I try not to get distracted by the one big curl that's popped out of the left side of her bandana. "I can do it," I say. "Really."

"There isn't any time tomorrow," she reminds me. "You've got interviews all morning, lunch with the governor, then there's your send-off celebration at the town hall, your autograph session, and—"

"I know," I interrupt. "Don't worry. I'll get it done."

My mom side-eyes me as she bends back down to finish putting my shirts in a suitcase. "All right, then. Now, are you going to tell me what's been bothering you or not?"

"Bothering me? Nothing's bothering me."

"Miranda."

I silently walk back across the room.

"Is this about learning who your fellow astronauts are?"

I go back to cleaning the shampoo spill. I'd been hoping to avoid this particular conversation. "No, they seem pretty cool." I give an indifferent shrug. "Though I don't know much about Rahim, I really thought Deepa Kaur had the medical officer thing in the bag—"

"I'm not talking about Rahim. I'm talking about Anna."

I flinch, remembering Anna Koubek's cold gray eyes as we shook hands on the podium at last year's Youth Advancing Astronomy Competition. A bit of shampoo drips off my nightstand.

"You didn't think I'd remember your—ah, what did you call her?—'nemesis' from Austria?" Mom asks.

"She's not my nemesis," I say. "She's just the girl I tied with."

Mom smiles. "That's the right attitude. Keep being the bigger person, Miranda. If anything, being teammates for Mars should prove to her how much you deserved to win first place with her, right?"

I scrub at my nightstand a little harder. "I hope so."

Two mornings later, a bump jolts our van, and I blink my eyes open.

"Sorry, pothole," my dad says.

It's still dark outside as we make the turn into the airport. I must've fallen asleep for most of the ride. The terminal entrance is lined with people waving good luck signs, American flags, and giant cutout Mars shapes, which makes me smile a little. At least, until I catch sight of all the reporters lined up beyond them. I groan, running my fingers over my face. I must look like a zombie, but the news people aren't going to care that I'd rather not be recorded right now.

"Emmaline, sweetie, wake up," my mom says as we pull the car to a stop.

"But waking up means Miranda's gonna go away."

Now that it's officially sunk in for her that me *winning* means me *leaving*, Emmaline's excitement has done a 180. My dad unbuckles her seatbelt, and I pause for one last moment of peace in the car. Then I dutifully undo my own seatbelt and open the door. The shouts from the reporters are immediate.

"Miranda! Is it true you turned down the limousine Governor Hull sent so you could spend your final hours with your family?"

"How does it feel to be the face of America as our nation rebuilds its reputation?"

"What do you think about China refusing to broadcast your send-off celebration yesterday?"

"Are you worried about working with Rahim Mahmoud, given Pakistan's alliance with Russia during the war?"

"Don't answer any of them!" Mary orders, having just climbed out of a black car with Michael. They rush to push the media back.

Ignoring the reporters, I walk around to get Ruby's box out of the back of our van. My mom straightens my sister's rumpled shirt. Several members of the airport staff help my dad unload my suitcases. I exhale, my breath fogging in the chilly January air. "Here we go, Ruby," I whisper. Then I turn and nearly drop her box.

The president of the United States waits in the doorway to the airport.

"Hello, Miranda," President Nelson says. Cameras flash faster than my eyes can keep up, and my parents both have their hands over their mouths. "It's wonderful to finally meet you in person."

It takes a moment, but I find my flabbergasted voice. "Nice to meet you, too."

Reporters cram in as close as they can get. Men in dark suits come to the aid of Mary and Michael, holding the media back as I approach the president.

"It'd be a shame to let our national hero fly off in a regular airplane," the president goes on to say. "So I would like to personally invite you to join me aboard *Air Force One*."

Air Force One?! The crowd around us roars with excitement that matches exactly how I feel inside, and my mom grasps me by the shoulders.

"Miranda, this is wonderful!" she exclaims.

"I . . . I don't know what to say," I stammer.

"She says yes!" my dad answers gleefully for me.

I laugh, and so does everyone else. Well, everyone except for Emmaline. I try to give her a grin, but she's got tears in her eyes, and my smile falters. She leans into my side, clings to my coat and shakes her head, as if refusing to believe any of this is happening.

"Can I have someone take that for you?" President Nelson gestures at Ruby's box, and I pull it tighter to my chest.

"No, thank you," I reply. "This is my carry-on."

Laughter ripples through the crowd again, and my face flushes. *What did I say?*

"You'll find *Air Force One* has a few different rules concerning luggage." President Nelson chuckles.

"Yes, but you still have to go through security," one of the men in suits says. "Your family can follow you to that point. So if you please, let's get moving."

We all enter the airport, escaping the chill outside. Emmaline puts her small hand in mine, but unfortunately, the president walks quickly, and it's not long before I lose my sister. I glance back to apologize, but my dad's already got Emmaline scooped up. Her face is buried in his shoulder as they walk down the carpeted hallway together.

It takes barely any time at all to reach security, and that means that somehow, it's already time to say good-bye.

I set Ruby's box down, shaking out my left arm, which has admittedly gotten a little tired. "Guess this is it," I say.

My mom pulls me in for a giant hug. I'm just tall enough now for my face to be above her shoulder, and her frizzy hair tickles my nose as she holds me tight. "Be safe," she says. I nod. The first tear finally manages to slip out and trickle down my face. "Have fun. Learn a lot. Teach me everything when you come home to visit."

"I will, Mom." It'll be two and a half months before I'm home again. Each Mars cadet gets four two-week vacations a year to visit family, which sounded like a lot back when they told me about it, but now that I'm actually leaving . . .

Two and a half months. Seventy-eight days. One thousand eight hundred and seventy-two hours. My mental math just makes it sound worse and worse, so I lock that part of my brain up.

"I love you, my little astronaut." My mom lets go of my shoulders and steps back, allowing Emmaline to come forward.

"Hey, Emmaline." I kneel down. My sister's face is covered in tears, and she definitely needs a tissue for her nose. "It's going to be okay."

"You're coming back, right?" she asks, sniffling.

"Of course," I tell her. "I promise. I'll be back to visit before you know it."

"But you won't live with us anymore."

I pause. "No. I won't."

At that, Emmaline dives forward into my arms, completely losing it.

"Be good for Mom and Dad." I bite back my own tears. "I'll vidchat as often as I can, okay?"

Emmaline nods into my shirt, wrapping her arms around me even tighter. After several moments, I slowly stand up, unwrap Emmaline's arms, and reluctantly step away from her.

Then my dad moves in and hugs me. "This is going to be such an amazing adventure for you."

I nod silently into his chest.

"Love you, sweetie. We'll see you again soon."

"Love you, too," I reply. Then we release each other, and I retrieve Ruby's box from the floor, wiping at my eyes.

I watch my family for a moment, all huddling together and

clutching tissues in their hands, before realizing that they aren't going to walk away.

I have to.

Air Force One is high-tech, plush, and everything I'd dreamed it'd be, but it's also kind of lonely. There's no one really to talk to. I managed to chat a little with President Nelson earlier, but then she disappeared to take a conference call with China.

I glance at my droidlet. That was over four hours ago. Long conference call.

Just when I feel my eyes about to close and sleep threatening to take over, Mary and Michael enter the main cabin, talking loudly with a man I've never met before.

"Miranda, this is Jason Erwich, secretary of state," Mary says, gesturing to the tall man.

I quickly stand up, shifting my weight to balance as we hit a touch of turbulence. "Nice to meet you, sir."

"Pleasure's all mine, Miss Regent." He takes a seat and gestures for me to do the same. "I want to take this opportunity to talk to you away from the prying eyes of the press. We're in a delicate situation, as you well know. You were chosen as a cadet over the Russian candidate, Sasha Oskev."

I nod, trying not to make any squeaking noises as I sit back in my leather chair.

"I don't know what the ISECG was thinking, selecting candidates so similar to each other from our two nations, but they have told us repeatedly they are less concerned with international politics and more with finding the best team' for the job." He shakes his head. "At least they had the good sense to set up your training facilities in neutral Antarctic territory. They're not *completely* clueless."

I'm not sure if I'm meant to agree with him or not, but I'm not prepared to bad-mouth the ISECG, so I just keep quiet.

"Regardless, what's done is done." Mr. Erwich searches my face, pausing for a moment before continuing. "This is a time of peace, but that doesn't mean it's necessarily *peaceful*. Please, whatever you do, always talk with Mary and Michael here before making any sort of public statement. And make sure to tell me straightaway if you ever feel threatened in any way, whatsoever."

"Yes, sir," I say. "Actually, about that . . ." I fiddle with the screen of my droidlet, opening my Wirldwindo account. Hiding my mystery message from my parents is one thing, but hiding it from the secretary of state feels like another. "I did sort of have this weird note pop up just after I won."

Mr. Erwich's brow furrows, and he takes my droidlet from my wrist. Then he snaps his fingers, and one of the suited security men steps forward. "Let's get this analyzed, Parker," he says. "Don't worry, Miss Regent, this is probably just an alarmist attention-seeker. But we'll look into it and make sure."

His tone is reassuring, but I suddenly feel way less certain than I was before about the troll status of the messenger. I'm grateful when Mr. Erwich finally heads back into a different part of the plane with my PR team.

I'm left alone for the rest of the flight, except when a security person returns to give me my droidlet and inform me that I will no longer have access to my Wirldwindo account. He explains that the CIA will monitor it on my behalf to track any more threats made on it.

"Wait, so I can't—?" But he's gone again before I can finish my protest.

I frown, twirling Ruby's flashcard.

"Okay, then. No Wirldwindo, I guess."

After that it's not too much longer before we touch down on the Falkland Islands, and I've talked myself into the lack of Wirldwindo being a good thing, so I won't be distracted during astronaut training. President Nelson emerges to join me in the main cabin once the plane comes to a full stop.

"Ready?" the president asks, straightening her blazer.

"Yeah." I pick up Ruby's box up from the seat next to mine and make a face. "There's going to be more media, isn't there?"

"Almost certainly." She smiles sympathetically. "It's never fun, but you'll get used to it."

I nod. There are a few things I'm learning I'm just going to have to get used to. Security comes back with the all clear, and we're allowed to exit.

It's cloudy outside, casting the island in an odd gray light, which its rocky nature only adds to. Stepping down the airplane stairs, I wave and smile at the crowd that—sure enough—has gathered to greet us and take a deep, calming breath. The air is different here. It smells saltier, which I know makes no sense, because sodium chloride is odorless. But still.

"*Hola*, Miranda!"

I stop at the bottom of the stairs with my security guards. The shout came from a small group of people, separate from the much larger mass that wraps around the landing strip. I peer into the group to see one boy in particular jumping and waving.

It's Esteban Castillo, and he's being escorted over with his own entourage of suited men. Cameras close in around us, documenting what I'm certain the reporters are describing as a momentous meeting.

"Hello, Esteban." I reach forward to shake his hand.

"Isn't this exciting?" Without warning, Esteban takes my hand and yanks me in for a hug. "It's like we're family already!"

My eyes fly open, and I can hear President Nelson laugh behind me as I'm pressed into an embrace with my fellow Mars cadet. Ruby's box gets squashed between us.

"Yeah," I say.

Esteban finally releases me, his face one huge grin. "Welcome to South America! I would show you around, but I'm not from the Falkland Islands, so I wouldn't know what to show off," Esteban rambles. His accent is noticeable, but it doesn't stop me from understanding what he's saying. "Now, if we were in Peru, I could show you all kinds of things. Though I'd be useless once again when we reach Antarctica."

He laughs, and I can't help but laugh a little with him. Whether it's because what he said was actually funny, or I'm just that nervous, I'm not sure. But my laughter makes him beam even brighter.

"I like you, Miranda!" He slaps me on the shoulder. "We're going to be good friends, I can already tell. Now for pictures!" he exclaims, spinning us toward the crowds. "Say cheese!"

To my horror, I actually do.

Esteban is a bundle of energy I can't hope to keep up with, but he drags me along anyway. President Nelson waves at me as we get separated. "Oh, have you met Mr. Burnett yet? He's American, too! Look, there he is!"

Before I know it, I'm being steered in a new direction across the tarmac. Cameras and security agents continue to follow our every move.

"Miranda, this is Mr. Burnett," Esteban tells me, motioning to the man in front of us. "He's with the ISECG and is going to be our teacher."

"Sort of." Mr. Burnett gives me a friendly nod. "I'm actually a grad student of Dr. Schuber's. I do programming."

"It's nice to meet you," I say. His messy hair makes him look younger than he actually is. He could almost pass for one of the high schoolers.

"And it's great to meet you," he replies, shaking my hand. "I feel like I already know you, thanks to all your interviews. Sounds like the other professors and cadets will be catching a different boat from South Africa, so we'll have plenty of time to officially chat on our boat to the training base."

"Which is where we get to go next!" Esteban says, gesturing to the left. I peer at the ocean in the distance. "Best day *ever*, am I right?"

I managed to escape Esteban's boundless enthusiasm after we'd left the harbor. He got distracted by our new tablet scrolls that we were given upon boarding.

"Amazing! Full 3D definition, fourteen-point-two-terabyte hard drive, multicore processors . . . Miranda, the software! They already have HID and STAR loaded on!"

Inside my cabin, I unroll my tablet scroll and fold the stand off the back. The material locks in place, allowing the screen to sit upright on its own. As I slide the arrow across the lower horizontal section, a keyboard unravels out from the bottom edge, flattening before me. Its buttons rise up as it settles, the memory material lighting up around each letter and number.

Okay, so maybe Esteban was right to geek out.

A knock sounds on my door. "Miranda?" I hear Esteban call from the other side.

"Come in," I say, setting my tablet down. I was going to call home to see some familiar faces for at least a moment, but I suppose that can wait.

The metal ship door swings open, and Esteban walks in, holding his tablet at his side. It's in 2D mode and opened to some website. "I thought you should see this."

His voice lacks its earlier brightness, as he holds up his tablet and I read what's on it:

Rahim Mahmoud Attacked En Route
to Mars Training Base

There's a picture of the smoking remains of a car under the words, and next to that a picture of Rahim being hoisted away by several medics. He doesn't look severely hurt, but I read on just to make sure.

"But why?" I finally manage to ask, unable to take my eyes off the images.

"I don't know," Esteban answers. "This was hours ago. Why didn't anyone tell us?"

"Another good question," I reply, my mind racing. "Maybe they don't know?"

He looks at me. "Maybe."

I shake my head, rejecting my own hypothesis. "No, that's just stupid. They have to know. Maybe they just didn't want to scare us—"

Before I can finish my thought, my words are cut off by a huge *boom*.

The ship jolts to one side so quickly that Esteban and I tumble straight into the wall, lose our footing, and collapse on the ground, just in time for the ship to rock back the other way again, sliding us across the floor.

My ears ring from the noise, but above the ringing I hear screams. Three words stand out amid the rest:

"WE'RE UNDER ATTACK!"

CHAPTER 3

"What's going on?" I scramble to my feet, clutching my tablet.

"It sounded like an explosion!" Esteban exclaims. "Come on!" He yanks the room's swinging metal door wide open, grabs my hand, and runs.

I don't question his plan. Running is exactly what my body is telling me to do right now. Run. Get away. It's only after a couple of minutes of racing through the lower corridors and reaching the stairway that I remember we're *on a ship*. There is nowhere to run.

We dash up the stairs anyway, and nearly collide with a group of men wearing suits. I gasp, stumbling backward. A dozen of them dart by, each holding a gun. Two stop when they notice us and bodily heave us back through the door from which we just emerged.

"Stay inside!" one of them orders gruffly. "We'll get you when it's safe!"

My stomach feels like it's dropping straight out of me. *Safe?* There's a high-pitched engine shriek and then a huge splash that sounds more like a thunderclap. The ship rocks again dramatically, and Esteban falls into my side. We struggle to remain upright, and then race back down the stairwell.

"What do we do?" he asks when we reach the bottom, both of us still running.

I stare at him as my feet pound down the narrow hall. "You're asking *me?*"

"*Kids!*" Mr. Burnett exclaims, rushing over to us as he rounds a corner. "Thank god you're okay!" He grabs us each by a shoulder. "We need to—"

Outside, several consecutive bangs go off.

"They're shooting," I whisper.

Mr. Burnett looks as pale as I feel. "Don't worry. Don't worry. It's going to be fine. They aren't . . . they won't hurt us . . ."

He might be right if it's only our security agents shooting, but what if it's the attackers? Hurting us is obviously their entire goal.

"Let's get you both to a safer room," Mr. Burnett says, pulling us after him. The shooting continues outside. I smell smoke inside.

Esteban and I stumble after Mr. Burnett. Crew members rush past, some with fire extinguishers. The smoke smell gets worse, and it isn't long before it starts making it hard to see.

"What's on fire?" Esteban asks.

"I don't know," Mr. Burnett says. "I don't know. This isn't . . . I don't . . ."

The poor guy loses his ability to speak and instead just pulls at his messy hair. We all stop in a hall as Mr. Burnett bends over, putting his head between his knees. He looks like he's about to throw up.

The smoke gets thicker around us, and I start coughing. "Mr. Burnett, we have to keep going," I say between coughs. My fingers tighten around the object in my hand, and it's only then that I realize both Esteban and I are still gripping our tablet scrolls. "Esteban." I turn. "We need to look up a floor map. We have to get above deck or we're going to suffocate."

We both unroll our tablets and start scanning.

"Here!" Esteban exclaims, pointing at his screen. "There's a back staircase this way! It should keep us away from the side with all the fighting."

I roll my tablet up and switch it to flashlight mode, attempting to illuminate a path through the smoke. We follow the corridor, and I just have to hope the floor map is accurate.

Even through the haze of the hallway, it soon becomes evident that it is. We reach the stairwell, but then another giant crashing splash sounds outside, and all three of us lose our footing. The ship lurches once more, and we topple violently down the stairs.

I drop my tablet scroll and grab desperately for the stairwell handrails, just managing to catch onto them and stop myself from falling all the way to the bottom. Esteban and Mr. Burnett are farther up the stairs above me, tangled in a pile together. I wince as my tablet bounces down, *kathunking* every time it hits a step. Loud shouts and bangs continue on deck above us.

Then the gunfire stops. There's a strange silence. I can hear my own shallow breathing; I'm a little wheezy. Even though the smoke stings my eyes, I can't bring myself to release my hold on the rail yet, so instead I just stare down the murky stairwell.

Two large hands grip me on the shoulders and pull me upright. I scream.

"Hey, hey!" a man shouts at me. His face is obscured by smoke, but I can tell he's wearing a security agent suit. "I'm not going to hurt you!"

I look over and see three other suited men helping Esteban and Mr. Burnett to their feet.

"Everything's okay," the man reassures me. "It's under control. Drone attack. It's shot down now. It's fine."

The ship's central air system kicks on, and I can hear fans whirring, dispelling the smoke. Slowly, the air begins to clear.

Drone attack.

I lick at my lips, which are incredibly dry. My eyes still sting, and it takes a lot of willpower to keep from rubbing them. The security agent stays at my side, holding my shoulder to keep me standing.

"We're getting our medics down here," he tells me. "You need to be checked out."

"Why . . . ?" I manage to ask.

"Smoke inhalation, for one thing," the man says.

I shake my head. "No, I mean, why was there a drone attack? Was it one of the ones guarding us?"

He looks at me, grimacing. "I am not at liberty to share my suspicions."

"You're in danger. Trust no one." My mind reels back to the anonymous message from my Wirldwindo account, and the next thing I know I'm on a gurney and they're pushing me through the halls. Esteban and Mr. Burnett follow me, each on their own gurney. It's like some sort of emergency parade.

Next to us, one of the security agents is speaking into his wrist. "They're fine. Everyone is fine. No casualties. Crew is working on ship repair, but the main engines weren't damaged and no major holes ruptured in the hull, so we're afloat and moving."

I'm desperate to keep listening, but a coughing fit overtakes me, and I miss whatever else he says.

An oxygen mask is shoved over my face, and someone tells me to breathe normally. A medical worker shines a penlight in my eyes. Another takes my blood pressure. Esteban and Mr. Burnett receive similar treatment. I realize that we aren't in a hall anymore, we're in a white room. It's like a doctor's office, which seems out of place on what is essentially a small cruise ship. There isn't much smoke in here, however. The fans must be working overtime.

Esteban is talking, but it's hard to hear him through the mask. He must realize that, because he removes it. "What about the others?" he asks.

"Put your mask back on!" a medical worker instructs.

"What about the others?" he insists.

"*What* others?" a security officer asks.

"The other Mars cadets," Esteban replies. "Rahim was attacked. Now us. What about the others?"

The room falls silent. Eventually, one of the security agents responds. "They're fine. There've been no other attacks. Though their security has increased tenfold, as will yours."

I let out a sigh of relief.

"Oh. Good," Esteban says. He puts his oxygen mask back on and lays down on his gurney.

The doctors have cleared me to breathe on my own, so I head outside to stand on the deck, stare at the waves, and try and process, well, *everything*.

"Ever been to this part of the world before?" a voice asks, and I turn.

"Mr. Burnett!" I stumble a bit. The waves are relentless, and it makes it tricky to regain my footing. The sounds of calling sea birds mock me as I grip the railing.

"Sorry, didn't mean to sneak up on you," he replies. The cold wind blows his hair every which way, making it even more messed up than before. "Just trying to make some conversation that doesn't involve oxygen masks and explosions."

I don't answer. I can't think of anything that doesn't involve those topics right now.

"I hear you won last year's International Practical Robotics Challenge," Mr. Burnett eventually says. It's a little hard to hear him over the wind, but I nod. "Nice."

"Yeah," I say. My hand goes to my throat for Ruby's flashcard, but stops when I remember I'm wearing a coat. Then the ship rocks more, and I grab onto the rail so I don't topple over again.

Mr. Burnett doesn't seem to notice. "You must have an interest in programming, then. If you ever have any questions, you can come ask me. Dr. Schuber is great, of course, but he and the other scientists can be a little intimidating until you get to know them."

I nod again, trying to ignore the security drones flying overhead, even as one of their shadows passes straight over us.

"Well, anyway, I'm going to go check in on Esteban," Mr. Burnett says, much to my relief. "You might want to come inside, too. The crew says it's going to get pretty rough out here."

"Rougher than what happened earlier?" I ask.

Mr. Burnett laughs. "Good point."

It isn't until we disembark the next day that I fully take in the damage to our ship. The entire starboard side is scorched, and large sections are bent inward. Several fighter jets swoop over our heads, and I'm escorted down the dock by two security agents. Relentless Antarctic wind punches my body, beating the warmth right out of me.

I clutch Ruby's box in my arms, trying my best to stop shivering uncontrollably. She doesn't need to be shaken any more than she already has been. When I found her after the attack, her box had clearly taken a tumble from all the jolting about the ship had done.

I went through it piece by piece during my call to my parents last night to make sure everything was okay. It took forever to reassure them about the extra security we now had, and that I would be much safer at the training island than I would be in an Ohio suburb. It was a long talk. Sasha texted me in the middle of it.

Yikes, Regent. Take care of yourself.

I promised him I would, and told him that the news was making the attack out to be worse than it was. But as I stare at the scorch marks on the side of the ship, I kind of feel like I've lied to them all.

The wind blows past us, and I shield my eyes as a blast of ice stings my cheeks. "Wow," I finally say, *really* glad that my parents can't see what I see. "Just look at it."

"I know," Esteban says. At first I think he's agreeing with me, but then I realize he's looking in the opposite direction. "It looks *amazing.*"

I turn to look at what he's taking in, and inhale sharply. It's our training base, and it's better than I could've even imagined.

The size of the base isn't what's impressive—it's the structures that make it up. The main building is shaped like a dome and has windows that appear to be made of solar glass. Out to the edges, past the rocks, is a series of smaller structures with dark exteriors. To the other side of the island, there's a hangar bigger than most of the buildings in downtown Columbus. And directly ahead of us, way in the distance on a separate island, I can make out the outline of a launchpad.

No way are we launching from here! My eyes go wide. *The weather is terrible, way too windy, and we're nowhere near the equator. The linear velocity would be awful. We'd waste so much fuel.* Then another thought strikes me. *Or maybe it's just for training. That would make much more sense.*

"Welcome to your private island," Mr. Burnett says, catching up with us. "You like it?"

"It's so cold!" Esteban laughs. "Just like Mars. It's perfect!"

A van labeled "ISECG" pulls up as Mr. Burnett continues to talk. "The other cadets are already here, as are most of the scientists and engineers you'll be working with. Sounds like we're going to meet in the hangar first. Dr. Mayworth will take your luggage to your rooms."

A woman in a huge parka climbs out of the van and introduces herself as our calculus professor. I really want to keep Ruby's parts with me, but my fingers are already numb in their gloves and holding the box has become impractical, so with great reluctance I hand her over.

"Have fun with the surprise waiting in the hangar." Dr. Mayworth winks at me as she takes the box.

"What surprise in the hangar?" Esteban asks Mr. Burnett.

My brain loops through the possibilities. "Oh, no way. It can't be a spaceplane already!"

Mr. Burnett just smiles mysteriously, and Esteban leaps into the air.

"Are you serious? A spaceplane?!" He lets out a whoop and I laugh, scarcely believing still that this is all happening. Yesterday we were attacked by drones. Today we get our own *spaceplane.* What kind of strange dream is this?

As we walk to the hangar, any notion of this being a dream gets slammed aside by the biting cold. *Come on, walk forward. It's worth it for a spaceplane!* I force one foot in front of the other, fighting the air that pushes back on me. Even though the temperature is well below the freezing point, there isn't nearly as much ice as I thought there'd be on this island. It's really mostly all rock. Big gray boulders lean against jagged cliff faces, and the ground itself is made of smaller bits of the same stone, broken up and scattered. There's the occasional patch of long, brown grass getting blown over sideways in the wind.

When we finally reach the main hangar doors, Esteban doesn't hesitate in yanking them open. Without even waiting for our security team or Mr. Burnett, he bounces down the halls. Less than ten seconds after we enter I hear him shout:

"OUR SPACEPLANE IS INCREDIBLE!"

It takes every ounce of self-control I have not to run after him. Instead, I walk like the professional Mars cadet I am, unzipping my coat and flexing my fingers in the sudden warmth of the indoors. But when I round the corner, dignity goes out the window, and I let out a squeal.

She's beautiful.

Behind a massive pane of glass, our spaceplane sits in the middle of the hangar, her outer shell partially built and shimmering in white. The lights of the hangar reflect off the spaceplane's surface, giving her a glow that I can't tear my eyes away from. Broad wings stretch out from her sides, turning upward in the style of the Dream Chaser plane that NASA uses. Her main body is nearly four times as long, however, and the far end of this spaceplane has the biggest set of engines that I've ever seen.

"Who's building her?" I ask.

"No single company," a voice next to me says. It's Dr. Schuber, head of the ISECG. It's the first time I've seen him in person since my interviews. Looks like he's wearing almost the exact same casual sweater with maybe the exact same blue jeans that he had on three months ago. "It's a collaboration," he continues. "We borrowed engineers and programmers from top aerospace manufacturing companies worldwide. This is a very special spaceplane, after all. Only the best of the best would do."

I'm only half listening. My attention is on the men and women in white full body suits working on the spacecraft. They look so miniscule next to the enormous vehicle.

"When will she be done?" Esteban asks.

"The skin will be completed by your first practical exam, and she should be operational within six months for short-distance travel," Dr. Schuber answers, as Mr. Burnett catches up to us.

Down below, a technician moves a large panel to the far side of the ship. "Do we get to help with her?" I ask.

Dr. Schuber and Mr. Burnett exchange glances.

"Perhaps," Dr. Schuber says. "Especially if you get assigned as flight engineer."

Which I should be, I think to myself. *That has to be why they picked me for this program, right? To work on the spaceplane? This beautiful, amazing spaceplane?* Her glow makes it seem like she's already out there, reflecting starlight as she zooms through the dark vacuum toward Mars. A tingle goes down my spine, and I have to check and make sure I'm not drooling.

"So this is your surprise." Mr. Burnett's eyes twinkle. "Hope you like her."

"We're calling her *Ambassador,* by the way," Dr. Schuber says. "We thought it was fitting."

I continue to nod along as they talk, until I notice something at the far end of the hangar that actually manages to draw my attention away.

The other cadets are here. From the end of their makeshift lineup, Anna Koubek's gray eyes lock on to mine.

CHAPTER 4

"It's so good to meet everyone!" Esteban gushes once we've walked over to the rest of the team. He immediately pulls Anna into a hug, and her eyes bug out. Then Esteban moves down the line, embracing each Mars cadet in turn.

Do I need to hug them all now, too? I squirm a little where I stand. I shouldn't have let Esteban go first.

Luckily, Anna saves me by holding out her hand. "Congratulations," she says.

"Yeah, you too," I reply. Just like at the Youth Advancing Astronomy Competition, her expression isn't exactly friendly, but we're not off to as bad of a start as I'd feared we would be.

Najma comes over to me next. "I'm happy to meet you, Miranda."

Before I can reply, Matsuo Tomoki steps in front of Najma,

grabs my hand, and shakes it firmly. "Hey, welcome!"

"Thanks. To, uh, both of you." I smile. Tomoki gives me a wink, and my face flushes. I knew that as a famous solar car racer, he'd be somewhat intimidating to meet, but I wasn't prepared for him to literally look like the epitome of awesome. His hair spikes up, and he's got a bleached arc of it curving over his left ear. Both ears are pierced with silver studs.

And then Rahim walks up. He's the cadet I know the least about, and he seems to be Tomoki's opposite in every way. Wearing a button-down shirt with khakis and shiny dress shoes, Rahim slouches slightly as he shuffles forward to offer me his hand.

"Nice to meet you, Miranda," he says.

"Nice to meet you, too, Rahim. How are you feeling?" I ask. He's got a bandage covering his other hand.

"I'm fine. I wasn't in the car. We were just walking to it." The tone of his voice sounds as automated as the one my droidlet's GPS uses.

"Oh," I reply. "Well, I'm glad that you weren't hurt too bad."

"I'm glad none of you were seriously hurt!" Najma exclaims. "So many attacks!"

"Yeah," I say. "We were lucky."

"We're beyond relieved you're all safe." Dr. Schuber walks up to join our little circle with Mr. Burnett. "That was quite a scare you three had."

Esteban, Rahim, and I nod, and then Mr. Burnett claps his hands. "Well, terrifying explosions aside, welcome everyone! I haven't been introduced to most of you yet. I'm Owen Burnett, Dr. Schuber's graduate student."

"And I've already met each of you," Dr. Schuber says. "So how about we take you to your dormitories so you can settle in before dinner?"

Zipping up our coats, we leave the hangar, heading back out into the intense cold. The frigid wind fights us each step of the way to the main building. Once we're finally there, Dr. Schuber punches in a code at the door and there's a whooshing noise as it slides open. We nearly fall over ourselves trying to get inside.

"That temperature shouldn't be allowed to exist," Najma says, shivering next to me.

I nod, rubbing my arms. I can't imagine what this would feel like to someone raised near the equator. To the far end of our group, Tomoki and Anna both struggle to look composed. Rahim rubs at his arms, same as me, and says nothing.

"What do you think our rooms will be like?" Esteban asks as we head through the maroon carpeted entranceway.

"Probably awesome." Tomoki shrugs off his parka. "I mean, we're the Mars cadets. Our rooms *need* to be awesome."

"Our rooms don't need to be anything but practical," Anna chides from ahead of us, not even bothering to turn around. She follows Dr. Schuber through a double set of doors.

The walls in this hallway are covered in pictures of previous astronaut crews, satellites, and several of the old space shuttle launches. We meet back up with Dr. Mayworth in front of a door, and Dr. Schuber pauses. "Mr. Burnett, would you mind showing the boys their quarters? Dr. Mayworth can take the girls to theirs. I need to go get Dr. Singh settled in."

"Sure thing," Mr. Burnett replies, swiping his droidlet up against the door we've stopped in front of. It swings open. Tomoki and Esteban nearly smash into each other, each trying to get through the door first. Mr. Burnett follows them, and Rahim trails behind.

"So cool!" Esteban shouts.

Najma and I catch each other's eye, then simultaneously try to peer into the room. But Dr. Mayworth swipes her droidlet and the door shuts before we have a chance to see much. Anna *tsks* from behind us.

"Come on, now, let's get you three to your rooms," Dr. Mayworth says.

The tall, gray-haired professor then walks with us on a new path through the halls, asking us a little about ourselves as we go. After a couple of minutes of awkward conversation, Dr. Mayworth swipes her droidlet at a new door. "Home sweet home," she says, stepping back.

The door opens to reveal a big room with a massive window off the back, and now I can see what Esteban thought was so great. Comfortable armchairs surround a large interactive tabletop. Every wall is a programmable touch screen. I can see the faint traces of solar glass built into the window, probably powering the bulk of the room's lighting if I had to guess. It's like someone took all the newest home tech and prototyped it in this one space.

And we get to *live* here.

"The three rooms to the left are your bedrooms," Dr. Mayworth explains. Then she gestures to the right. "The bathroom is opposite them, over there. It's shared, but you'll need to get used to sharing among yourselves for your mission, so why not start now?"

We all wander farther in. "Do we have assigned rooms?" Najma asks, looking at the trio of bedroom doors.

"No," Dr. Mayworth answers. "It's entirely up to you three to pick your own."

I turn to the girls to see how we want to decide who gets what, but then Anna just up and says, "I'll take this one." She walks to the door farthest from the dormitory entrance without looking back.

"Well, okay then," I say. "Um . . ."

"Mind if I take the room on the left?" Najma asks, fiddling with her fingers. "I mean, you can have it, if you'd like, but I'm not sure I want to be in the middle."

"No, it's fine," I find myself saying. "All yours."

And then Najma's gone, too, and I'm left in the common room with Dr. Mayworth.

"Looks like you're stuck in the middle." The professor smiles at me. "Hope that's okay with you. I put your robot's box under the center table, by the way."

I thank her, and gather up Ruby to head into our room.

"Middle it is, huh, Ruby?" I say, shutting my new bedroom door. Silence greets me on the other side, and I stand still for a moment, feeling strangely alone. "I really shouldn't have taken you apart," I say to the box in my arms, as I stare at my piles of luggage. "You could have helped me unpack."

Daylight shines in through the gym's windows as I run around the indoor track. That same daylight woke me up at odd hours all last night, since I didn't notice until this morning that there were polarizing filters I could adjust on my solar glass to block out the sun.

Antarctica in January is really, really strange.

I guess I have to be grateful to the ever-lasting sun, though. Waking up on repeat helped me escape the nightmares I kept having of the boat attack.

I stop running and do a few stretches. I know the only way to get the sounds of those drones bombing us out of my head will be to keep myself busy and distracted. Which shouldn't be too hard—after all, I am here to train for the coolest space mission since Apollo 11.

As I head back to the dorm, Anna pushes past me in the hall, beelining it to our rooms after her kickboxing session, probably so she can beat me to the shower. I'd initially hoped Anna wouldn't be as standoffish as I remembered, but I tried to knock on her door last night and was completely ignored. And the only thing she said to me this morning was some sort of uppity grunt when I first entered the gym.

Back in my room, I sit down at my desk. Anna's a quandary to sort out later. Right now there are two symbols on my tablet telling me I have an incoming call and also a voice message.

I peer closer at the incoming call first. It's from Sasha. Reaching forward, I tap the bouncing symbol with my finger, smiling at the prospect of seeing a familiar face. "Hello?"

Sasha's image pops up in front of me, and in the back of my mind I remember that I haven't showered yet. *Oh well.* Sasha's sandy hair sticks up in all directions and he's wearing the same T-shirt he's always in, so I'm sure he's not judging.

"Regent," Sasha says. "Been a busy few days for you. How are you doing?"

"Hey, Sasha," I reply. "It's . . . yeah. Been kind of a whirlwind." Behind him, I can see his robot, Comet, skitter up his wall. Looks like he's doing a set of diagnostic exercises. Normally, I'd point out that Ruby runs those faster, but I figure that might be kind of rude now that I've won the biggest competition we've ever been in together.

"You're an international star now." Sasha stretches back in his desk chair. "Random attacks probably come with the territory, no?"

"Do they really?" I ask, rubbing my face with my hand.

"Glad you're okay," Sasha says. "How's Ruby?"

"In pieces, but not from the attacks. I'm upgrading her nano-wiring."

"Again? Scared I'm going to get an edge on you now that you've got all this astronaut training to do?" Behind him, Comet slides back down and spins, and I'm sure Sasha's having him do that on purpose just for our vidchat.

"Don't think I'm going to slack off," I retort. "You better not, either."

"Wouldn't dream of it," Sasha replies. But then his expression changes and his voice gets quiet. "Um, so, just so you know, we didn't do it."

"Do what?"

Sasha clicks a remote, settling Comet into a resting position. "The attack. It's not Russia. Americans think it is. They're protesting. People have actually sent me threats."

"What?!" I stare at him.

"Could you say something maybe? Something to calm Americans down? My parents are getting scared," Sasha continues. "They keep talking about the war, and I need to get them to shut up. I promised I would ask you."

"Yeah," I reply, nodding. "Yeah, I'll do what I can. Sorry."

"It's fine," he says.

"No, about everything. I . . . well, you would've deserved this just as much as me."

Sasha snorts. "Don't worry about *that*. I'll find some other way to outdo you, Regent."

I smile. "If that's how it's going to be, you're on."

"Actually, I'm off," he says. Then the screen goes dark. I laugh, until I see the second bouncing dot and remember that I have a message. I flick it open.

It's from Mary and Michael. Just the people I need to talk to.

"Did you know people are blaming Russia for the attack on us?" I ask Esteban as all six of us file into the dining room for breakfast.

"What? Why?" he asks.

"People think they're still sore about a US nominee getting picked when their own didn't."

"But Rahim was attacked, too!" Esteban grabs Rahim by the shoulder of his dress shirt. "Why would Russia be angry with Pakistan? They were allies!"

Rahim's eyes are as big as moons. He struggles out of Esteban's grip. "I don't know," he says, smoothing his shirt. "But there are many others who could have wanted to attack me."

"What others?" I ask.

"I'd rather not talk about it," Rahim replies. His tone is grim, and he says nothing else as he takes a seat at the table. On the other side of the table, Najma and Anna sit down together, and Tomoki stretches in his chair. Despite his yawning, his hair is perfectly spiked, so he clearly hasn't just rolled out of bed.

"Hey, Anna, what are you so sad about over there?" Esteban asks.

"Sad?" She looks up sharply.

"You haven't smiled even once yet this morning."

I wince, watching this unfold.

"I'm not sad," Anna says. "I just don't feel like smiling."

"Why not?" Esteban gestures around the dining room. "We're here to train for Mars! And we're making new friends! Life is pretty much amazing right now!"

Anna stares at him. "I haven't made any friends yet."

Esteban's eyebrows knit together. "But what about—"

"Esteban." I catch his eye. "It's fine. We'll all become friends in time."

"Possibly," Anna mutters. Something inside me tenses up. Luckily, Esteban didn't seem to hear her, because he's already moved on to talking to Najma.

I watch Anna carefully. I guess I don't mind her being rude to me too much, but being rude to Esteban is an entirely different matter. *He's like a puppy,* I realize, watching him show Najma how to fold her napkin into various geometric shapes. *Would Anna really kick a puppy?*

Almost as if she can hear my mental train of thought, Anna looks straight at me. "Are you ready for our first lesson?" she asks.

I finished all my reading for our astrophysics class last night. It was pretty intense stuff, but I kept up. I wonder if Anna or any of the others were able to do the same. "Yes. Are you?"

"Of course," Anna replies.

The kitchen window opens into the dining room, and breakfast is laid out for us to pick up as we choose.

"Hey, did you guys hear that we'll be getting mentors?" Esteban asks, shoving his face full of waffles and continuing to be oblivious to the mood of the room. "How awesome is that?"

He blabbers on for the rest of breakfast, hypothesizing about who they've brought in to mentor us cadets. I eat my eggs, mentally running through my astrophysics notes in preparation for our first class.

"Congratulations," Dr. Singh says.

All six of us sit in a row in front of the professor and a touch screen. We've each got our tablets open, and I'm determined to take the best notes I can. My mom's an astrophysicist, and it's one of my favorite subjects.

"You are here because you are smart," Dr. Singh says. "You work hard. But you are here with five others who work hard and are smart, too. I want the best from each of you in these studies. This is difficult material. Do not expect yourself to know it already."

We all nod. *Don't worry, Dr. Singh. I never give less than my best.*

"We will begin with a review of quantum mechanics and conclude with a treatment of the multiparticle Hamiltonian." And then, he starts.

It's only a few minutes in, when I already feel something I've never felt in school before: lost. My hands can't seem to move fast enough across my tablet keyboard. Dr. Singh begins using symbols that I can't even find the buttons for. There's no time to search for them, so I have to use scribble mode to draw them in myself. After fifty-three minutes of mind-melting lecture, Dr. Singh asks each of us to do a practice set of problems focusing on Coulomb potential energy.

My hands freeze over my tablet. I've never worked with Coulomb potential energy before. Has anyone else? I glance around, but no one else looks panicked. Either they're hiding it well, or . . .

"The problems can be moved to your tablet," Dr. Singh says, and I reach out to make a pinching motion toward the touch screen, pulling the file down to my tablet screen. "You'll be timed, so I can get a sense of where each of you are."

Upon hearing that, we all dive straight in. I work furiously, ignoring the cramping in my hand as I scribble through each problem. Five minutes tick by. Ten minutes. Fifteen minutes.

Anna finishes first, earning her a glare from Tomoki and almost one from me, as well. *How did she . . . ?* But then Najma finishes second, and Tomoki as a rushed third. I'm barely halfway done with my set, and can feel my forehead crinkling around beads of sweat. *Come on, Miranda, you can figure this out. The sum over j is . . .*

"Done!" Esteban exclaims, high-fiving Tomoki. "Phew!"

Come on . . . !

And then Rahim finishes, too.

I'm last.

"Anytime, Miranda," Anna whispers, just loud enough for me to hear.

My face is flushed with held-back tears that I want to release but know I can't. I stubbornly finish my set, knowing everyone is waiting for me. Submitting my answers earns me a big pat on the back from Esteban, which threatens to knock a tear loose. Najma moves to come talk to me, but as soon as we're dismissed, I head back to my room and shut myself in.

CHAPTER 5

I don't cry. I take a lot of deep breaths, but I don't cry.

Instead, I try to wrap my brain around what just happened. My forehead presses against the solar glass of my window, the cool touch helping to numb my emotions. I thought I'd prepared well for class, but clearly I hadn't prepared well enough. I swear, Coulomb potential energy wasn't anywhere in our readings. I look over at my dresser, which I turned into a pseudo-workbench last night.

"All right, Ruby," I say to the pile of parts strewn across the surface. "I'm going to fix this. I'll study harder. We've had a busy few days with a lot of stuff to distract us, haven't we? We can do better."

I swallow. Ruby, of course, doesn't answer. I imagine her whole again, her spider legs bobbing her blocky body up and down and her optical sensors winking at me cheerfully. I hug myself with my arms, stepping away from my window, deciding then and there that I need to rebuild her ASAP. Then my droidlet pings, interrupting my pity party. It's a text from Esteban:

Our mentors are here! Our mentors are here!!!!! THEY'RE GOING TO MEET US AT LUNCH! BEST DAY EVER!

I have no idea who our mentors might be, but I can only hope they haven't talked to Dr. Singh about how badly I did in astrophysics this morning.

I sit in the dining room, only half listening as Esteban talks to—or rather, *at*—Rahim, continuing his speculation from breakfast as to who could be our mentors. Rahim's two chairs down from me, and Esteban is in the chair next to me on the opposite side, so it's kind of hard to ignore their one-sided conversation completely.

"Do you think it will be someone from the rover teams? Maybe from JPL? ESA? One of the ISS astronauts? Oh man, I hope we get astronauts!"

Tomoki wanders in, taking a seat on the far end of the table and flipping a small solar cell around his knuckles like a coin. Najma enters next, sitting across the table from me, and Anna joins us last, sitting beside Najma, which leaves only two chairs empty—the ones directly between me and Rahim. I straighten up, realizing I'll be sitting next to one of our mentors.

There's a knock at the dining room door. It's Dr. Schuber, in his sweater and blue jeans. "Hope your first lesson went well," he says. We all watch him expectantly, and he laughs a little. "I can see there's no distracting you. Without further ado . . ." He steps aside. Two figures walk through the doorway.

All six of us promptly gasp, shriek, or manage some combination of the two.

"Vladimir Kreshkov!" Tomoki leaps to his feet. The solar cell he'd been playing with falls to the floor.

My tongue feels so big in my mouth I can barely get a word out, but luckily Najma has less trouble. "Lizzie Donaldson!" she exclaims.

"Hi, everyone," the woman in the doorway says, waving.

I'm still speechless. *We get* Lizzie Donaldson *as our mentor?!*

"So, what's for lunch?" the Russian man asks, walking over and pulling out the chair next to Rahim. That means . . .

Sure enough, Lizzie Donaldson—*the* Lizzie Donaldson— takes a seat next to me. I'm barely listening as Dr. Schuber explains their roles to us. *Lizzie Donaldson has been to space eight times. She's spent 744 days outside Earth's atmosphere. That's 17,856 hours. Oh my god.*

Keep it together, Miranda. Don't say anything stupid.

"So you must be Najma," Lizzie Donaldson nods across the table.

Najma squeaks out a "yes," her hands cupped over her mouth.

The astronaut turns to Anna. "And Anna, correct?"

Anna gives her a curt nod, but I can tell even *she's* rattled. Her gray eyes are absolutely gigantic.

Then Lizzie Donaldson turns to me. "And that makes you Miranda."

"Yes." I feel like I should say something more, but I keep my mouth shut. I managed my first word to Lizzie Donaldson without screwing up, and I don't want to jinx it now.

"Esteban Castillo, Rahim Mahmoud, and Matsuo Tomoki?" Vladimir Kreshkov asks the boys.

Tomoki just stares at the cosmonaut, his solar cell lying forgotten on the floor. I feel a bit better about my own reaction, knowing even celebrities like him can be stunned silent when they meet their idols.

And then there's Esteban, who is incapable of silence.

"Yes, sir!" Esteban says. "What an honor to meet you and Ms. Donaldson!" He reaches over me to shake Lizzie's hand, then climbs up on his feet and leans even farther over to shake Kreshkov's. I have to bend way to the side to avoid getting squashed into Esteban's chest, and only just stop myself from leaning into Lizzie Donaldson's lap. "This is so great!"

It's like he's trying to win the world record for longest handshake. I bore my eyes into the table. *Okay, Esteban. Anytime now...*

When he finally sits back down, I waste no time in straightening up and bending away from the astronaut next to me. "Sorry about that," I mumble.

Lizzie Donaldson laughs. "No problem!"

"Now that you've been introduced, I'll let you all get to

know each other," Dr. Schuber says. "If you need me, I'll be in my office." Then he leaves, and a staff person brings us each our lunch.

I'd ordered grilled cheese after my astrophysics disaster, hoping the cheesy goodness would take my mind off things. But now, with Lizzie Donaldson right next to me, I can't help but wonder if grilled cheese looks too childish. Eventually I decide that *not* eating would be even weirder, so I go ahead and take a bite.

"Before we begin our meal," Kreshkov says, standing up.

I pause, clutching on to my sandwich. Slowly I pull it back, using my teeth to sever the strands of melted cheese stretching from the bread to my mouth.

Kreshkov looks around the table. "I would like to say a few words." Like Sasha, his *w*'s sound more like *v*'s. "First, I want to say that I'm sorry some of you were attacked on your way here. I'm relieved that no one was seriously hurt."

I glance at Rahim, who's tracing one finger over his bandaged hand. Esteban pats me on the shoulder, and Lizzie Donaldson smiles at the two of us. My face must be as red as the tomatoes on my sandwich by now.

"Second, I know there has been some suspicion over Russia and the attacks. Let me say on behalf of my country, that we would never wish harm upon any of you. Ever." He looks directly at me, and I'm reminded of Sasha's words earlier today. *"We didn't do it."*

Kreshkov's eyes are like two dark asteroids, barreling through space toward me. *Why not look at Esteban and Rahim, too? Come on, I wasn't the only one attacked!*

"We'll be staying here with you guys up through your first practical," Lizzie Donaldson says. "Then we'll leave to spend time with our families. But we'll be back again." She gives me a reassuring smile. I go back to staring at the table.

And why did Lizzie Donaldson look at me instead of the others, too? Maybe I just seem like the one who needs the most coddling.

"What do you mean, *practical?*" Tomoki asks.

"Well, every two and a half months, you get to go home for a couple of weeks to see your families, right?" Lizzie puts her napkin down on her lap. "Before you go home, you'll be given exams, including a practical exam. The first few practical exams will involve taking the spaceplane over to the launchpad island, where you guys will get quizzed on lift-off procedures."

"All right!" Esteban exclaims. Tomoki gives him a fist bump from across the table.

"We're already going to start training on launch procedures?" Najma asks.

Kreshkov nods. "Yes. Preparing for space travel is what you're here for, after all. Speaking of, have you started lessons yet?"

Rahim nods. "We had our first lesson today. Astrophysics."

"And how did it go?" the cosmonaut asks next.

I want to sink under the table.

"Very interesting, sir," Anna answers. "I believe we all have a lot to learn."

I stare down at my sandwich. I can feel Anna's eyes on me,

but I refuse to acknowledge her. *I'll study even more tonight. I'll get better.*

"How about physical training?" Lizzie Donaldson asks. "Is anyone interested in trying out the vertical treadmill with me tomorrow? Learn how to jog in space?"

I look up at her. Now *that* sounds fun.

Mechanical engineering goes better than astrophysics, and my spirits cautiously lift. Dr. Bouvier doesn't pull any tricks or throw material at us that I've never heard of. We spend the time designing reentry capsules that we'll get to build models of next week. Four o'clock rolls around, and before I realize it, class is over.

I walk back to our dormitory with Anna and Najma. "Either of you want to work on our engineering homework together?" I ask.

"I don't need any homework help," Anna scoffs, heading straight for her bedroom.

"I didn't mean that you needed help," I say, even though she can't hear me since she's already shut her door. "Or that I do," I add under my breath.

"I don't understand," Najma says. "Is she like this just because you two tied at that Advancing Astronomy competition?"

"I guess." I sigh, loading my reentry capsule design onto our touch table. Najma follows my lead and does the same. "I'm pretty sure Anna is convinced she should've won clear out. That was the first time they'd ever declared a tie, after all."

"I'm sure you earned it," Najma reassures me. "Why else

would they give the prize to you both?"

I don't know how to answer that—which apparently is a theme with me today.

After we get our work done, Najma turns in for the night. Despite mechanical engineering going okay, I'm not sure how easily I'll be able to sleep with my astrophysics failure in the back of my mind. So instead, I spend some time working on Ruby before heading to bed myself. People can say what they want about robots, but there's no arguing that they're fantastic listeners.

Morning arrives much more quickly than I'd like it to. At seven I find myself in the gym, lying in a harness of straps and metal posts. If it wasn't so absurdly uncomfortable, I'd be falling back asleep.

"Are all of these really necessary?" Tomoki asks, pulling at one of the straps near his elbow.

"Sure are," Lizzie Donaldson says. "Trust me, floating away when you're trying to exercise is one of the most annoying sensations ever."

I laugh. It comes out a bit awkwardly, and I can't tell if it's because I'm lying on my back or if I'm just being doofy in front of Lizzie Donaldson again. We start running on the vertical treadmills while Tomoki grills our mentor on what blasting off into space feels like.

"I actually get the same feeling every time," Lizzie Donaldson—Lizzie—answers. She asked me to call her by her first name, and I keep forgetting. "First time, second time, eighth time . . . all the same. It's scary and exhilarating. Everyone gets the shakes at least a little, but I wouldn't trade the feeling of shooting upward at eighteen thousand miles per hour for anything."

"I can't wait," Tomoki replies.

"I've talked to the ISECG about letting you guys actually do a short space trip in a couple of years," Lizzie says. "A preparation trip. Maybe to the ISS 2."

"You mean we'd get to go to the new International Space Station?" I ask, craning my head to look at her.

Lizzie laughs. "I don't see why not. No better training than actual space flight, I'd say."

"Awesome," Tomoki says, and I have to agree.

A bubbling burst of determination fills me, and I push my legs even harder.

Unfortunately, later in the day I'm back to feeling soul-crushed again.

Calculus is just as embarrassing as astrophysics was yesterday, and programming isn't any better. In both classes, we're asked to take pop quizzes that I very clearly take the longest working on. And what's worse, in programming Dr. Schuber streams live feeds to show what our codes are doing in front of the whole room. Najma's and Esteban's run the smoothest, but mine has a bug somewhere I just can't pinpoint. My screen remains frustratingly empty.

By the end of the session, I'm the only one with nothing to show for my time. Mr. Burnett passes out data cards to each of us on our way out and I have to be careful not to crush mine in anguish.

"Homework," he tells us. "Dr. Schuber asked that I make these for you guys. It's BoS translated into a new, experimental programming language. Play around with it tonight."

BoS? I cringe. No one else seems concerned, but I barely know that language. Before I can even start a groan, Esteban and Tomoki race past me in the hall, jumping and hitting at each other's heads.

"Taller!" Esteban shouts.

"Not now!" Tomoki replies.

"Yes, now!"

"They act like children," Anna comments beside me. I look over at her, honestly a tad surprised she's choosing to talk to me at all after watching me awkwardly flail through two classes today.

"Well, they are boys," I reply. "We can't expect them to be as mature as us."

"Annoying, isn't it?" Najma says, joining us.

Anna cracks a smile. It's not a big one, but it's the most I've seen from her yet. Maybe she is human after all.

"It is," Anna agrees. "But maybe it gives us the advantage for better assignments."

I'm about to shake my head, but then I realize she has a point. Maybe I'll get to be flight engineer despite how classes are going, as long as I keep up a higher level of maturity.

"So what mission job do you guys want?" I ask, trying for conversation.

"Programmer," Najma immediately says, falling into step with us as both Anna and I turn to head to our rooms.

"Oh, good, I want to be a flight engineer," I reply. Programmers and flight engineers work closely together to keep everything operational on their spacecraft, and I can't think of anyone I'd rather work with more than Najma. "What about you, Anna?"

"I wouldn't like to say." Anna's expression is back to being stony.

"Why not?" Najma asks. "We won't care if you want the same as us."

Anna just hurries to walk faster. Najma and I look at each other, then both speed up.

"I think she wants to be mission commander," Najma says to me, as if Anna isn't standing between us. "What do you think?"

"Maybe," I say. "Or maybe she can't decide."

"Maybe," Najma considers. "Or she's waiting to see what one of the boys gets."

"That's ridiculous." Anna shoots a glare at Najma. "I know what I want. I just don't think I need to tell you two."

"I wouldn't be too sad if a certain boy and I get the same job." Najma shrugs.

I train my eyes on her. Anna does the same. "Do you have *interests* in a boy here?" Anna asks.

Najma averts her gaze and rubs at her arm. "Maybe."

"Who?" I ask.

Najma glances around our hall. "Maybe I'll tell you in our room—hey!" she shouts, as Anna and I pick up the pace. We reach our dorm, push open the door and sit down, staring at Najma as she trails in after us.

"Well?" I ask.

Najma takes a seat in one of our big armchairs, fiddling with the edge of her shirt as she sinks into it. "Oh, fine." She glances one more time back at the door to make sure that it's shut. "It's Esteban. But you can't tell him!"

"You like that silly boy?" Anna scoffs. "Really?"

"Yes," Najma says. "He's nice! He makes me smile."

Anna crosses her arms. "He's always so *happy.*"

"He is," I agree. "But that's not a bad thing."

"Speak for yourself," Anna says. With that, she stands up and walks out of the room.

Najma looks at me with big, expectant eyes. I pull at a string on the edge of my chair. I wish I knew what else to say in a situation like this. I end up landing on, "So, do you think he likes you back?"

Luckily, Najma goes with it and starts talking more. I lean backward in my armchair to listen. Anna's a lost cause, Ruby's in pieces, and Sasha is in an entirely different hemisphere. It feels nice to make at least one new friend.

CHAPTER 6

"Okay, we're teaming up!" Lizzie claps her hands together, looking devilishly around the gym at all of us. Our first week has come and gone, and today our mentors asked us to join them for a special training before dinner, but refused to give details. I'm really close to being done with Ruby's reassembly and had planned on using the time before dinner to finish her, but when *Lizzie Donaldson* asks me to be somewhere, I can't say no.

"Each of you must learn to work perfectly in sync with one another if you are to be a successful unit," Kreshkov says. "Today you will act in teams of three in order to complete a challenge Lizzie and I designed."

Around us and overhead there's a whole mess of ropes and pipes dangling from the ceiling in loops and knots. Tied up among them are various pieces of mechanical equipment. I glance at Najma, who is glancing at me. I try to casually step closer to her and Esteban, mentally willing our mentors to group us together.

"What is the goal?" Anna asks.

"To build a basic station hatch door," Lizzie explains.

"Without your feet ever touching the gym floor," Kreshkov adds. "Touch the floor, and you'll be disqualified."

My stomach clenches at that.

"Will we be timed?" Tomoki asks.

"What does the winning team get?" Anna asks at the same exact moment.

My athleticism is very ground based. Running, jumping—that I can handle. Climbing?

I fiddle with Ruby's flashcard. *You'll be fine. Remember, you passed all the ISECG's physical examinations.*

"You will be timed, but the team that completes their door faster is not necessarily the winner," Kreshkov answers. "The door that seals most securely to its frame will win."

Rahim is nodding next to Esteban, but Esteban looks puzzled.

"Time won't factor in at all?" he asks.

"I didn't say that," Kreshkov replies mysteriously.

Anna frowns, but I've already spotted the tube of epoxy sealant, and I think I know what Kreshkov is getting at. Assembling the materials will require us to pay attention to the time, because if we don't move quickly enough, the sealant will harden before the pieces are all in place.

Not going to lie, I'm more than ready to rub that discovery in Anna's face if she somehow loses and I win.

"Okay," Lizzie brings our attention back after we all start murmuring to each other about how we're going to do this. "Team Antares is Esteban, Najma, and—"

I step closer to them.

"—Rahim."

My heart drops.

"And Team Spica consists of Miranda, Anna, and Tomoki." Kreshkov gestures for us to group up. "You'll have five minutes to plan before we start."

"Good luck." Lizzie smiles, and I fight back the protest that's building inside of me.

Anna doesn't look any happier than I feel. Meanwhile, Tomoki stretches lazily, sauntering away from us. "You two lucked out," he says. "If I could have picked anyone to be on my team, I would have picked me, too."

"*Mein Gott,*" Anna mutters. "What did I do to deserve this?"

The two of us follow Tomoki over to the spot on the gym floor marked in blue, for Spica's star color, and I set my shoulders, determined not to let my teammates intimidate me. Building things is what I'm best at, and if we're going to win, I know my help will be critical. The ISECG picked us all for a reason. This one has to be mine.

"Okay," I say. "First, let's make a list of what we need to collect—"

"Lists are a waste of time," Tomoki interrupts me. "I work

better when I can improvise. Just grab all the best pieces, and I'll figure out how to use them once we've got them."

"What we *need* to do is make a schematic of the door plan," Anna says. "From there, we can—"

"Anna, I already know how to make the door," I say. Her eyes flash at me. "It's super easy. We just need to get the appropriate supplies and make sure not to miss any."

"We're going to miss out on the good stuff if we waste time making lists and drawing stuff," Tomoki says. Then he points. "Look, let's start by getting that big piece over there before the other team grabs it. That'll cut down on our assembly time."

"Not if that piece doesn't fit with anything else." I try not to roll my eyes. Tomoki is supposed to be the hotshot solar car engineer; how can he not understand *organizing*? "We should be looking for parts of equal size with interlocking fittings. If we're smart about which supplies we collect—"

"If we're smart, we won't let our weakest link take charge of this mission," Anna says.

"Oh ho!" Tomoki laughs, raising a hand to high-five Anna. She doesn't take him up on the offer.

"Listen," I half growl, determined not to let my first real chance to prove myself pass me by. "Just because I haven't been as fast as you two with our quizzes doesn't mean I don't know what I'm talking about here. Engineering is what I *do*."

"It's also what Tomoki does, and planning is what *I* do," Anna says. "We need to establish team roles to operate efficiently. I will organize the mission. Tomoki will be lead designer, since he ranks higher than you in class. You will build what we tell you to and try not to get in our way."

"Sounds good to me," Tomoki says. "As long as *both* of you stay out of my way when I'm gathering supplies. I don't need anyone slowing me down."

I open and shut my mouth, trying to find the words to respond. My eyes land on Lizzie, and I wonder if I can ask her to step in and make my team listen, but then Anna's talking again.

"Going to pout to the teacher?" she asks.

I flush. "No."

"You two ready to trounce Team Antares?" Tomoki asks before I can come up with a better argument. "Looks like Kreshkov is about to tell us to start."

Sure enough, Kreshkov clears his throat, drawing our attention back to the center of the gym. I set my shoulders.

"Okay, teams," Kreshkov says. We all change our stances, eyeing which ropes above we're going to grab to haul ourselves up. "The challenge begins. Your feet need to be off the floor and up in the ropes in three . . . two . . . one . . ."

We jump into the air, pulling ourselves up into the artificial jungle of supplies. Ever the show-off, Tomoki does a backflip, dangling from his rope and grabbing another before moving toward that big chunk of door he talked about earlier. Anna goes for digital draft paper, and I'm paralyzed for a moment, still unsure what I can possibly do for a team who doesn't seem to care if I'm on it or not.

Then I spy a small control panel, about the size of a dinner plate, with wires sticking out the back.

"Where are you going?" Anna demands, as I haul myself—embarrassingly slowly—toward the panel. I really wish this challenge didn't involve climbing.

Out of the corner of my eye, I spy Tomoki ripping the door chunk out of its ropes, just before Rahim gets to it. "Team Spica for the win, Rahim!" he taunts, before heading back to Anna. He snatches the epoxy sealant on his way, and some rubber hosing and hardware, so I have to begrudgingly admit that his improvisation technique probably *does* work for him.

Anna begins scribbling on her paper, giving up on me entirely with an audible scoff. That's fine by me. Better to make the panel on my own and just add it in when they finish.

"Oh, hey!" I hear Esteban. I turn, and he's giving me a huge smile. "Nice idea, Miranda!" He gestures to the piece of equipment I'm untangling.

"Thanks!" I say, wishing even harder than before that I'd been put on the other team.

I get to work on my own project, not bothering to go back to Anna and Tomoki as they start their door. Without me to focus on, Anna's full attention is on Tomoki, and their bickering gets so loud Kreshkov actually has to go over to remind them that they're meant to be working together.

Looks like Lizzie got the job telling me the same. "Miranda," she calls up from the gym floor below. "This is meant to be a team-building exercise."

"Yeah, well, my team voted me off," I say, using wire strippers to get some clean points of connection between two wires I need to reroute.

"First of all, they can't do that," she says next. "And second, things are devolving pretty quickly without you there to mediate."

Anna's shrieks draw my attention. "*Idiot!* Now these pieces are stuck permanently!"

"It's not my fault!" Tomoki squeezes the tube of sealant so hard I'm worried it's going to burst. "I thought Miranda would be back to add the frame support, but she's off doing her own thing!"

Team Antares stares incredulously in our direction, and my face reddens.

"Then you're both responsible for making us fail!" Anna glares. "We are going to lose. I refuse to be held accountable for your mistakes."

"That's enough—" Kreshkov tries to intervene.

But that last comment clearly pushes Tomoki over the edge. "*My* mistakes? Do you even know who you're talking to? I'm Matsuo Tomoki! I don't make mistakes, I make things *happen*. If you would bother to help, instead of bossing us all around—"

I can't take this anymore. "Guys," I yell over, twisting the wires I was working on together. "Hey! Stop it. I'll come help, just hold on a sec."

Below me, Lizzie smiles. "You're making a very mature decision right now, Miranda. Very proud of you."

As annoyed at all of this as I am, Lizzie's words do warm the cold attitude I'd been letting control me. I tuck the panel under one arm, reach out for a rope to pull myself over—

And miss.

Losing balance, I tumble out of the mess of ropes and land on the gym floor. A loud echo of my fall sounds around the room, and my back seriously smarts as I lay there, stunned. The control panel is in my grip, luckily not broken. But the rules were to not touch the gym floor . . .

Anna breaks the silence. "Way to go."

Lizzie and Kreshkov rush over to check if I'm okay. Which I am. At least, as okay as I can be, now that I'm disqualified from the challenge.

Tomoki groans, and if my body wasn't still in shock, I would run as far away from everyone as I could.

Team Antares won, which was no surprise to anyone other than perhaps Anna. When we got back to the dorms, just before shutting herself in her room, she muttered something about how she would have won if she had been allowed to do the challenge on her own. Funny—that's exactly how I feel. But instead, I once again look like the failure of the group.

I set down my soldering iron and take off my goggles to wipe at my face. Everything is so backward here. I've never been the worst before. And while I've certainly had challenges making friends in the past, I've never had this much trouble doing group work for school. Usually I just do it all, and everyone's happy with that. But here . . .

I take a deep, determined breath. At least there's one part of my normal life I can bring back.

Ruby's red outer casing shines from the far side of the table, and I reach for the next piece, cracking my knuckles and continuing with my task. Sasha once said Ruby looked like a giant crab with a sledgehammer sticking out of its back. *Puh. Sledgehammer. Like Ruby's optical unit is anywhere near as heavy as that.* Besides, Ruby has ten legs that can *each* rotate up into arms, rather than just the front two—so not like a crab at *all*.

After I finally get her casing in place, I untie her flashcard from around my neck. It's kind of weird not having it there anymore, but Ruby needs it back now.

I insert the card, close up the covering over it, and take Ruby off her charge pad. Each of her optic sensors has a tiny white light blinking inside, letting me know she's charged. I connect two plugs on the back of her wiring column. The lights stop blinking and stay on.

I hold my breath.

"Ruby, movement check," I say.

Ruby bobs her head in acknowledgement of the command. Her five legs on her right side ripple. Then the five on the left. Then she rears up on her back legs, leaving the front ones to spin and rotate, each reaching out in turn from side to side. She scoots around in a circle on her hind legs. Her head swivels. Her wire column bends left, then right, then forward, then backward. Finally, she lands back on all ten feet, gives another head bob, and sends a message via my droidlet.

:TASK COMPLETE. WAITING FOR INSTRUCTION:

I gather the robot up in my arms and give her a gentle hug. "Oh, Ruby. It's good to have you back."

Programmed to copy what I do and say, my mechbot wraps her front limbs around me. My droidlet pings once more.

:GOOD TO HAVE YOU BACK:

CHAPTER 7

"I heard things didn't go great yesterday," Mr. Burnett says to me after class. I'd been trying to pack up in a rush to get back to my room to show off Ruby to Najma, but that plan is now thwarted.

"I fell," I say. "I'm fine now."

Mr. Burnett sighs. "I heard it was a bit more than that. You should talk to Lizzie. I know she wants to help."

Lizzie has texted me several times, trying to set up a time for us to talk, but I've been ignoring her messages. I don't deserve her help. And talking isn't going to change anything, anyway.

"I know." I shove my tablet scroll in my bag and move to leave.

"Hey—" Mr. Burnett steps forward, blocking my exit ever so slightly. "Hold on a sec." He runs a hand through his messy hair, then rubs the side of his face, obviously having no idea what to say to me. He's just trying to do the adult thing, and it's only getting more awkward by the moment.

I shoulder my bag, but don't make any more effort to leave. I'd feel kind of guilty not hearing him out, since he's trying to help.

"Did you know that the first two times I applied to work with Dr. Schuber, I got turned down?" Mr. Burnett asks.

I shake my head, not really sure I'm ready for Mr. Burnett to share his personal story, but realizing that's exactly what I'm in for.

He nods. "Yep. Flat-out rejected. Twice. I just wanted to get my PhD as his student, but instead had to go get a job for a while out in the real world. Scary!"

He laughs, like this is something I should also find funny, so I offer a small smile.

"I ended up working for Valorheart Industries—they're a big military supplier who was hiring a lot during the war. Do you know them? Maybe not. Anyway, I did programming for them for two years before the peace treaty got signed. Then I got let go. Another failure." Mr. Burnett sighs again, this time overly dramatically, clearly watching for my reaction.

I mentally run through a list of what I can respond with. "Well, if they fell apart because there wasn't a war to make stuff for anymore, that's not really your fault—" I start.

"Exactly, Miranda!" Mr. Burnett beams. "You see? Circumstances can sometimes make you feel like you've messed up, but it's not always that simple. And the happy ending to my story is that I then reapplied to work with Dr. Schuber, and this time was accepted!"

"That is a happy ending," I agree. I can see Najma in the hall waiting for me, and I really want Mr. Burnett to finish his pep talk and let me go.

"Just keep doing your best," he says next. "You're a genius, and your team is going to need you at the top of your game. Whether they recognize that or not."

"Yeah, thanks," I say. "Anyway, Najma's kind of waiting . . ." I edge toward the door.

"Oh yes, of course."

I escape to the hall, where Najma asks me what Mr. Burnett wanted. We start walking, and I spill the whole mega-awkward conversation once we're out of earshot of our classroom.

Najma laughs. "Aww, it sounds like he was just trying to help!"

"Yeah, but he's worse with social cues than *I* am," I say, as we head back to the dorm together. "I was trying to leave, and he just kept telling me his life story."

"How difficult for you." Najma's words sound sympathetic, but I can tell she's still secretly laughing at me. "Too bad mind reading isn't real. Imagine how much easier things would be if we all knew what everyone was thinking."

"Oh yeah? You want to tell Esteban what you're thinking?" I grin in her direction.

"Hey!" Najma protests. "That's not what I meant!"

"Hi, Esteban." I bat my eyelashes at his imaginary figure in the hall. "My name's Najma, and I want to have a big space wedding with you some day."

"Stop it!" Najma smacks me. But she's also giggling, and after a couple more ridiculous lines from me, we both are.

Then we round a corner and nearly run straight into Rahim.

"What's so funny?" he asks, straightening up and adjusting the cuffs of his sweater. But we're laughing too hard to answer, so we just flee in the opposite direction, leaving a very baffled Rahim behind.

Looping back around to get to our dorm, we burst into the common area, somehow laughing even harder than before. Anna's there, sitting at the touch table, the light from our solar glass windows gleaming off her blond hair. She looks up, staring back and forth between the two of us.

Najma and I quickly shut up, frozen in the doorway. No one speaks for several moments. Then Anna breaks her stare, gathers her things, and disappears into her room, slamming the door.

I wince. "Think she's still mad about yesterday?"

Najma's expression drops, and so does her voice. "I don't know. But Miranda, I think she was crying."

A lone crumpled tissue lies on the chair where Anna had been moments earlier. My eyebrows furrow. *Crying? Anna?*

Rahim isn't the only confused cadet at this base right now.

That night I spend some time talking to my family. After Emmaline gets done saying hello to Ruby, I tell them about what we're learning in class, about the physical challenges our mentors have issued us, and how I'm hanging more with Najma. I don't tell them anything else, but my mom is perceptive and insists she stays on the screen with me after Dad takes Emmaline to read her a bedtime story.

"You know you can talk to me if things aren't going well," she says.

"Things are fine," I lie. "I'm kind of tired, though, so I may go to bed."

Ruby hears the phrase *go to bed* and scuttles off to fetch my toothbrush.

"Are you still shaken up from the attack?" Mom asks. "It's okay if you are. What happened to you was very scary, and that fear can linger. It's nothing to be ashamed of."

"Mom, astronauts don't get scared."

"Yes, but—"

"It's not that. It's . . ." I take my toothbrush from Ruby, who holds it up toward me from the floor by my desk. "I'm just tired. Training is hard work."

Mom doesn't seem convinced, but she doesn't press it further. "Okay. Just know I'm here if you want to talk."

I'm the worst cadet here, and everyone knows it.

I'm trying hard, but I just can't keep up.

One of the girls I live with actively loathes me.

"Thanks. I'm fine, though. Really."

Sunlight glints off the ice as Tomoki and Esteban race each other across the rocky terrain toward the hangar. We're practicing in the spaceplane for the first time today, and I'm hoping it will go better than everything else has been going. Especially since Dr.

Schuber himself is coming to oversee our first practice.

Off the coast of our island, I can see whitecaps roll over one another. A chunk of ice gets knocked underwater, only to bob back up to the surface with a splash. Our group trails Tomoki and Esteban. Najma and Anna chat with our mentors and Dr. Schuber, which leaves me to walk awkwardly with Rahim. He's just so *quiet*, which is absolutely no good for me today. The boat attack nightmares came back last night, and I barely slept. For once, I understand Esteban's need to jabber.

"Pretty exciting, isn't it?" I say, my breath puffing out in the air. "I mean, *I'm* excited. An actual chance to practice with real spaceplane controls? This is going to be amazing."

Rahim just nods. His black boots shuffle across the ground, and he keeps his hands in his coat pockets with his arms pinched tightly against his body.

I shove my own hands in my pockets. *Why won't he say anything? Is he just shy? Does he not want to talk to me?* "So . . ." I try to think up something else to say. *Anything* else to say.

"Do you know Sasha Oskev?" Rahim asks, startling me into looking over at him.

I shield my face from a sudden burst of wind. "Yeah. I do."

"I thought you might," Rahim says. "We're friends. Just online."

"Oh. Cool. Same here, mostly." We reach the hangar. Inside, Esteban is wheezing and Tomoki is celebrating his apparent win by pretending *not* to wheeze. Rahim and I are the last two in, and the huge hangar doors shut behind us with a *clang*.

I shiver in my parka, not yet ready to unzip it and give up its warmth after that trek. Dr. Schuber waves us on from up ahead, and we head farther into the hangar, past some engineers and technicians working on what looks to be one of the main thrusters.

"Did you know Sasha is Kreshkov's nephew?" Rahim asks next.

My mouth actually drops open, and I stop walking. "He's *what?*" I glance at the Russian cosmonaut, who's already reached the entrance to the cleanroom. *How did I never know this?!*

I want to ask Rahim more, but he's gone on ahead, and I'm left standing alone. Immediately I text Sasha, but then I have to hurry and catch up to everyone else at the cleanroom. There, we discard our boots and parkas, douse ourselves in sanitary sprays, and put on full-bodied white suits to keep the spaceplane's exposed panels free from earthly contaminants. I'm still waiting for a reply from Sasha by the time we head into the main hangar.

Our spaceplane glistens under the lights. My breath catches in my throat when I notice the Destined for Mars mission logo on her side. While classes and physical training have started to become routine here, every now and again I'm slammed with a reminder that *I am going to Mars*. That this is really, *really* happening.

"The *Ambassador* spaceplane will be your home for the eighteen-month round-trip to and from Mars," Dr. Schuber says, giving us a proper introduction to our vehicle as we gather around the stairs leading to her entryway. "Know her, love her, live her.

Within the next few months she will be ready for short-range space travel, and after another year of tests, we may allow you six to take her out for a spin."

Esteban shouts something gleeful and incoherent, and Tomoki offers him a low fist bump. I'm tingling from head to toe, and it's not just because my body is finally adjusting back to indoor temperatures.

"Now who wants to see the inside of your spaceplane?" Kreshkov asks.

Everyone cheers—even Anna, who I notice is gently trailing one hand along the belly of the ship as she moves to take her place in line.

Then my droidlet pings. I look down to see that Sasha's replied.

I never wanted it to be a big deal.

Exasperated, I text him back.

Sasha, your uncle has been to space eleven times! Other than robotics, becoming astronauts is all we ever talked about. Not once did you think I'd find this interesting?!

A moment later, as I'm inching closer in line to our spaceplane, I get another reply.

I actually worried you'd find it *too* interesting.

Good *grief.* I shake my head. There's no time to respond, since we're about to climb up into the ship. Our matching white shoes clunk against the metal stairs that lead us to the entrance hatch. Halfway up, Lizzie makes us all stop and turn to look down at her. She takes a picture, grinning.

"The world's going to love this one!" Lizzie says. "You guys don't mind if I send it to some news sites, do you?"

Lizzie could plaster it on every screen in existence, and I wouldn't argue. This is the single best moment of my entire life so far. I'm about to enter my *spaceplane*.

One by one, we reach the top of the stairs. I step through the hatch, reverently reaching out to trace my hand over the interactive paneling. We all squeeze together, moving as far in as we can so our mentors and Dr. Schuber can join us. Once we're all inside, Tomoki greedily eyes the cockpit, as Esteban flits around the crowded main cabin.

"We're actually inside our spaceplane! Best day *ever*!" Esteban grabs for Najma and her eyes widen as he jumps up and down. They knock into Anna, who stumbles and struggles not to topple over. After regaining her footing, she shoots a glance at our mentors and brushes off her white suit.

I notice that the flooring is grated and decide to program Ruby to walk in the width of the flooring patterns once I get back to my room. I can't *wait* until she gets to see this place.

"Now, I know you're all excited, and you should be," Lizzie says, motioning us through a narrow metal door. "But remember, we've got a job to do in here."

We enter the cockpit, and Tomoki whistles. We've all been working with three-dimensional projections of the cockpit for several days now, but actually seeing it in person is . . . *wow*.

Rahim moves a computer console closer to him to examine its design, while Tomoki helps himself to the pilot's chair. He wraps his hands around the controls, surprisingly softly. If I didn't know better, I'd say there were tears in his eyes.

"We'll rotate jobs today, just to give you all an overview of what each role entails," Dr. Schuber explains. "We've already got some positions in mind for each of you, as you've probably guessed, but we'll give everyone a fair shot to see if there are any surprises."

"To start, Rahim and Esteban, please take the pilot chairs," Kreshkov says. I can practically see Tomoki's head explode and have to cover my mouth so I don't laugh out loud. "Anna, you're at the first programmer console, Tomoki at the second, and Miranda and Najma, please sit in the flight engineer seats."

Flight engineer! My spirit soars. Next to me, though, Najma slumps her shoulders.

"Remember, we'll be rotating," I whisper to her. She nods back, smiling a little.

Anna takes her seat without question, her shoulders straight, held at attention, awaiting orders. I sit in my assigned seat, copying Anna's posture, determined not to mess up.

"Now to start, please turn on your spaceplane," Kreshkov instructs.

"I got this!" Esteban flips a switch up at the pilot's seat, and around us the cockpit comes to life. The noise fills me with such glee that for the next several hours, I don't think about Sasha's connection to our cosmonaut mentor even once.

Later that day we're back to our normal class schedule, and to my extreme shock, it's not just me frustrated in calculus. Dr.

Mayworth calls each of us up in turn to work out a problem, and so far none of us have succeeded.

Anna stands at the touch screen, gripping her stylus so tight that her knuckles have turned white. Esteban exchanges wide-eyed glances with Tomoki, who shakes his head and shrugs. Rahim has his arms crossed and is staring at his desk. He was up moments earlier. I was up before him, and Najma before me. Several minutes of staring later, Anna finally shakes her head, sets down the stylus, and takes her seat.

"Interesting," Dr. Mayworth says. "Nobody can solve this?"

We all sit in silence for several moments, and I exhale in relief. It finally isn't just me.

"Any idea why?" our professor asks. No one answers, so she continues. "It's because this problem doesn't have an answer. It's unsolvable."

I snap my head up sharply, and I'm not the only one. Anna looks like she's prepared to exact murder.

"Then why did you give it to us?" Esteban asks.

"She wanted to see how we would try to solve the problem," Najma says softly from her desk next to mine. "She wanted to see what we would try to do."

"Exactly," Dr. Mayworth replies. "This was a test in critical thinking."

Critical thinking?

"Did none of you question if there was an error in the problem after seeing your peers continuously fail?" she asks. "Your homework tonight is to think about this problem. Come in tomorrow

ready to explain which part is wrong and how you would fix it."
Dr. Mayworth waves her hand on the side of the board, shutting
it down. The math disappears, and the board fades back to white.
"Good luck."

CHAPTER 8

And almost overnight—other than the weird Sasha issue—things begin looking up. I still might be doing the worst, but I'm no longer alone in double-checking my homework and paying extra attention to readings. Ruby keeps me company when I'm shut away in my room, and Najma and I hang out on a regular basis now. Soon enough, there's just a week to go until our first quarterly exams, which means there's just over a week to go until we get to visit our families. I can't believe the time has flown by so fast.

:TASK COMPLETE. WAITING FOR INSTRUCTION:

Ruby trundles over to me after organizing my drawer of circuit boards, her multiple legs folding underneath her to look up at me in expectation.

"Thanks, that's all for now, Ruby. I've got studying to do. You can power down."

Her lights blink off, and I smile. Then I get up and wander out of my room to check if the kitchen has any instant cocoa packs. Ruby might get to rest, but I gave up on sleeping a while ago. I can't fail our exams. Studying needs to be my entire life.

It turns out I'm not the only one awake at one in the morning. Anna sits in the common room, using the touch table to project the spaceplane cockpit controls around her.

"Hi, Anna," I say, walking past her to the door, carrying my mom's "IT'S AN ASTROPHYSICIST THING: YOU WOULDN'T UNDERSTAND" mug. "Do you want any hot chocolate?"

"Does it look like I want hot chocolate?" Anna replies, narrowing her eyes and moving switches around on the projected image.

I keep walking. "Didn't think so. Just being friendly."

Anna doesn't say anything in return, which I've pretty much gotten used to by now. I head out of the dorm toward the dining hall. Night at our training base is as silent as space, so as I get closer to the kitchen, I'm surprised to hear voices murmuring.

". . . tough to be in that situation," a woman's voice says. "But that's life. Sometimes you just have to do what your supervisors say, even if you don't agree with it. Schuber's a good man; I'm sure whatever he wants done is worth your time."

"But what if it isn't?" a man's voice asks.

"You have to trust that it is. For instance, NASA wants me here, but I know the ISS 2 is in trouble and needs a team of specialists up there with the next set of equipment. They have a leak. I could help them, but—"

I round the corner to find Lizzie and Mr. Burnett chatting over steaming mugs. They stop talking and stare at me.

"Uh. Hi," I say, sidling into the kitchen. "Just, uh, getting some hot chocolate." My face is red. *Of all people to run into on a midnight-snack run.*

"No problem." Lizzie smiles at me. "Still hitting the books?"

"Yeah," I say. "Trying to at least." *What was that about the ISS 2? Does Lizzie not want to be here with us?* I start calculating the rate of the rising steam from their mugs in an effort to derail that upsetting train of thought.

"Well, don't let us interrupt," Mr. Burnett says.

At that, I scamper by them, finding some cocoa mix and milk and adding them to my mug as quickly as possible. Then I head back to my room.

"See you in the morning for spaceplane practice," I say to Anna as I pass on by.

Anna replies with a grunt, and I close my bedroom door.

Quarterly exams are officially the worst thing to happen to me since our boat got bombed. If I thought I'd been embarrassed earlier about how poorly I was doing compared to the other cadets, it's nothing next to having my scores posted live for the whole base to see daily.

"So if we've got thirty pascals of pressure on Mars, and we're coming in at thirty one thousand, two hundred kilometers per hour, and we need to slow up by . . ." I trail off, tapping my stylus on my palm. It's still sweaty from our calculus exam earlier that day. I know I did awful, but focusing on that won't help me pass the next test, so I force myself to concentrate.

Najma types quickly into her tablet. "Remember, the main parachute isn't functioning."

"Right," I sigh. "No main chute, and we're coming in at top speeds. . . ."

Across the way, Anna's door is shut tight. She's been studying on her own this entire time. I can't help but wonder how she's been scoring better than everyone, even Najma. It's no shock she's beating me—everyone is. My one remaining hope to prove I'm the best at something, *anything*, is mechanical engineering. But even there, I doubt I'll beat Tomoki.

My droidlet beeps, interrupting my thoughts, and I pull it out to see a text from my PR team, Mary and Michael.

WE WILL DEBRIEF YOU SOON RE: SITUATION IN RUSSIA.

IN THE MEANTIME, TRY NOT TO WATCH THE NEWS.

DON'T MAKE ANY PUBLIC STATEMENTS UNTIL WE TALK!!!

What situation in Russia? Is everything okay? I think about Sasha and squeeze my hands into fists. "Najma?"

"Yeah?" she replies, engrossed in her notes.

"If someone tells you, 'don't turn on the news right now,' what's the first thing you'd want to do?" I try to keep my voice casual.

"I don't know," she answers. "It'd depend on who it was telling me."

I squish up my mouth, biting back words. That isn't what I wanted her to say. Oh well.

I switch on the breaking-news app on our touch table. It syncs to a live news feed from some city I don't recognize. People are forming a mob in the streets, holding up signs in Russian. Before I can even start to translate them, I hear the chanting. While I'm rusty on written Russian, their spoken Russian is simple enough for me to follow.

"MIRANDA, GO HOME! MIRANDA, GO HOME!"

Each time they say my name, it's like they're clubbing me in the head.

"SASHA WAS ROBBED! MIRANDA, GO HOME!"

More people join in by the second, and what looks like an American flag burns behind the original group of protestors. It's practically a full-on riot.

A news reporter talks over the footage. "Protests continue in Russia as new evidence comes to light that Miranda Regent—US Destined for Mars nominee and ISECG-chosen cadet—may have been shoehorned into the program by the American government. President Nelson is denying these allegations, but this is only adding to the tensions between nations, as many in the United States still believe that Russia was responsible for the attack on young Regent's ship several weeks ago."

Najma isn't stuck in her notes anymore. Instead, she stares at me, her mouth just as wide open as my own. "That's got to be a lie," she says. "They wouldn't have done that. They couldn't have."

A ball of ice rolls around inside of me, like a tiny lost comet. *Shoehorned in . . . ? As in, the United States might have forced the ISECG to pick me?*

"I refuse to believe that you didn't earn your way onto this team," Najma declares.

I swallow, trying to fight back the idea, but it *hurts* and I can't. "I . . . I don't . . ."

"Well, it makes sense to me," Anna says, walking up behind us. "She *is* the worst of us all. You know that as well as I do, Najma."

The comet inside me tears into pieces. I feel like I'm out there with it in space, unable to catch a breath.

Najma switches off the news feed. "No, I don't! Why would you even say such a thing?"

"Because it's the truth, and she has to hear it." Anna's eyes bore into mine. "Everyone else in the world knows why you got picked, Miranda. It's not because you're a great astronaut cadet, and it's certainly not because of that stupid robot you're always working on. It's because of what country you're from. America and NASA weren't about to let this program happen without their cadet involved. You shouldn't *really* be here, and you know it."

"That's not true!" Najma stands up, blocking Anna from me. "Leave her alone!"

"Oh, grow up, both of you," Anna says, pushing past me and heading back to her room. "If you don't believe me, I'll guess we'll just have to see how Miranda compares to the rest of us on our remaining exams. Including our spaceplane practical."

*****

Anna's words burn in my brain for the next twenty-four hours. The main exams are over, and there's no denying it now: I'm the worst of the six of us. But we still have our spaceplane exam to get through, and I'm determined to make up some points today.

There are three helicopters heading to the launch island, and they split us and the staff up between them. I learn, to my surprise, that all of our staff are flight certified, including the professors. Dr. Singh is our pilot. Apparently that was one of the requirements of working here.

Speaking of the staff, one of them—no one would tell me who—decided I should ride over with Anna, so there is *no* talking during our time aboard our helicopter. Thank goodness it's a short trip.

"You know, this would all be more convincing if we had real astronaut suits," Tomoki says once all three copters have landed and we've unloaded onto the island.

"Next time we'll have them," Najma says. "That's what Mr. Burnett told me on the ride over."

"At least they cleared us to use the plane without those clean-room suits," Esteban says. "Those just made me feel like I was in a hospital!"

"They're only letting us go without them because all the remaining sensitive parts are cordoned off in the rear of the space-plane," Anna says. "Eventually, the whole plane will be accessible without special attire."

We walk as a group now, heading toward the launchpad.

Ambassador has been set atop several booster rockets, and she looks even more massive sitting upright than she did when she was on her side in the hangar. I shiver. This is what she's going to look like in nine years when we actually go to Mars. They've set everything up today to be as realistic as possible, and I try to shake the fear that this is the only time I'll get to experience a launch simulation. It's hard not to wonder if the protestors are right—if I really was just picked because I was the American candidate. And if so, if I'll get booted from the program once the truth is found out.

I hold back a nervous laugh. *Either way, after this practical I'll get to go home and see my family.*

We enter the launch structure and get in the elevator that will take us up to the entry level for *Ambassador*. It's warmer inside, and I flex my fingers to get the blood flowing. If only they'd let me bring Ruby along. I always do better with her at my side. But they denied my request to have her join us, on the premise that they wanted to see what I could do on my own. No pressure or anything.

"You guys all set?" Lizzie asks.

"Absolutely!" Esteban immediately replies. The rest of us nod. The elevator doors open up, and then we're on the gangplank walking to our spaceplane, over two hundred feet above the ground.

Here we go, Miranda, I tell myself. *You're supposed to be here. Prove it.*

Each step we take clangs on the metal grating below our feet.

There are chunks of ice falling from the boosters below—all from the enormous amount of frost built up on the tanks. The wind is relentless up on the gangplank. The hatch opens, and we all clamber in. Walking forward onto the gray floor of *Ambassador*, I turn to the left to reach for the ladder that will take me to my seat. Rahim follows behind me, and everyone else climbs up after him.

We had to decide in advance who would sit where for this first practical. Tomoki immediately claimed the pilot's seat. Anna chose to sit next to him as copilot. Najma got dibs on programmer, positioning herself closest to the main computer consoles, which leaves Esteban, Rahim, and me in the back seats, each at a generic console station meant for the flight engineers and the secondary programmer. I'm between the two boys.

We sit down, leaning back into our seats horizontally like I've been doing each morning for my running sessions with Lizzie. Rahim is the picture of seriousness, clipping on his wireless headset. On the other side of me, Esteban can barely control himself.

"Best day ever, best day ever, best day ever," he keeps repeating.

Lizzie and Kreshkov get to sit upright behind us on the divider between the cockpit and the rest of the spaceplane. I can hear them whispering to each other and wish I knew what they were saying. I wonder if Lizzie has told Kreshkov that she'd rather be on the ISS 2 than here with us.

My stomach churns. I hate when I can't control where my thoughts go, especially during times I need to concentrate. I begin mentally reciting the procedure clock.

"Ambassador, can you hear us?" a voice calls over the speakers.

"Mission Control, we can hear you," Anna replies. We each repeat after her, confirming that our communication systems are online.

"Commencing MCLC," the voice says. *MCLC.* We had to memorize a whole list of acronyms. This one was Main Cabin Leak Check. We wait for them to report back.

"MCLC complete, commencing preflight alignment."

That's our cue. Najma starts typing at the consoles, getting the computer systems online. Tomoki and Anna work on activating flight controls. Esteban, Rahim, and I take turns running diagnostics on the various systems. Next time we do this, we'll have official roles: a pilot, a lead programmer, a planetary geologist, a medical officer, a communications officer, and a lead flight engineer. One person will also be named mission commander, and some of us will get secondary roles to provide support for the lead roles. One of the flight engineer roles—I don't even care if it's lead or secondary—*has* to be me.

My fingers fly over the keyboard. I will *not* mess this up. The numbers flash in front of me, disappearing just as quickly as they're displayed.

Liquid hydrogen tanks at -253°C, opening at 3.2 m/sec. Closing at 9.3 m/s. Liquid oxygen tanks at -183°C, opening at 2.1 m/s. Closing at 5.7 m/s.

That's too slow.

"*Ambassador* to Mission Control, LOX close speed three decimal three meters per second too slow," I announce into my headset.

"Mission Control to *Ambassador,* good catch. We'll update you on its repair status," the voice says over the speaker in my ear.

Rahim takes over the diagnostics, and I strain my ears to hear if Lizzie and Kreshkov are talking about what I discovered. I'm sure I earned points for catching that error. The liquid oxygen, or LOX, is one of the main components of the rocket fuel, but too much too fast and the explosions will get out of control and blow our boosters straight off. Then we either fall from the sky or explode with the boosters. Neither is a good option.

After diagnostics continue for another forty-five minutes, Mission Control lets me know the fix has been made and the launch can proceed. It's T minus twenty minutes to launch, and time to close the vents. Najma works with Mission Control to get the computers all set to launch configuration. Tomoki and Anna line up the fuel cells.

Even though they're no longer important, the diagnostic numbers idly flash by as Esteban enters the command codes on his console to shut the vents. I watch them, since I have nothing else to do at the moment.

LOX open 2.1 m/s.

LOX close 4.8 m/s.

"Wait," I say. I pull my own console closer to make sure I'm seeing what I think I'm seeing. "Mission Control, diagnostics showing LOX closing rate slower than before, not faster."

Anna can't turn around to face me, but her voice sounds in my ear. "Miranda, you're sure?"

"Completely," I reply.

"Mission Control to *Ambassador*, our tests showing nine decimal oh meters per second."

I shake my head. "Four decimal eight here, Mission Control."

"Really?" Esteban asks next to me. His fingers type quickly, going back through the running diagnostics. "Oh wow. Yeah."

Rahim pulls my console toward him, since his isn't on the right screen. My neck creaks. I wish I could just sit up straight— this lying backward stuff is really going to take some getting used to.

"*Ambassador*, our tests still showing nine decimal oh," Mission Control says.

"Do something back there," Anna orders.

I'd *love* to do something and earn more points, but what? *If Ruby was here, she could go down and take real measurements. Hmm . . . that's a thought, actually.* "Mission Control, permission to virtually access cryo systems?" I ask.

There's no response for several minutes. Esteban reaches for the console Rahim's looking at, and there's a tug-of-war over the top of me.

"Really, guys?" I ask.

"Let me see it!" Esteban says. "I want to double-check the numbers!"

"I haven't finished!" Rahim replies.

Exams. Ugh. Three competitive people is two too many for

this job. I twist my head, trying to see past the console they're yanking back and forth. The countdown clock has stopped at T minus sixteen minutes.

"Mission Control to *Ambassador*," they finally answer me. "Permission granted."

"Thank you," I say. I get up from my seat, pushing past the two boys to get back to the ladder. I climb up a couple of rungs, clinging on to it until I'm next to Najma. It's nice to be vertical again. "Najma, can you get me in?"

"Already done," Najma says. She swivels her main console toward me. The screen has a virtual view of the oxidizer locker. I hook one arm through a ladder rung, using the crook of my elbow to hold on. Triggering the motion sensor, I then use my hands to guide the video feed. Liquid hydrogen is above, liquid oxygen is past a safety wall below. I virtually push through the wall to check out the other side.

There. The open/close mechanism. I bite at my lower lip, zooming in closer. *What's wrong? Physically, it looks fine. Maybe there's a faulty connection in the electronics?*

"Mission Control, what powers the closing mechanisms?" I ask.

"Lithium battery, three point seven volts," Mission Control responds.

"Connectors?"

"Silver-plated nanowire, seven count," they reply.

"Four are out," I reply, doing a quick mental calculation. "Four wires must be out."

Mission Control is silent. So is our crew, even the whispering Lizzie and Kreshkov. The countdown clock remains frozen at T minus sixteen minutes.

"Mission Control, do you copy?" I ask.

"*Ambassador,* we copy," they answer. "We're aborting the mission. Please standby."

"Aborting?" Tomoki takes off his headset and slams it down. "No!"

"Really?" Najma stares at the console. "They are aborting it? But this isn't real. Why can't we just make a note at this point and continue?"

Everyone starts talking at once, and I shrink back, climbing down the ladder to where Lizzie and Kreshkov sit. I turn away from them, staring at the still-closed exit hatch. The complaints continue behind me, and my face gets hot, even as I wonder if this catch will be what saves me from flunking completely.

"Settle down!" Lizzie shouts. "Seriously, settle down! This is a good experience. This sort of thing happens all the time."

"If they notice something dangerous, they abort the mission," Kreshkov adds. "This is meant to be a realistic practice. They could not ignore such an error and continue with the simulation."

"They could have if Miranda had stayed quiet," Anna points out.

"Now we're not going to get another chance to do this for three whole months!" Tomoki pouts. "Two weeks at home, two and a half months of more classes before our next quarterly exams . . . Way to ruin the best thing we've gotten to do so far!"

I stare even harder at the door. *Please just open. Please just open, and let me out.*

"Would you rather your crew member ignore a potentially fatal flaw in your spaceplane?" Lizzie asks. "Is that what you'd prefer?"

No one answers. I hold my breath, not daring to turn around.

"I thought so," Lizzie says.

"If this were real, Miranda would have just saved all of your lives," Kreshkov says. "First lesson of space travel: things don't always go as expected. I'm sure the examiners set this up so that you would learn what often happens at launch—that something or other delays you."

I want to go home now more than ever. Lizzie and Kreshkov treating me like a teacher's pet isn't going to make anyone any happier with me. Even when I do something right for once, I still mess things up.

"I think you all owe Miranda an apology," Lizzie says next.

"No, they don't. It's fine." I turn around. "Really. I'm sorry everyone. Mission Control was trying to go on like everything was fine to give us a chance to finish up our practice, and I got too obsessive. Maybe I would've lost some points for ignoring the problem, but we all could've continued anyway and gained more experience. I should've consulted with the whole team before acting."

"Miranda, don't apologize for being thorough," Kreshkov says. "This is exactly what an astronaut—"

The airlock hisses and our exit hatch opens back up to the

gangplank. I don't wait to hear what Kreshkov's saying. I dart out the door.

I'm going to go pack. Ruby and I are going home tonight. I'm going to get away from everyone who doesn't think I should be here, everyone who's mad at me for wrecking our first chance to do a realistic run-through, everyone who's—

A deafening triple boom hits my ears and the entire gangplank shakes under me. I fall, gripping on to the frigid, metal mesh floor. Sirens sound. I twist myself around, flipping over to try and climb to my feet.

"Miranda!" Lizzie shouts from inside the spaceplane. She jumps out, running to help me up. "Are you all right?"

"What was that?" I ask. My ears are ringing, and it's hard to hear Lizzie's response now that she isn't yelling. But I don't need to hear her. I can see what made that noise.

On the northern side of the island, a giant plume of smoke rises. The helicopter that brought Anna and me to the launch island is in mangled, blazing pieces.

CHAPTER 9

"Get them inside!"

"Move, dammit!"

I'm dragged bodily off the gangplank by several guys in suits. I do my best to keep my feet on the ground and walk on my own, but they're having none of it.

"Out of the way!"

They shove aside all the tech staff inside the launchpad complex. It's not just me being dragged, either. Burly men have grabbed each of us. I can hear Tomoki in the back yelling that he can walk on his own. I catch Anna's steely gaze and look away quickly. Esteban gets shoved up next to me, and we exchange glances. It's just like before. I can even smell the smoke.

The men set us down at the top of the stairwell. Najma and Rahim are pushed in front of us, and we're all rushed down the steps. No elevators now. The guy shoving me talks into his droid-let. "Get everyone to the bunkers. There may be more bombs on the main island. This is not a drill."

Bunkers? More bombs? I swear my heart misses a beat. *Ruby*.

"Wait!" I yell. "I have to get to my room!"

"No," the man says, gripping me by the shoulders and directing me down the staircase. "Your dorms aren't safe."

"I know, that's why I need to—"

"No," he repeats.

"But my—"

"Whatever you've got in your room isn't worth dying for," he growls at me.

Tears spring to my eyes. *Ruby . . .*

I'm not the only one crying. Najma has tears streaming down her face, too. We burst out the doors into the wind. The men in suits form a circle around us, rushing us across the empty landscape. The cold stings my damp eyes and I wipe at them, trying to get the teardrops off my face before they freeze there.

Ahead of us, a double set of thick metal doors open. The security agent lets go of me and I wonder briefly if I'd be able to escape and successfully find a way back to the main island. I envision my room exploding, Ruby's parts flying . . .

My leg muscles twitch. I have to run. But the circle of guards just won't give me the gap I need to get away, and now they're shoving me into the bunker. Lizzie, who I didn't even realize was behind me, gives my shoulder a squeeze.

"It'll be all right," she says.

Staff from the launchpad continue to file in, guided by the guards. I squat down on the floor just to the edge of everyone else. Tomoki paces back and forth. He's the only one of us not sitting. Anna is on the ground with her arms crossed. Her stare is blank, much like Rahim's across the way from her. I wonder what he's thinking. He's been through this already, too, just like Esteban and me. But he had to handle it alone. Is it easier for him this time, with the rest of us involved? Somehow, watching him sit in silence, I don't think so.

"It'll be over soon," Esteban says. "With all these people helping, it has to be."

I nod, not really listening as he continues to spout his eternal optimism.

"This is the second time they've tried to get us, and they've missed again! Whoever they are, they aren't very good at this attacking thing."

"Not us," Anna says. "They aren't attacking *us*." She locks eyes with me, and I shrink back.

"What do you mean?" Esteban asks.

"Isn't it obvious?" Anna says. "They want to kill Miranda."

My fingernails bite into the metal floor. *No.*

"Now, that's just speculation," Lizzie tries to calm the conversation. "She's not the only one who's been attacked."

Rahim glares at the back of Anna's head. "No, she is not."

"What, you don't think someone would target her?" Anna turns to ask Rahim. "Really?"

"No, I think they would," he says, carefully.

Rahim! I want to shout. I thought he was going to defend me, but now . . .

"Anna, it was your helicopter, too," Najma says. "Who's to say it wasn't a bomb meant for you?"

My heart swells. *Thank you, Najma!*

"Common denominator." Anna crosses her arms. "Esteban and Miranda were attacked on the way here, and now Miranda and I had our helicopter targeted. You don't have to be a genius to see the connection."

"Explains how you figured it out," Tomoki says, tossing and catching that solar cell he's always playing with. He must have brought it to the spaceplane practical.

Anna glowers, and Esteban laughs, but I'm shaking even worse than before. I tear my eyes away from the solar cell as Tomoki catches it once again, my mind shielding itself with mental math about its changing velocity. "Was anyone in the helicopter?" I ask Lizzie. "You know. When it blew up?"

Lizzie hesitates. "I don't know, Miranda," she says. "But if they were, you can't blame yourself for this. No matter what anyone else suggests."

That's it. I can't hold back my emotions any longer. I failed my exams. I messed up our training run. Ruby might be destroyed any second now. And I might've . . . it might be my fault that people might be . . .

I climb to my feet, retreat to the corner of the bunker, and cover my face so no one has to watch me cry.

*****

An hour goes by in slow, torturous fashion. The only thing keeping me from completely falling apart is that I haven't heard any more explosions. Ruby is still safe. And from what I've gathered, military personnel are flying in from all over the world to guard the islands, and the ones already here are doing a giant sweep looking for more bombs. Dr. Schuber has been speaking furiously into his droidlet, demanding that the main island be checked multiple times before anyone sets foot back on it.

A hand falls on my shoulder. I look up, expecting Lizzie, but it's Mr. Burnett. His face is scrunched in worry. "Miranda? How are you doing?"

I clear my throat. "I'm all right."

He sits down next to me. "I've got some good news for you."

I look at him out of the corner of my eye. *What could possibly be good right now?*

He coughs. "Well, good news and bad news."

That's what I thought.

"Which do you want first?" he asks me.

I hate that question. "I don't care," I reply. "Whichever." He's quiet for several moments, staring at the floor. "Fine, tell me the bad news first," I say, just to get him talking.

He nods slowly. "All right. The bad news is . . . well, it's bad news. There's no easy way to say this: there have been casualties."

So people have *died.* "How many?" I whisper.

Mr. Burnett hesitates. "I don't know if you really—"

"How many?!" I ask, loud enough for most of the bunker to turn and stare at me.

"Well, honestly, we were pretty lucky for the size of that explosion," he says. "There were only two."

Only two. ONLY two.

"But you can't blame yourself." Mr. Burnett's voice drops even quieter. "You didn't do this. It was completely outside your control."

Two people. Dead.

"Your trips home have all been postponed until they figure out what's going on and feel assured they can have you guys travel safely," Mr. Burnett continues. "I'm sorry, you won't be able to see your family for a while longer than originally planned."

My ill stomach cements inside me. Those Russian protestors were right. I'm not meant to be here. If I'd gone home like they'd said, this wouldn't have happened. But now I can't leave. None of us can. Everyone is stuck in Antarctica because of me. I shut my eyes and feel my eyelashes dampen once again.

"Do you want to hear the good news?" Mr. Burnett asks.

"Sure," I manage to croak out.

"Because of this, we're giving out mission assignments early."

I look at him sharply.

"They're subject to change," he continues, "but at least for now, you'll be training as lead flight engineer." Mr. Burnett gives me a shaky smile, as though hoping this will cheer me up.

"Are you sure?" I guiltily fight down the excitement that threatens to bubble up inside me. "You're still going to want me here? After everything?"

Mr. Burnett hesitates. "Why wouldn't we, Miranda?"

"I . . ." I glance across the room at the other cadets.

"Dr. Schuber just finalized the list and gave me permission to spread the word to you all. I decided you should know first. Give you something positive to think about," Mr. Burnett says.

"Thank—thank you."

"You're welcome."

Mr. Burnett stands up and heads over to the rest of the cadets, and I'm left with my foggy thoughts. My brain retreats from thinking about the attack and latches on to a safer topic. *I wonder what everyone else's jobs are?* I watch, my face feeling numb, as Mr. Burnett gathers everyone around to make the announcements. *They're all finding out together. They're all going to know what everyone got. And I'm going to have to go around and ask or something else embarrassing.* I wrap my arms over my knees, hugging them to my chest.

"What?!" I hear Tomoki shout. He shoots me a glare, and I freeze.

What just happened? Did he want flight engineer? I thought he wanted pilot!

But then everyone's looking my way, some more furtively than others, and it dawns on me: they must be learning that we're all stuck on this island for who knows how long. And blaming me. *Or are they blaming me for those people who died?*

Lizzie walks over to me with several other adults. "Miranda, I understand you found out your assignment?" she asks.

I nod, tearing my eyes away from the cadets. Esteban is gasping, and Najma has her hands over her mouth in horror, and I realize that *now* they must be finding out about the deaths.

"Well, here are the lead engineers for the spaceplane." She gestures to the four people at her side. "They'll be working with you in your training. You're welcome to spend any time you want with them outside of lessons."

I nod again and climb to my feet to shake their hands. "It's nice to meet you all," I say on complete autopilot, even though Dr. Bouvier is one of them, and I've been taking classes from him for two months.

"We understand you've got a pretty high-tech mechbot," one of the engineers says. "We could use a good one to help us on the spaceplane. Think you could bring her by whenever you come to work?"

Come to work. The shadows over my mind inch backward. "Yeah," I say. "I mean, assuming she's okay. She's back in the dorms right now . . ."

"Oh, that's already all clear," Lizzie says. "They've just sent word in. Now only the professors' buildings need to be inspected, and we can get out of here."

The shadows retreat farther back. *Ruby is safe.* I lean against the wall and close my eyes. Somehow, things will be okay. Ruby is safe.

They gave us the all clear and shuttled us back to the main island about an hour ago. I still have no idea what jobs everyone else got, but I don't care right now. My teary call home haunts me, and I need to throw myself into something. I'm going to pack up Ruby, and together we're going to go work on the spaceplane.

"We love you and miss you, but would rather you be safe on your island than risking coming home to see us."

"Your mom is right, sweetie. We love you very much. It's hard to not have you here. But to think if you'd been on that helicopter when it . . . when it . . ."

My dad actually broke down crying on the vidchat. I think my mom would've, too, but she had Emmaline hugging her tight and was clearly doing her best to look okay for my sister.

I zip up my parka and power Ruby down, preparing to head out. But then my droidlet buzzes to let me know I have a call coming in. For a moment, I wonder if it's my parents calling me back, but then I read the ID. It says, "Washington, DC."

Oh boy. I brace myself for a conversation with my PR agents. I really should have seen this coming.

"Hello?"

The video projection pops up, and my eyes widen. It isn't Mary and Michael. It's the secretary of state, Jason Erwich.

"Miranda, so good to see you're unharmed. How are you feeling?" Mr. Erwich says, straightening his tie.

"As okay as I can be," I say, quickly recovering from the shock. "How are you? Uh, sir?"

"How I am doesn't really matter right now," he says. "What matters is that you're safe."

I am. But two other people aren't.

Mr. Erwich leans forward in his office chair. "Miranda, I wanted to let you know personally that your Wirldwindo account has gotten more anonymous warning messages. There was a lot of debate as to whether or not we should tell you. But one of the messages came in earlier today."

"It did?" I gape. "You mean you knew that helicopter was going to be attacked? Why didn't you stop it?"

"We knew there was danger, but we didn't know what it was referencing," Mr. Erwich admits. "The messages have all been extremely vague, including this most recent one—which is why we've decided to have you take a look at them. They might mean more to you than us."

I nod. If there's anything I can do to prevent a future attack, I'll do it. "Send them over," I tell him. "I'll look at them right now."

"Okay, hold on." Mr. Erwich presses something on his tablet. "There. Emailed. Let me know your thoughts once you've had some time to consider them. Good luck, Miranda."

"Thank you, sir," I say.

Mr. Erwich ends the video call, and I open the email that's just come in. I'm not sure if I want the messages to make sense to me or not. If they do, and I didn't see them in time . . .

But as it turns out, the messages mean nothing to me.

YOU ARE STILL IN DANGER.

GET OUT WHILE YOU CAN.

ANOTHER ATTACK IS COMING.

I hang my head. They're just as generic as Mr. Erwich said they sounded. What am I supposed to report back to him? That I have no clue at all?

I close out of my email, a growl rising up inside me.

Picking up Ruby, I leave my room and head somewhere I might actually be of use. Two men in suits follow me with every step I take, and I don't even care anymore. So what if I need to be constantly guarded so I don't get blown to bits? I'm a flight engineer. I've got a job to do and that's all that matters.

Once I exit the building, wind blasts tiny ice crystals into my face. I don't care about that, either. Let it be freezing. I'm going to Mars where it's always frigid. Cold temperatures are just going to be my life from now on.

Shifting Ruby in my arms, I trudge down the rocky paths of our training island. For once, sunlight isn't blinding me as it reflects off the ocean waves. *Huh.* I look up into the sky.

"What do you know, Ruby?" I say, even though she can't hear me. "It's actually getting dark out."

I shouldn't be so surprised. As the seasons change, the days and nights will become equal again. I take a trembling breath and pause to count the stars.

One.

Two.

The more my eyes adjust, the more I can see. Behind me, my security agents wait. I'm sure they want me indoors, but they're just going to have to deal and give me a moment.

I look around, taking in the unfamiliar constellations. The Southern Hemisphere's sky is so different from the one I'm used to. I look north. Mars will be north from here, instead of south like back home. Really, everything is north from here. I train my eyes in that direction. Home is north on our planet, and Mars is north in the sky.

Both might as well be equally as far away right now. The wind whips past me, pushing strands of hair across my face. I tear my eyes away from the stars above. Still cradling Ruby, I start marching again, straight past the generators and into the hangar.

"Hello?" I call out, once inside. "Anyone here?"

"Miranda, is that you?" I hear Dr. Bouvier ask.

"Yeah," I reply, walking around the corner. There she is. Our spaceplane. *Ambassador.* I wonder how long it took for them to pull her back in this afternoon.

Two people work on the left wing. It looks like they're adjusting the heat-resistant paneling. Just hearing the sounds of the welding equipment calms my nerves.

"Can I help with anything?" I ask.

Dr. Bouvier smiles. "Of course! It's great to see you here so soon after receiving your role assignment. And bringing your mechbot, too!" I can tell he's being overly enthusiastic, for my sake.

I follow Dr. Bouvier toward the spaceplane, hefting Ruby in my arms. "What can we do?" I ask, determined to prove to Dr. Bouvier, and to *everyone*, that I can carry on like a professional.

"Owen is working on hooking up the navigation computer. Why don't you give him a hand? He's in the back cabin."

I nod and then head into the spaceplane, remembering to step up over the lip on the floor where the hatch attaches. They're still installing the sound-dampening tiles, so for now, each footstep I take echoes through the spaceplane's interior.

"Hello?" I ask, entering the back cabin. "Mr. Burnett?"

"Hello, Miranda." Mr. Burnett stands up from where he was crouching. "Thought that might be you. Here to help?"

"Yeah," I reply. "I brought Ruby, too."

"Great!" Mr. Burnett reaches down to grab a metal box and then passes it to me. "Have some nanowires then," he says. I take the box awkwardly with my right hand, tucking Ruby under my left arm. "Think you could piece together some converters for me?"

"Sure," I say. I sit down on the floor, turning Ruby on. She starts her movement tests as I begin sorting through the wires. "Do you want Ruby to install them? She's more precise than we'd be."

Mr. Burnett raises his eyebrows. "That'd be great." He gives the robot an impressed nod.

Moments later, I hand off the first converter to Ruby, who walks over to the gaping hole in the wall where Mr. Burnett's working. She scans the open paneling of wires until she registers the end of the set that needs a converter. Then she gets to work, her front two legs acting as pinpoint precision pliers and welders, installing the device in seconds flat.

Mr. Burnett whistles as Ruby spider-walks her way back to me. "That's the fastest mechbot I've ever seen."

I smile politely. "Thanks."

We repeat the process. As Ruby and I work on the wiring, Mr. Burnett gets out his tablet and connects it into the paneling.

"Dr. Schuber wants me to get some initial navigational codes installed," he explains. "Not the most exciting coding ever, but I suppose that's why he's making me do it and not him."

"Are you guys going to have Najma help with the coding?" I take a casual stab at which job Najma was assigned. Ruby bobs her head beside me, accepting the newest converter and tottering off with it.

"Sure will," Mr. Burnett replies. "She's lead programmer, after all."

"Oh, good," I say. "I know she wanted that job." I tighten a converter cap to the point it almost snaps. "Just wish she could've found out about it in better circumstances. I sort of messed that up for everyone, I guess." My voice has turned into a mumble.

Mr. Burnett stops what he's doing and looks at me. "Miranda . . ."

"No, it's fine." I can't look him in the eye.

"Miranda, stop it. Don't blame yourself." His expression turns pained. "The fault lies with whoever around here actually sabotaged that helicopter."

That makes me look up. "Whoever around *here?*"

It's Mr. Burnett's turn to look away. "What?"

"That's what you said." I watch him carefully. "You think someone here did it?"

Mr. Burnett looks down at his tablet, typing out code that I'm sure doesn't require his full attention. "I meant . . . I mean . . . no. No, I need to stop talking."

"Mr. Burnett, this is the second time I've almost been blown up," I say, adrenaline surging at the prospect of answers. "I need to know everything I can! People *died*. Do you really think someone around here is involved?"

Mr. Burnett types in silence for several more moments. The only sound is the click-clack of his keyboard and the whir of Ruby's legs as they reach up to grab another converter.

"Maybe," he finally answers. His voice is so quiet I barely hear him. "And if they were . . . Well, Miranda, there are certain countries that are less than happy about you getting picked for this. I'm pretty sure you understand that already."

I do. Or I thought I did.

Ruby nudges me, making me jump. She's programmed to tap me with her front leg if I get off task for more than ninety seconds. My droidlet pings.

:TASK COMPLETE. WAITING FOR INSTRUCTION:

"Sorry, Ruby." I hand her the next converter.

"If you really want to know what's going on, think about who's been attacked and think about what it'd mean if certain countries began disagreeing." Mr. Burnett's eyes plead, as if he's trying to tell me more than he's able to say.

My face blanches. *Could the world actually go back to war?*

Mr. Burnett must notice my expression, because he quickly adds, "Well, don't think about any of it *too* much. I don't want you to worry yourself over this when you should be concentrating on your studies."

I nod. *Don't worry about it. Right.*

CHAPTER 10

For three days, I bury myself in spaceplane work. Mary and Michael call almost hourly, and I pretend I don't get service in the hangar.

For three days, I weld pieces of our ship together, using the hypnotizing light of the molten metal to forget that we have zero idea of when any of us will see our families again.

For three days, security agents guard me. They stand awkwardly in *Ambassador's* half-built chambers, ignoring Ruby as she occasionally crawls straight over them to her next task.

And for three days, I manage to avoid almost every single person at the training base. But Lizzie has caught up to me today. She sits at our dorm's touch table, directly between me and my bedroom door. There is no escape.

"So." She drums her fingers along the table edge. I sit in my chair, unwilling to look her way. After a moment of intense staring, Lizzie unrolls her tablet and slides it across the table to me. "Faulty timer."

"Faulty timer?" I ask.

"Read it," Lizzie instructs.

I pull Lizzie's tablet closer and press the edges of it flat against the table. It's a full analysis of the helicopter explosion. I scan past the rundown of the trace chemicals until I get to the mechanical overview, and there it is:

CONCLUSION: DETONATION TIMER IMPROPERLY SYNCHED. EXPLOSION OCCURRED ONE HOUR TWENTY-FOUR MINUTES EARLIER THAN INTENDED.

My face stays neutral, but inside I feel sick. "It was definitely meant for me, then."

"Well," Lizzie starts. I wonder if she's going to try to tell me that the explosion could've been meant for anyone onboard the helicopter during the time it was supposed to take us back to the main island. But then . . . "I'd say yes. Probably."

I stiffen. "Why are you telling me this?"

"Because you have a right to know what the evidence is piling up to suggest," Lizzie replies. "You aren't a baby. You're thirteen, you're training to be an astronaut, and you're one of the smartest people on the planet."

"No, I'm not." I push her tablet back at her.

Lizzie frowns, leaning forward in her chair. "What do you mean, you're not?"

I cross my arms. "I'm not the smartest. I shouldn't be here. Everyone knows it. I'm just here because the United States had too much influence and forced the ISECG to take me. And that's probably why I'm being targeted." Everything I say bites into me, chipping away at the emotion-wall I've managed to build over the past three days. "Honestly, it'd be better for everyone if I left. But . . ." I trail off, unable to finish the thought without my wall collapsing.

Lizzie's eyes are steady. "But what?"

"But . . ." I can feel a lump forming in my throat. "I . . . this is . . ."

I swallow. I've spent three days blocking out the paranoia and guilt. Three days staying numb. Lizzie waits patiently, and sure enough, being forced to talk about it completely demolishes my wall.

"I don't want to leave," I gasp as a panicked sob escapes me. "I want to go to Mars! Even if I'm not meant to be here. Even if I'm not the best. I don't want to lose this. It's everything I've ever dreamed of! But if people are dying because of me and my stupid dream, then maybe it isn't worth it—"

Lizzie slams a hand down on the touch table. "Okay, that's it." She stands up and pulls me up with her. "Come on." She starts walking, leaving the common room. I've never heard her voice this stern before, and my feet automatically follow hers.

We walk through the hallways at a brisk pace. She grabs her parka out of a closet, and tosses me mine as well. Bewildered, I put it on. "Where are we going?"

"Come on," is all she says in reply.

I'm not sure how long we're going to be, so I message Ruby her power-down code. From my room, she messages back her confirmation:

:10-4, ASTRONAUT REGENT:

I cover up my droidlet, hoping Lizzie doesn't see the new cheesy confirmation code I programmed Ruby to send me in a pathetic attempt to make myself feel better. But Lizzie isn't looking at me. She's opening the door to the outside.

I follow her, zipping up my coat. As we exit, two security agents immediately begin tailing us, as I've become used to whenever I leave the main building. The only reason they're not glued to me while in the main building as well is because of all the bomb-sniffing dogs and armed guards that patrol the halls in there all day, every day.

I have to jog to keep up with Lizzie's pace. It's clear straightaway that we're going to the hangar, but I have no idea what Lizzie could possibly have to show me in there. I've practically lived there since the attack.

We enter the hangar, Lizzie still leading the way. But instead of going down the hall to the right like I normally do, she turns and goes left toward the offices. Now my curiosity is sparked even more. The guards position themselves at the door to the office we head into, and Lizzie stops by a quadrangular arrangement of empty desks, smacking her hand against a clipboard on the wall.

"The log sheet?" I ask, staring up at the paper on the clipboard.

Lizzie takes the board off the wall and pushes it at me. "You like data, don't you? Well, here's some for you. A record of productivity for the past three months of spaceplane work. Notice anything about the numbers for the last three days?"

I flip through the log sheets, scanning the numbers. When it hits me, my eyes widen.

"Exactly," Lizzie says. "Ever since you've been assigned as lead flight engineer and have started work on this spaceplane, productivity has—to coin a phrase—skyrocketed." She smiles at me. "Everyone's talking about it. Much more than they're talking about any connection between you and the attacks. Not a single person doubts that you're meant to be here."

"But . . ." I read through the numbers again, making sure I understand them right. Sure enough, things have really begun moving along ever since I joined the engineering team. Still, though. "I did worse than everyone else on the exams, remember?"

Lizzie takes the clipboard from me and hangs it back up. "Yeah, but do you see any of the other cadets down here day in and day out working on this spaceplane? Do any of them have a working mechbot that is already being fitted for thrusters?"

I flush. *So she knows I've been outfitting Ruby for space travel.*

Lizzie smiles again. "Miranda, you were chosen to be here. For really, really good reasons. Not because you're American. Not because of anything political. You were picked because we need someone like you."

I try to process this.

"So you'd better not quit on us." Lizzie pokes me in the shoulder. "Whatever's going on with these attacks and threats, you can't let them get to you. You're going to be a great astronaut."

I nod slowly.

"No quitting," Lizzie repeats, poking me again. "Got it?"

I look up at her. "But what if you do?"

Lizzie's eyebrows furrow. "What are you talking about?" The clipboard behind her is still swaying slightly on its nail, rocking back and forth.

I clench my fists, forcing myself to plow on. "I heard you and Mr. Burnett talking. You said the ISS 2 has a leak and needs help, and that you'd rather go and help them than stay here with us."

Lizzie's eyebrows pinch together even harder. "Miranda . . . no. That's not at all what I meant."

"Then what *did* you mean?" I'm starting to shake. With everything else going on, I thought I'd gotten past this. It shouldn't be this big of a deal. But somehow, it is, and I can't reason myself out of it.

Lizzie sighs. For a solid minute, she says nothing, and we stand in silence in the empty office space. Eventually, she sits down in someone's chair and puts her chin in her hands.

"I think we're too similar sometimes."

Out of anything I was expecting her to say, it wasn't that.

"What?" I take a step back and knock into another chair. It rolls into its desk.

Lizzie spins to face me square on. "Miranda, the ISS 2 does need a repair crew. And yes, I could help them. I'm trained, I'm ready, and it would be faster just to send me up there rather than get people with less experience ready for the task. But they aren't sending me. You know why?"

I shake my head.

"Because the International Space Station is a team effort, and I've pulled a lot of the weight on that team for too long," she explains. "If I don't step back and let others learn, then what happens when I'm too old to fly anymore? Who will take my place? Just because I *can* do it all, doesn't mean I should. What I should be doing is passing my knowledge on to the next generation. Which is why I'm here, with you."

I frown. "But it'd be so much more efficient if you just took a month off from here and went and did the repairs."

Lizzie laughs. "Yes, yes it would."

"Have you explained that to them? Tell them we're fine with you going for a while, as long as you come back! Maybe then they'll see—"

"Miranda," Lizzie cuts me off. "The decision is already made. And I'm okay with it. Really."

I open my mouth to argue again. "But—"

"Maybe once you're my age, you'll understand." Lizzie gets up from her chair and cracks a half smile. "It took me this long, after all."

Back in my room, I'm getting another lecture. But this one's from thousands of miles away.

"Honestly, Regent, instead of working on that spaceplane,

you should try and figure out who's attempting to assassinate you," Sasha says. "I think that takes priority." He crosses his arms, tapping a wrench against his T-shirt.

I settle back, getting comfortable as Sasha goes into one of his rambles. Next to me, Ruby nudges me with one of her spidery arms, attempting to get me back on task. We'd been working together on her new shielding when Sasha called, and Ruby isn't programmed to handle interruptions very well.

"Clearly the people officially in charge of the investigation are doing a terrible job of it," Sasha continues. "The Miranda I know wouldn't sit back and take that." He points his wrench toward the camera, shaking it. "If you're not going to try and solve this mystery, then you give me no choice but to solve it for you. And I know you'd hate it if I did it before you did."

His gaze is challenging, but there's a touch of concern in his eyes that I'm not used to seeing. I straighten up. "Like you'd really be able to figure it out from halfway across the world."

He recrosses his arms. "I could."

"No way." I let out an unimpressed laugh, and next to me, Ruby mimics the motion, bobbing up and down. "I have literally every advantage in this situation."

"Then what's stopping you?"

I lean forward, getting another retort ready, and Ruby leans with me. But I can't think of anything to say. *What* is *stopping me?*

My mind churns. "Mr. Burnett knows something," I muse. "I think, at least. He let it slip that someone around here might be involved. But he wouldn't tell me any more than that."

"Break into his office," Sasha suggests. "Look for clues."

I shake my head. "There are way too many guards wandering around. I'd definitely be noticed. Though . . ." An idea strikes me. "Maybe we could break into his *files*."

"I thought you said Burnett was a programming professional? Since when can you hack professionally encrypted files?" Sasha raises his eyebrows.

"I can't. But I know someone who can."

I exhale. I've got everyone sitting around in one of our study rooms.

"Okay, so," I start awkwardly, looking at the five cadets. "I've brought everyone together because I wanted a chance to apologize."

Tomoki stops tossing his solar cell.

"What are you apologizing for?" Esteban frowns.

"First, for messing up our first practical exam," I say. Esteban opens his mouth to argue, but I cut him off. "Really. I was too caught up in the moment and trying to prove myself. I'm sorry I just ended up ruining it for everyone."

No one says anything, so I continue.

"Second, I'm sorry that we're all stuck here. I know that I'm being targeted by someone. I'm really, really sorry that this delayed everyone's visit home. And especially sorry for putting you guys in danger." I look at Esteban and Anna in particular.

"No," Najma says.

I blink at her, startled.

"Don't be sorry for that. Thank you for your apology, but it's us who should be sorry." She glares around the room, her eyes staying on Anna the longest. "It's not your fault that people are trying to attack you. It's not your fault those people died that day. I'm sorry we weren't more considerate to you after all that happened."

Tomoki nods. "Yeah, some of us were pretty big jerks about that." He coughs pointedly, also glancing Anna's way.

"There's no way that was your fault!" Esteban says. "I mean, it'd be as much your fault as mine, then. Or Anna's! Right, Anna?"

Anna doesn't respond. Not even a sarcastic snort. I grimace, unsure how to set things right with her. But then Rahim speaks up.

"You can't ever blame yourself for someone else's actions," he says. "People die because other people are bad. Not because you exist."

That makes me pause. *Did anyone die during the attack on Rahim months ago?* I realize with growing alarm that I don't actually know. *Has he been dealing with this same guilt? Oh god, is that why he's always so quiet?* I have no idea how to bring that subject up with him, so I just say, "Yeah. I've been figuring that out, too. But here's the thing," I get back to the original point of the conversation, "I want to find out who's doing this. We've had three attacks now. We're six of the smartest people on the planet. We should be able to figure this out." I let that sink in for a moment, then continue. "I think Mr. Burnett knows something and has been hiding it. We need a way to get that information. But as a professional programmer, his files are probably super encrypted."

I give Najma a significant look.

One by one, each cadet turns to her, even Anna. It takes a moment of everyone staring, but eventually Najma taps her chin, thoughtfully. "I might have a way."

"I thought you might," I reply.

CHAPTER 11

Najma's fingers fly across her keyboard in our darkened dormitory common room. I stare intently at her screen. The code flashes by faster than I can follow.

"Any progress?" Tomoki asks. His 3D face floats on the touch table, with Esteban and Rahim hovering behind him in their own common room.

"Yes," Najma replies.

"Really?" Esteban pushes forward.

Najma nods. "Progress, yes. Answers, no."

Esteban's expression falls, and he scoots back behind Tomoki once again.

"Give her time," Anna orders. "She's working as fast as she can."

The fact that Anna has joined in at all gives me hope.

After several more minutes, Najma gives one last button push and smiles. "I'm in."

"Yes!" Esteban shouts. Rahim and Tomoki shush him. I quickly turn the volume down on the touch table.

"Is it impossible for you to keep your mouth shut?" Anna hisses.

"Sorry!" Esteban apologizes, almost as loudly as his first outburst. I wince. There aren't any adults in here with us, but who knows who's wandering the halls.

"Are you sure Mr. Burnett won't notice you've broken into his system?" Rahim asks.

"He won't," Najma assures him. "Once I run my erasure code, this will be untraceable."

"How do you know that?" Tomoki asks.

"Because I've hacked into Dr. Schuber's system before."

Anna's eyes fly open. "You've what?"

Najma shrugs. "It took days—way longer than this. But he's the best in the business, and if he didn't notice, no way Mr. Burnett will."

"When did you do this?" I ask.

Najma stops typing for a moment, her eyes drifting toward the far wall as she considers. "A couple of months ago," she finally says. Then she's back to typing.

Sounds to me like Dr. Schuber isn't the best in the business anymore—Najma is. I watch over her shoulder as she quickly scans through the inbox. I see emails from Valorheart Industries flash by several times, and I grimace. I forgot about Mr. Burnett getting fired before he came here. And now, here we are, breaking into his email. Poor guy.

"Here we go," Najma says, opening up an email from Mr. Burnett to Dr. Schuber. It's from the day after our training run—the day after the deadly attack. "Do you have your remote desktop up?" she asks the boys.

They nod, but I'm already reading.

> Robert—
>
> I've been thinking. Shouldn't we come forward about the backups? Making the list public might help narrow down who's behind the attacks. It doesn't seem right, withholding information.
>
> —Owen

As we all finish reading, we exchange glances.

"What backups?" Esteban asks.

"What list?" I ask.

"Is there a reply?" Anna asks.

Najma scrolls through. "Here."

> Owen—
>
> Revealing the list will just create more problems. Think about it logically.
>
> —Robert

"Well, that was shot down fast," Tomoki says.

I reread the email several times, trying to see if there are any clues I'm missing.

"Maybe Mr. Burnett has the list saved in his files somewhere," Esteban suggests.

Najma chews on her lower lip.

"Could you do a file search?" I ask.

"Yeah, I could," she says. "But I don't think it will help. This list could be anywhere, under any file name. It might not even be on his cloud. In fact, if it's top secret it probably isn't."

"Check his sent mail again," Rahim says. "I have a hunch."

I look over at him, but his face reveals nothing about his thoughts. At least, the slightly grainy 3D projected image of him doesn't.

Najma goes back to his sent mail. "Now what?" she asks. "There aren't any more messages to Dr. Schuber about that topic."

Rahim scans through. "No . . . no . . ." He shakes his head. "Try his messages to Kreshkov."

On the far side of Najma, Anna lets out a soft exclamation of understanding. "Rahim, you're brilliant."

I'm still lost, but I don't want to admit that in front of the others, so I lean in with Anna.

"There," Rahim says. "March eighteenth."

Najma opens it.

Vlad—

After these latest attacks, I really think it's important that you be up front with the information I told you earlier this year. You don't want it to come out in a negative way later.

—Owen

"Whoa." Tomoki blinks.

"Find the other messages," Anna orders.

Najma scrolls. "There isn't any reply from Kreshkov, but it looks like Mr. Burnett emailed him one other time before this." She brings up an email from January ninth.

Vlad—

We haven't had a chance to get to know each other too well, but I'm sure we will soon. I'm Robert Schuber's grad student and will be working with the cadets at their training base. I've been entrusted with some information that I feel you should have.

If you didn't already know, your nephew is Miranda Regent's official replacement. Each of the cadets has one. They've been kept relatively secret so far, but seeing as you'll be acting as a mentor to Miranda, it's only right that you know. I hope you won't harbor any ill feelings toward her. It was a very difficult decision to choose who would be the primary cadets and who would be held in reserve.

—Owen

I can feel my mouth drop open. We have official replacements. And Sasha is mine.

"It makes sense," Anna says. "It's smart to have backups. Any of us could end up sick, or maybe we quit or die during training—"

"Cheerful," Tomoki raises an eyebrow and cuts her off. "Interesting how there's a specific one for each of us, too. Makes you wonder who yours is."

"And there's really no reply from Kreshkov?" Esteban asks.

Najma shakes her head. "Nothing."

"Well, we now have a motive behind the attacks," Anna says. "Replacing Miranda."

My mind reels. "Mr. Burnett said that someone here might be involved . . ."

"Not Kreshkov," Tomoki says. He gives me a glare so strong that I don't dare finish my thought out loud.

"Conceivably any of us could get targeted, if people learn who's replacing us and want to make it actually happen," Najma says quietly. "Maybe that's what happened to you, Rahim."

I'm only half listening. *Sasha is my official replacement. If I get booted, he gets in.*

Anna crosses her arms. "We need to find out who else knows about these replacements. Dr. Schuber's head of the ISECG. He'd be most likely to have a record of who's in on the secret." She turns to Najma. "You broke into Schuber's system before. Could you do that again?"

"Probably," Najma says, "But it took days the first time. This isn't going to be a quick job."

Does Sasha know any of this?

Esteban shrugs. "We can be patient, if you're willing to try."

Najma smiles at him, then cracks her knuckles. "Okay. I'll do it. But I think we've learned what we can from Mr. Burnett. I'm going to close the connection for now and run my erasure code so we can stay secret."

Everyone parts ways. The boys end their video chat, and Anna and I head back to our rooms to let Najma finish her task without distraction. I close my door, letting out a breath.

I need to call Sasha. It's only fair.

"Ruby, could you bring me my tablet?"

Ruby totters across my floor, climbing up onto my desk with my tablet in tow. She sets it down next to me and bobs her head. My droidlet pings.

:TASK COMPLETE. WAITING FOR INSTRUCTION:

"Thanks. That's all for now, Ruby." I pick up the tablet and unroll it, flicking the side to lock it into its open position. "Call Sasha," I say. I watch the circle spin around the picture of his face and wait for him to answer.

Eventually he picks up. "Hey, Regent; hey, Ruby." Half his face is covered in oil or grease or something, and Comet lies in pieces across his desk. "Little busy right now, actually."

"Um, what are you doing?" I stare at the strewn-about parts.

"You upgraded, didn't you?" He wipes his hands on a rag. "If Ruby's gotten a boost, Comet needs a bigger one." Sasha glances toward Ruby, and I narrow my eyes, quickly angling the vidscreen away from her.

"No cheating," I warn.

"I don't need to cheat, Regent," he replies, setting down the oily rag. "So what's going on? Did you find out who's behind the attacks?"

I shake my head. "Not exactly. But we did learn something . . . interesting."

"Oh? What?"

I take a deep breath. Then I tell him everything.

*****

Now that I know he's officially my replacement, it's impossible not to imagine Sasha taking my place in everything I do. Today, instead of classes, we're trying on the first layer of our spacesuits, and I wonder what Sasha would think of the design.

Spacesuits are given the technical name of Extravehicular Mobility Units, or EMUs for short. To get us used to the feel of them, we're going to get new official suits designed for us every year. Sliding into the first layer of the EMU feels like slipping on butterfly netting all over my body. It's bizarre, but a good distraction from the mind-numbing programming quizzes Dr. Schuber gave us yesterday.

I wonder how Sasha would have done on my quiz.

"Okay, now, buckle together the tubing," Kreshkov instructs as Lizzie helps Najma get her first clasp done.

My eyes track Kreshkov as he walks around the room, inspecting each of us. During our conversation yesterday, Sasha insisted that his uncle would never try anything to hurt any of us. I want to believe that. I really do. Kreshkov has been nothing but supportive of us. But so far, he's the only person we know of with motive for attacking me.

"This tubing is your air conditioning," Kreshkov continues, straightening out Esteban's sleeve. "Keeping cool is critical, so never underestimate the importance of this layer."

I nod along with his explanations, perhaps overly enthusiastically. Paranoia is making me a bit too smiley around Kreshkov this afternoon.

"Space is cold, but your suits are designed to trap in body

heat, so there's always the chance you'll *over*heat. Any questions?"

A million. But none I actually have the guts to ask.

"I still don't see why we had to miss geology just to practice putting on *this*," Anna mutters, plucking at her netted suit layer. "Seems like a waste of time. Most of us won't even need to wear this in space. Just Miranda and Tomoki."

"Tomoki?" I ask, as I adjust my netting over my left wrist.

"Well, yeah, me," Tomoki says. "I'm not just our pilot, you know. I'm your number one flight engineer assistant!" He gives me a mock salute.

I file this information away, trying to hide any surprise that made its way onto my face. "Oh. Well, uh, at ease, soldier," I say, returning his salute.

Tomoki lets out a laugh, leaning back in his chair and putting his hands behind his head. *So Tomoki is my secondary. I should have guessed. Of course they would give him multiple roles—he'd never be content in just one.*

Would have been nice if someone had told me, though.

"Anna, the reason you need to get used to these things as soon as possible is because your mission is so much longer than anyone's before," Lizzie explains. "You'll want to feel like these suits are your second skin. Most astronauts only spend a few months in space, and even they need that level of familiarity. And yes, Tomoki and Miranda are the two most likely to space-walk for repairs, but did you think you wouldn't need EMUs on Mars itself?"

Anna's face goes red.

"All right, now it's time for our lesson on the control module," Lizzie says, tapping the touch screen behind her to bring up an interactive image.

Before we get to Lizzie's lesson, Mr. Burnett bursts into the room. "Good news from Dr. Schuber!"

Everyone looks over, wrinkling up in our EMU netting.

"What is it?" Tomoki asks.

Mr. Burnett waves at Lizzie and Kreshkov. "Sorry for interrupting," he says. "Anyway, since we still don't have clearance to have any of you travel, after your next quarterly exams, we're bringing your families here!"

Lizzie and Kreshkov look at each other, eyebrows raised.

"Really?" Tomoki asks.

Esteban lets out a whoop of joy, turning to double high-five an ecstatic Najma on his right and a startled Rahim on his left. "We get to see our families after all!" he cheers.

I feel a grin spread across my face, and I find myself glancing over at Anna for her reaction. Naturally, she isn't smiling, but her lack of a smile seems more like a frown than usual.

She gets up, takes off her EMU netting, and glares at each of us. "I don't understand why any of you are happy. All this means is that our families are more expendable than we are. They'll let *them* risk traveling, but not us." Anna dumps her spacesuit material on the touch table. "I'm going to do something actually useful: study. Have fun playing astronaut."

With that, she's gone, and I'm left desperately trying to grab on to the shreds of happiness I felt moments ago.

I'd only just begun to get over my attack nightmares, but Anna's point about the danger our families might face throws all that progress straight out the window.

That night I wake up clutching sweat-sodden sheets, images of Emmaline, Mom, and Dad in huge explosions reverberating through my head. To my dismay, the dreams only get worse as the week goes on.

Unable to handle the horrific images my brain comes up with every night, I end up programming Ruby to nudge me awake whenever my droidlet senses my heart racing. That does manage to help during those hours, but daytime distractions are few and far between. Najma is too busy with her secret task, which is clearly taking up far more time than she'd originally estimated. Esteban invited me to study with the boys, but after a couple of tries I couldn't handle their ridiculousness and opted to study alone. Sasha hasn't answered my vidchat requests ever since I told him that he was my replacement.

There's a bitterness growing inside me that I don't like.

Sasha would do better here. Sasha could handle anything. He probably knows it, too. That must be why he's stopped talking to me. I don't want to admit how much I miss talking to him, so I stop trying to call. Instead, I throw myself even more into working on our spaceplane. If Lizzie is right, that's at least one place where I'm making a real, positive difference.

Ruby and I spend more and more time in the hangar, and the

days tick by one by one, counting down until our families will begin their journeys here.

As we make our way through what I would normally think of as spring, the never-ending Antarctic sun begins to change into the never-ending Antarctic dark. The cold grows sharper, but that doesn't stop Dr. Schuber from marching us all out into it today.

I'd complain, but he did so for good reason. The full spacesuits we were measured for a month ago are ready for us to wear, and we need to get photographed in them for the media.

Sleep deprivation can't ruin this one. We. Have. *Spacesuits*.

"This is one of the proudest moments of my life," Dr. Schuber proclaims. The head of the ISECG puffs up with pure delight, his usual relaxed attitude forgotten as he watches his team walk around, dressed for space for the first time. Rahim and I wait with him outside one of the smaller buildings on the island complex, under a portable shelter with heaters cranked as high as possible. Ruby is clipped to my side, powered down for the moment.

"Pictures in SPACE!" Esteban gleefully bounces in slow motion toward the little building in front of us. Dr. Schuber beams at him through his scarf. I can tell by the way his eyes crinkle.

"Proudest moment of his life," Rahim says quietly to me, with a small gesture at Schuber and Esteban.

I smile. Rahim is growing on me. Sasha *does* have good taste in friends. Even if he isn't talking to me now.

Najma leaves the building, squeaking quickly past Dr. Schuber. My smile fades. Najma's the youngest of us all, and we've put a lot of pressure on her. But if anyone is going to break into Schuber's files without him noticing, she'll be the one to do it.

"How did the pictures go?" Rahim asks her.

"Fine," Najma says, before flitting away so she doesn't have to talk to Dr. Schuber.

Esteban disappears into the building for his turn with the photographer, and I wait outside with Dr. Schuber and Rahim. Anna and Tomoki already had their turn earlier, and a few minutes ago headed back to the main complex. Or rather, *Anna* headed back and Tomoki tagged along to bother her instead of waiting for his dorm mates. Sometimes I actually feel bad for Anna.

Sometimes.

After a few minutes, it's my turn. Ruby and I head to the building, leaving our warm shelter for a brief, but difficult, sprint through the cold Antarctic air. My security agents follow me, stopping just outside to guard the door. Once I get inside, I let out a massive shiver. I should have worn my helmet on the way over instead of carrying it, because I know my cheeks must be bright red from windburn.

This is it?

I look around the building. It's essentially just a small room, crowded with equipment. I wonder if Dr. Schuber knows that his prize astronauts are getting photographed inside a glorified broom closet.

144

I wake up Ruby and look to the ISECG photographer for instructions.

"This way, please," she says, positioning us where she wants us among her props. I hold my helmet under my arm, sitting on a tall black stool in my bulky suit. It's definitely awkward, but far too cool to complain about.

The photographer moves back to her camera and tells me to smile, but I don't need the reminder. I'm in my actual EMU—or at least, the model that will fit me until I grow some more. True giddiness bubbles inside me for the first time in ages, and I more than oblige her requests.

This is a suit meant for *me* and me alone. Not Sasha. *Me.* Like I'm actually meant to be here. Like I'm equal to all the other cadets. Our grades aren't pinned to our suits. Just our mission logo.

"Head more to the left," the lady instructs.

I do as she says, even though shifting even slightly is tough in these heavy outfits. Ruby clings to special straps on my side. Mimicking my posture, she's bright-eyed and awaiting action, just like when I start her up for spaceplane work. Behind us to the side, there's that umbrella thing they use on picture day at school.

"Okay, now look up and to the right, like you're stargazing," the woman requests.

I glance up toward the white ceiling, and Ruby does the same.

"Perfect." She clicks her camera rapidly. It reflects off the backdrop behind me, illuminating the entire tiny room for a brief moment. "Now do the same to the left."

I twist my head again, feeling the weight of the suit rub against my shoulders. In space, without gravity to worry about, the suits will definitely be more comfortable. It's been a while since I've let myself dream about our actual Mars mission, what with everything else going on. It's a relief to just have a moment to remember the amazing experience I'm going to have in a few years. I look up at the ceiling again, readying for the next string of pictures.

Then the photographer's camera explodes.

CHAPTER 12

Haze. Blurry, gray haze. And a pungent smell that makes my lungs seize up. That's what I notice first.

Someone's shaking me. No. Pushing me? Prodding me.

I groan, blinking my eyes, which are inexplicably desert dry and tearing up all at once. Everything's orange. *What's going on? Who . . . ?*

The prodding continues, at a neat, regular interval. Poke. Poke. Poke.

Oh. Of course.

Through the smoke and firelight, Ruby jabs me with one of her utility arms. I blink harder, tremors going through my body. "Ruby?" My voice shakes as much as the rest of me, and all that shaking knocks my memories into place.

The blast!

I sit bolt upright. Ruby stops her prodding, and my droidlet pings.

:WAITING FOR INSTRUCTION:

"Ruby!" I gasp, grabbing her. The entire room is on fire. The camera is completely incinerated. And the photographer is nowhere to be seen.

Behind me, the ISECG flag tips toward the floor, engulfed in flames. I scramble backward, clutching Ruby as embers fling toward us. One catches me on the forehead, and I yelp. The pole hits the ground, clattering in the inferno.

I stand up and then immediately duck back down in a fit of coughs. The smoke is too thick. *Where's the door?! Where's the photographer?!*

Getting to my knees, I drag myself across the floor, under the smoke. My suit weighs on me like a collapsing star, and in the intense heat I almost feel like I'm in one.

I can hear people shouting outside over the crackling of the flames. The backdrop from the photo session falls to the floor, sending a *whoosh* of fire straight out.

RUN! My brain screams at me.

Smoke or no smoke, I pull myself and the impossibly heavy suit up and slam bodily into the door. The flash of fire comes straight at me, and I throw my hands up to block it.

The door doesn't budge. My gloves ignite.

Ripping them off, I grab for the door handle and let out a shriek. It *burns*. It's almost molten hot. My skin prickles up, and I recoil, until another swath of fire forces me back.

Everything's moving. Everything's in flames. I can't see. I can't hear. I can't *anything* anymore. *I have to get out of here!*

Now people are pounding outside. I feel the vibrations through the door.

"Ruby!" I order, my voice dry against the smoke. My head feels as heavy as my suit, and I know that if I mess this up, I'm going to run out of time. "Open!"

Ruby spins on the side of my suit toward the door, as I mime what she needs to do. She extends one of her arms forward, twisting out a pair of supersized pliers. Latching onto the handle, she turns . . .

. . . And the two of us collapse through the Antarctic air, face-first onto the gray rocks outside.

"Miranda!" I hear someone—*Dr. Schuber?*—yell. I don't hear much else before everything goes dark once again.

Aside from a few first- and second-degree burns— and another bout of smoke inhalation—I'm otherwise undamaged. The photographer hasn't been found, but according to the news she's an internationally wanted assassin, so that's . . . fun.

"Can I ask the obvious question?" Tomoki says from the chair next to mine. We're in one of the common study areas. Almost everyone has been taking turns hanging out with me after this latest attack, which I've appreciated more than I've been able to say.

"Yeah?" I answer, looking up from the work I'd been doing on Ruby.

Tomoki flips his solar cell into the air. "Why aren't you dead?"

I raise an eyebrow.

He catches the little disc as it falls back down. "Don't take that the wrong way," Tomoki says. "I'm glad you're not. But if a famous assassin was sent to kill you, why *aren't* you dead? You can't just be that lucky."

I go back to polishing Ruby's outer armor, attempting to get the last of the scorch marks off her red exterior. "Not sure I'd call myself lucky," I mumble, staring at my bandaged hands.

"But you *are*," he insists, leaning back in his chair. "You've been targeted three times and survived. Probability says that doesn't make sense. Come on. At least one of those times you should've been exploded into fleshy little pieces."

"Can we *not* talk about all the times I've nearly been blown up?" I ask, scrubbing even harder at Ruby's plating. "Believe it or not, it's not fun to think about."

Tomoki shrugs. "Fine, new topic. Is Najma any closer to getting into Dr. Schuber's account and finding out who knows about the replacements?"

I don't even try to hide my exaggerated sigh. "Tomoki. When she knows, you'll know."

After a few minutes of silence, my droidlet beeps to remind us to get to programming. I put away Ruby's polishing cloth, and Tomoki and I head over together. Rahim offers me a sympathetic smile when I enter. I smile back and take my seat, tucking Ruby under my chair.

I try my best to concentrate through Dr. Schuber's lecture and practice exercises, but my hands prickle and even the slightest of noises make me jump. Every time I outwardly show any sign of nerves, I know Anna must be rolling her eyes from the desk behind mine. At least I'm not alone in my frazzled behavior. Poor Najma is almost equally as jittery, though for entirely different reasons.

"Miranda, can I talk to you for a moment?" Dr. Schuber asks after class wraps up. "Najma, don't go far, this concerns you, too."

Everyone looks at us from our two rows of chairs, obviously all thinking the same thing: *Oh no, he knows what we've been up to!*

Slowly, the other cadets file out, with Najma giving me one last, wide-eyed look before she steps to wait just outside the door. I get up from my seat and walk up to Dr. Schuber at the touch screen.

"Is everything okay?" I ask, rolling up my tablet and clasping it behind my back. Outside in the hall, a bomb-sniffing dog makes its rounds with its handler, who pauses once to look at me and then continues down the corridor.

"I've noticed you're having trouble in this class," Dr. Schuber says.

My face pales. An entire new set of butterflies migrates into my stomach, and I barely find myself able to respond. "A little," I admit.

"Listen, I know you've had some rough times lately," Dr. Schuber says, scratching the top of his graying hair. "I mean, really rough times. It's no secret that all these attacks are affecting you. It's okay to feel upset, you know."

I nod along, not sure what else to do.

"If you need some time to compose yourself, we could probably arrange things to get you safely home," he continues. "No one is supposed to leave the island, but I could pull some strings if you want to get out of here."

I stare at him. *Wait. Is he saying I should leave?* Sweat stings the wounded palms of my hands. *Is this some roundabout way of kicking me out?*

"I'd rather stay, if I can," I answer slowly. "I'll work harder. I promise." I'm not really sure *how* I'll work harder than I have been, but I'll find a way. Maybe I just won't sleep. Quarterly exams are coming up again, and I'll be up late studying for those, anyway, so I'm sure it won't make a big difference if I just cut sleep out entirely.

"Well, if that's the case, then it might be a good idea for you to team up with another cadet for a bit, as far as programming is concerned." Dr. Schuber leans back against the touch screen. "How about asking Najma for some help? I had Owen email you your quiz results. Maybe you can start with that. Have her help you learn where you went wrong."

I nod, probably a little too quickly. "Yes. Yes, I can do that. That sounds good."

"Let's call her in and see what she thinks."

I shake my head, desperate to keep Najma as far from Dr. Schuber as I can. "No, that's okay. I'll ask her myself."

"You're sure?"

"Absolutely."

Dr. Schuber considers me before responding. "Okay. Do let me know if you change your mind about heading home, though. Training twenty-four seven isn't for everyone."

"I can handle it," I say, clenching my fists tighter around my tablet scroll.

He studies me for another moment and then nods. I collect Ruby from under my seat and walk out of the room at a casual pace, but that turns into a dead sprint as soon as I reach the hall.

"Miranda!" Najma calls after me. "Miranda, wait!" She chases me down the hall, all the way to our dormitory.

I fling the door open, turning Ruby on for moral support.

"Hey, hey, calm down," Najma says on repeat, following me inside.

My bandaged hands are over my face as I throw myself into one of our plush dorm chairs. Ruby scuttles up one of the armrests, blinking her optical sensors in her quiet, reassuring way. "He wants me to leave!" I exclaim. "I didn't think I was doing *that* badly!"

"I heard your whole conversation, Miranda, and I don't think that's what that was about," Najma says. "I think he was just offering you a chance to take a little break."

"So he could prove I can't handle this!" I say, digging my fingers into my cheeks to stop any tears from leaking out. "Ugh! Why?"

"It's going to be fine," Najma says. "Why don't you let me take a look at that quiz? We can work through it tomorrow once I see what your code actually does."

"Are you sure?" I ask. "You already have so much on your plate with studying for exams and the whole file-hacking thing . . ."

"I think I've done about all I can with Schuber's files," she cuts me off. "So this really wouldn't be much trouble. Let me help you."

Her voice sounds guarded, so I hesitate, but only for a moment. Then I nod.

That night at dinner, Najma keeps clearing her throat and throwing us significant looks. She isn't the most subtle of people, I've noticed.

"Later," I mouth to her. We're surrounded by our professors right now, and if she wants to talk about what I *think* she wants to talk about, then she better stop hinting at it.

Unfortunately, this is where our language barrier comes into play.

"What did you say?" Najma whispers across the table to me. Of course, that just makes everyone look.

"Nothing," I answer quickly. Lipreading a foreign language probably isn't the easiest skill to pick up on the fly. But now that we all know something's up, all six of us start shoveling food into our mouths. Moments later, we get up and head down the hall together.

"Well?" Tomoki asks Najma. Our little herd rounds a bend toward the bio lab. We'd agreed it was a safe meeting place, since even with all the beefed up security, the camera feeds don't work in the cold storage. Apparently Esteban and Rahim found that out after they knocked over a tray of stem cells in there and never got blamed for it.

"Did you get in?" Esteban asks, pushing open the freezer doors.

Najma shakes her head once the doors close. "Dr. Schuber's system has changed. A lot." Her eyes drop.

Anna crosses her arms. I can see goosebumps on them from the cold. "How long until you can get past it?" she asks.

Najma looks up sharply. "Past it? I don't think you understand. He's got his system locked down. I don't think I *can* get past it."

"But then how do we learn who knows about the replacements?" Rahim asks.

Esteban shrugs. "We could always ask."

We all stare at him.

"What?" he asks.

"Esteban," I say slowly. "You want us to tell Mr. Burnett that we broke into his system?"

"Or Dr. Schuber?" Anna asks.

"Well, no." He goes a little pink. "They don't have to know *that*. We just need to ask them about what happens if one of us goes home and quits. And then when they tell us about our replacements, we'll ask who else knows. Boom! Suspect list made!"

"Never going to work," Anna shakes her head. "Dr. Schuber may already know Najma tried to break into his files again. Way too suspicious now."

"You're all acting like they're our enemies or something."
Esteban frowns. "I don't think they're against us."

"They might be," Anna says.

My mind flashes guiltily to Kreshkov. "We don't have any
real evidence for that," I say quickly, to myself as much as Anna.
"All we've established is that they're keeping something from us."

"Okay, so if we can't get into Dr. Schuber's system, why did
you drag us all in here, then?" Tomoki asks Najma.

"Because I found something . . . *shocking* in Miranda's quiz,"
Najma says.

Anna snorts. "What, a correct answer?"

"Shut up, Anna," I say, though I blush as Tomoki lets out a
laugh at Anna's quip.

"Listen." Najma glares at Anna and unrolls her tablet. "First
of all, Miranda's quiz was way different than mine. In fact, it was
a lot *harder* than mine."

I lean back against a shelf and groan. "Are you just saying that
to make me feel better?"

Najma shakes her head. "No. It's true. It was in a whole different language than what our quizzes were supposed to be in.
Look." Najma presses a button. "When I ran the code, this message appeared."

Words hover in the air above Najma's tablet:

GET OUT OF HERE IF YOU WANT TO LIVE.

THE WORST IS STILL COMING.

Tomoki lets out a low whistle. "Whoa. That's way cooler than
what my quiz's code did."

I'm shaking, and I don't think it's from the cold of the freezer. Another message. Like the ones from my Wirldwindo account. *Dr. Schuber put that in there?*

"Blunt." Anna nods, as if in approval. "Direct."

"Direct?" Tomoki snorts. "If Dr. Schuber wanted to warn Miranda of danger and get her to leave so we'd be safe, why doesn't he tell her all this to her face?"

Esteban for once is silent, furrowing his eyebrows in concern and looking over at me. Rahim watches me as well.

"Maybe he did," I say, barely louder than a whisper. My breath fogs in front of me. "Dr. Schuber just suggested I take some time off. That's what he talked to me about after class today. If I'd actually managed to crack this quiz on time, I would've had this warning before that photographer attacked me. But I didn't."

"Someone's been sending you anonymous tips ever since you got picked as a cadet, haven't they?" Najma asks. "Maybe it's been him."

"*Who* is he trying to warn her about, though?" Rahim asks.

"That is the real question," Anna says.

"Yeah," I agree, trying to get my trembling under control. "Seriously. It'd be way more helpful to know who's trying to hurt me, rather than all this vague 'watch out' nonsense I keep getting."

"If Dr. Schuber's been trying to warn you, it must be because he knows the danger you are up against but is prevented from revealing the culprit," Najma says. "Just like Mr. Burnett wouldn't give you a straight answer. Maybe they are afraid of someone here finding out, like—"

"We don't know for sure it's Dr. Schuber sending you all your messages, though," Tomoki says, before Najma can name Kreshkov. "This one, yes, but the others? Could be anyone."

"We should find a way to confirm it's been him," Najma says.

"Oh!" Esteban exclaims. "I can do that!"

We all turn.

"No, we're not just asking him to his face," Anna says.

Esteban ignores her comment. "Miranda, ever since I've found out about those warnings you get, I've been developing a social simulator to try to pin down who could be your secret messenger. If you give me access to the messages you've gotten, I could run them through and match their source code and word choice against messages from Dr. Schuber—and any of our teachers, for that matter."

"Esteban, that's awesome." I blink. "Thank you."

Esteban grins. "I might not be as good as Najma, but I do what I can."

Najma flushes at the compliment.

"That's one trail to follow," Anna says. "But finding out who's trying to save you doesn't answer who's trying to kill you. I'm going to examine past security feeds. It's time we learned for ourselves who was around our helicopter before it blew, and who that photographer was talking to here."

I nod. "Probably a good idea if there are two sets of eyes on the security feeds. And no, I'm not about to suggest me." I hold up a hand to stop her immediate protest.

"I'll do it," Rahim says.

I watch Anna. She can't really say no to *Rahim*, can she? Her face twists a bit, and I'm pleased to see that she can't.

"You keep trying to get into Dr. Schuber's files," Anna instructs Najma. "We need to know who else knows about Miranda's replacement. And you keep an eye on Kreshkov," she says to Tomoki. "He's top of the suspect list, still."

"Hey, there's no way Kreshkov's got anything to do with this." Tomoki's eyes flash.

"Actually," Najma interjects, cautiously. "Now that we're talking about it, the first time I broke into Dr. Schuber's files there were a lot of emails between him and Kreshkov." She hits one fist into her opposite hand. "Oh, if only I'd thought to read them!"

"Hold on, you hacked into Dr. Schuber's email account and didn't actually *read* any of his emails?" Tomoki asks.

"Of course not," Najma says. "Why would I invade his privacy like that?"

Tomoki stares at her. "Do you hear yourself?"

"Kreshkov's nephew does want to be a Mars cadet, so we can't ignore that they have motive," Anna says, getting the conversation back on track.

My eyes narrow at her word choice: *"they."* "Wait, wait, hold on." I feel my heartbeat kick up a notch. "You aren't suggesting that Sasha is involved, are you?"

At that, literally *everyone* stares at me.

"Uh, well, *yeah*, I mean . . ." Esteban trails off when he catches my wounded look. "Or not! That, too!"

"Clearly it's a possibility." Anna shoots Esteban an exacer-
bated glare. "What makes you think he wouldn't be?"

"Rahim." I turn toward the quietest member of our group.
"Come on, you're his friend, too! You know he wouldn't ever be
involved in anything like this."

Rahim shakes his head. "I hope he wouldn't. We haven't spoken much since I became a cadet, though. Anything is possible,
but I don't think this is very likely."

"It isn't!" I agree immediately. "He's not a bad person. He's
taking this whole thing really well, actually. We *have* spoken
since I became a cadet, and he's been completely supportive."
Well, we were *speaking until* . . .

"When was the last time you spoke?" Anna asks, as if reading
my thoughts.

"A month or two ago," I reply. "I . . ." I bite at my lip, the cold
of the freezer stinging it. Guilt creeps into my stomach. *I told him*
everything. My voice drops to a lower volume. "I, uh, explained
some of what we found."

Najma's eyes widen. "Miranda, what did you tell him?"

I look around helplessly at everyone.

"Did you tell him he was your official replacement?" Tomoki
asks.

"I . . ."

"Oh my god, Miranda! You're a bigger idiot than even *I'd*
imagined!" Anna spins away, slamming her hand into a wall.
"What made you *possibly* think that was a good idea?"

"He's my friend!" I clench my fists. "He's not evil, and he had

160

a right to know! What if he gets targeted next?"

"Was this before or after that photographer tried to blow you up?" Tomoki asks next.

"Before," I say, "But that doesn't mean it's his fault!" I add quickly, as Tomoki groans.

"Miranda!" he exclaims.

"Come on, guys, you have to trust me on this!" I look to Esteban and Najma next, but they're both just shaking their heads at me in unison. "Look, we'll call him right now! You guys can confront him, and then you'll see."

I pick out his contact information on my droidlet.

"Rahim knows. He's his friend, too," I ramble, poking at Sasha's icon. A circle spins around his face as the call starts. "He's a good person. Sasha wouldn't try to—"

But I'm cut off with a *bzz-bzz* sound. My droidlet flashes orange.

CONTACT UNREACHABLE AT THIS CONNECTION.

CONTACT MAY HAVE DELETED YOUR APPROVAL

FOR COMMUNICATION.

I gape.

"Gee, *that's* not suspicious at all," Anna says

"Sasha," I whisper. "No."

CHAPTER 13

I sit in our dining hall, prodding at my sandwich. Everyone chats around me, but I can't talk to them. No matter how I've tried to get in touch with Sasha, he still isn't returning any of my messages. I hate what that's made me start wondering.

But with our quarterly exams going on once again, I haven't had tons of time to try and solve this mystery. No one has, which is rough. Our families are flying here today, and since we still haven't figured out who's behind the attacks, we're all on edge worrying about their safety.

"Tomorrow you'll have your second practical exam," Dr. Schuber tells us from his seat at the end of the table. I set my sandwich down to listen. "After your families arrive, you'll have some time with them before the test. The exam itself will begin at fourteen hundred hours."

I glance at my droidlet. It's half past twelve. Our practical is in twenty-five and a half hours, but more importantly, my family will have left the house by now. They're already traveling.

They're going to be fine, I tell myself. *They've got loads of guards.*

"Please prepare as you would for a real mission," Dr. Schuber continues, setting his napkin on the table in a rumpled heap. "We will assess your performance throughout the day, and, unlike last time, you will be given a review."

I look over at Lizzie. She nods reassuringly from across the table. But then Kreshkov smiles at me from the seat next to her, and I suck in a breath, quickly turning away.

"What happens if we fail?" Tomoki asks.

"Yeah," Esteban chimes in. "Would you really flunk us out? Get replacements for us or something?"

Anna shoots the two boys a piercing glare before I manage to do so myself.

What are they thinking?! Way to fail at subtlety! I want to yell at them both, but they're giving each other smug looks. They must've planned this ahead of time. Ugh.

Dr. Schuber considers the boys for a moment. Rahim barely contains a groan, rubbing his face with his hands. I try to watch Kreshkov's reaction out of the corner of my eye, but his face reveals nothing.

"If you did poorly on this exam, we would assign you extra training time and take it out of your free time," Dr. Schuber simply says. "We want you to succeed."

I wonder if Dr. Schuber has me in mind when he's thinking

about someone needing extra training time. But I also wonder if he avoided the question about replacements on purpose. Has Esteban gotten any closer to figuring out if Dr. Schuber has been my secret messenger all along?

The professor scoots back from the table and stands up. "Best of luck today." As his eyes make contact with mine they seem to linger for a moment.

"All right, let's get you to your classroom." Lizzie claps her hands together. "Calculus exam next!"

I hide a grimace as Anna walks out ahead of everyone else, giving me one last haughty look. There's just way too much to worry about right now. My brain is going to go supernova.

Miraculously, my brain survives, but just barely. Quarterly exams wrap up, save for the spaceplane practical, and our families arrive, safe and sound.

"Mom! Dad! Emmaline!"

They dash forward to meet me after going through two separate security scanners. The military-grade heli-jets they arrived in power down in the dark at the edge of the island, and I fall into my mom's arms. Ruby gets squished between us.

"Miranda!" Emmaline yells, gleefully leaping up onto my side and clinging to it like a monkey. I tip over. Now I've got a robot on one arm and a six-year-old on the other.

"Whoa there!" My dad leans in to support Emmaline, wrapping his arms around me as well.

They're all here. I hadn't realized how much I'd missed them until this moment. Mom's hair is still messy, Dad's mechanical watch still ticks loudly, and Emmaline is still a little snot factory. I'd missed it all.

"It's great to see you, kiddo," my dad says, his breath fogging as he pulls Emmaline off my side. I can hardly believe how much she's grown in just a few short months.

"We've missed you so much," my mom adds. She rubs her arms for warmth in the Antarctic wind.

"I've missed you, too," I say. Then I laugh at my shivering family. "Not used to the temperatures here, huh?"

They laugh in return. Around us, the other cadets greet their own families in the soft starlight of Antarctic midmorning. I recognize Esteban's parents and his little brothers. Both of the boys are climbing on Esteban, and he's laughing loudly enough that it's practically echoing off the ocean. Behind him, Tomoki is chatting with his parents near the portable lights the staff are using to help unload luggage, and Najma is hugging her mom tight. What looks to be her dad and her older brother stand near her.

Off to my side, Rahim has an entire crowd of people. Parents, it looks like, and also maybe grandparents. Then there's a boy a bit older than he is and two younger girls. Finally, Anna stands a ways away from the heli-jets with her father. I recognize him from the Advancing Astronomy Competition. They aren't hugging. In fact, it looks like Anna's getting some sort of lecture, though it is hard to tell in the dark. Her head is lowered, and her dad is gesticulating wildly.

"Does Ruby know any new tricks since you rebuilt her?"

Emmaline asks, drawing my scanning gaze back to my own family.

I nod, hefting Ruby up higher. "Tons. I've been programming her to help build our spaceplane."

"Our flight engineer." My mom beams. "We're so proud of you."

My dad rubs my head, and Emmaline reaches toward my mechbot. "Can I hold Ruby?"

"Nope," I say, shifting Ruby up in my arms higher away from my sister.

"Aww!" Emmaline pouts. "Come on! Just for a second?"

"No way." I turn. "How about we go inside, where it's warm?" I suggest, starting to walk toward the main complex.

"Just for half a second? I'll be careful, I promise!" Emmaline begs as we all trek toward the big building. I'm relieved that my family doesn't mention the security agents who trail us. I wonder if they made Emmaline promise not to point them out, for my sake.

"Miranda, let your sister hold the robot," my mom says.

"No!" I look at my mom. "Ruby isn't a toy."

Emmaline throws her arms across her chest. "Fine! Then when you come home next, you can't play with my new engineering blocks!"

"Emmaline, do you see this place?" I gesture with my free arm at all the buildings we're passing. "Like I'd want to play with some little kid engineering blocks." I hold Ruby even higher after Emmaline tries to jump after her.

"Be nice." My mom sighs, exasperated, as we all enter the main building together. Bright lights greet us, and we unzip our coats. "Honestly, you two have been back together for all of thirty seconds, and you're already fighting."

"It's probably been closer to three hundred and thirty seconds," I say without thinking.

My dad starts laughing. "Is it weird that I missed this?"

We all laugh at that, heading down the hall toward my room.

Shortly after showing my family my dormitory, we regroup with some of the other cadets and their families in the lobby to continue the tour together. But before we can get far, we're intercepted by our mentors and a bunch of our professors.

"You still have the spaceplane practical to prepare for," Dr. Mayworth not-so-subtly reminds us.

"We'll take over as tour guides for now," Dr. Singh adds.

A frown creeps over my face, and I can hear Tomoki and Esteban in particular expressing disgruntlement from over by the Apollo mission posters.

"It's okay, kiddo," my dad tells me. Emmaline ducks behind him now that we're surrounded by a bunch of people she doesn't know. "We'll have plenty of time to catch up later."

I sigh. "I suppose so."

"You poor thing, having to go prepare for a launch simulation. Being a Mars cadet is quite the full-time job, isn't it?" my mom comments, grinning slyly at me.

"Yeah, okay, you've made your point, Mom," I say, shooing her away. "Just get going already."

My parents follow our professors down the hall, pulling Emmaline along behind them, and I can't help but smile watching them go. It really is good to have them here.

After our families disappear, the six of us gather together for a final pep talk from our mentors.

"This is different than your first practical," Lizzie reminds us once we're all seated in a semicircle setup of maroon chairs. Esteban fidgets next to me, and Anna's expression is unreadable next to him. "You'll need to suit up, go to your mission-briefing area, and take some fake press photos before even boarding *Ambassador.*"

Well, everyone but me will suit up. I awkwardly lean back, looking down at my hands. My burns may have healed, but my EMU was too badly damaged in the fire to wear for this run. It'd be a lie to say I'm not disappointed.

"We're doing our best to give you an authentic experience," Mr. Burnett says. "Prepare yourselves accordingly."

"Everyone keeps saying it's so you can feel ready for your mission in a few years, but personally I think we're also doing it for fun at this point." Kreshkov smiles at us. "So don't worry too much. We'll be watching from Mission Control."

"You won't be in the spaceplane with us?" Najma asks. "I thought—"

"Oh no," Lizzie says. "Vlad and I have done enough run-throughs and practices with you kids that you should be able to handle it on your own."

We all glance at each other. They start passing out the EMU

layers, and I shrink back even further as everyone stands up.

"Sorry again about your suit," Mr. Burnett says, stepping over to me. "It's a real shame you'll have to miss out on that part of the experience. Real shame."

"It's all right." I set my shoulders. He looks more upset than I feel.

Mr. Burnett bites at his lip. "Maybe we can—"

"Not so fast!" Lizzie darts over, her eyes sparkling. "Miranda, you didn't think we'd forgotten about you, did you?"

"Huh?" I ask. Mr. Burnett looks over sharply.

"Vlad!" Lizzie calls. The Russian cosmonaut walks over with a box in tow. His eyes sparkle, too, and I'm caught by surprise yet again at how much I can see Sasha in them.

"A new EMU, just for you!" Kreshkov says, thumping one hand on the outside of the box.

I gasp, jumping to my feet. "Really?!"

Mr. Burnett's mouth gapes wide open. "That's not possible. How did you . . . ?"

"It was our little secret." Lizzie winks at Mr. Burnett. "We didn't even tell Dr. Schuber. Miranda deserves this suit, especially after all she's been through. We couldn't let her go through the day without one. Not with her whole family here to see her."

"We put in a rush order," Kreshkov explains. "It's just as operational as all the others." He sets the box at my feet, and I finally find the right words.

"Thank you," I say. "I . . ." I look at Lizzie, then at Kreshkov. In this moment, I'm not sure I could suspect the man of hurting a mosquito, much less organizing a string of deadly attacks. A smile breaks over my face. "*Thank* you."

Next to them, Mr. Burnett's eyes shimmer.

"Mr. Burnett?" I ask. "Are you—?"

He clears his throat and smiles. "That was really thoughtful of you both," Mr. Burnett says to Lizzie and Kreshkov. "I'll go find Dr. Schuber and let him know the good news."

He retreats before I can question him any further. My eyes narrow. This is the last straw. Dr. Schuber's weird warnings and Mr. Burnett's jumpy behavior . . .

Does Dr. Schuber know Mr. Burnett suspects what's going on around here? Does Mr. Burnett know Dr. Schuber's been warning me? Either way, why haven't either of them done anything useful with their knowledge other than use it to freak me out?

My resolve strengthens. After this practical exam, I need to talk the team into confronting Mr. Burnett in person. It's time to get some straight answers, and I get the feeling we can make Mr. Burnett talk.

Two hours later, I zip up the front of my flight suit and look at myself in my mirror. I have to admit, I look pretty awesome. Well, except for my head. My CCA—Communications Carrier Assembly, or fancy phrase for "cloth helmet"—sits over most of my hair, but not all of it. A few strands stick out.

I straighten out the orange paneling along the front of my body. As I do, I can feel the light tubing in my first layer of net-like clothing shift. The rubber layer over it squeaks.

"Ready, Ruby?" I ask. My mechbot sits on her table, having just finished her diagnostics.

She bobs her head at me. I bend down awkwardly in the big suit, and she climbs onto my back, hooking four of her ten appendages into the special clasps Lizzie asked the suit engineers to include.

"I can do this," I say, taking one last look in the mirror. "I got this. I won't mess up." Mirror-me's expression isn't very reassuring, so I quickly turn away and walk out the door.

Anna is already in the common room, waiting. "We're going to be late," she says.

"I—" I start to defend myself, but then she glares at Najma's still-closed door.

"At least you're out here. I was sure you'd be last."

Najma walks out. "Are we all ready?" she asks. Her helmet is held under her arm, and her hair looks way better tucked into its CCA than mine does.

"We've *been* ready," Anna says.

Lizzie comes into the dorm. "Sounds like the three of you are set to go." She beams at us. "You all look awesome. Just plain awesome. And Miranda, I can't wait to see you in your full EMU. You ready for the quick change?"

I nod. Now that I've got my suit again, Tomoki and I will be graded on putting on our full Extravehicular Mobility Units during the practical, while the others get graded on helping us. Honestly, that's the part of all this I'm least nervous about.

Lizzie snaps a quick picture of us with her droidlet. "Great!

I'll walk you over. I'm excited to see you all work as a team today!"

Anna opens our door and heads out, scoffing under her breath. I ignore her and follow Najma out the door. Lizzie drops in step behind us.

We walk through the halls to the lobby, photos of past astronaut teams flanking us. As we step out into the cold and the dark, mock paparazzi take our pictures, and an entire security task force surrounds us. Tomoki and Rahim approach from behind, and I look around once they've joined us. *Where's Esteban?*

"Miranda!" My little sister calls out. She and my parents stand off to the side in a crowd with our professors and the other families. Emmaline dashes toward me in her thick purple coat. A security agent steps forward to stop her, and I shoot him a glare. He notices and retreats back a couple of paces to give us room.

"Sorry. Reflex," he mutters.

"Hey there, Emmaline!" I set down my helmet to grab my sister and lift her up into the air. I regret my decision about half a second into the lift. My flight suit is heavy enough, and my sister isn't nearly as light as she used to be. I set her back down quickly. "You ready to watch your big sister blast off?"

"You're not really blasting off." Emmaline struggles to get out of my grip as her feet land back on the ground. "Mom said so. She said this is just practice."

"And she's right," I say. The other cadets pause around me, and I throw them a sheepish grin. "Just a second, guys." Then I kneel down with Emmaline. "So, are you ready to watch your big sister *pretend* to blast off?"

"Yes! But next time, you need to come home, okay? It's weird that it's night in the middle of the afternoon. And it's too cold!" She shivers dramatically, and I laugh again.

"I will if they let me." I put my helmet over my sister's head. "There. Now you look like you could lend us a hand. Ready?"

"Hey!" Emmaline giggles. "I can't see in here!"

"Miranda," Anna says. "Come on. We can't waste time."

"Let her have her moment," Rahim says. I look up at him in surprise. He smiles as Emmaline takes my helmet off. "She's cute."

I glance over to where his family stands, my eyes falling on Rahim's two little sisters. "Okay, Emmaline." I turn back to her. "I've got to go now."

"Okay, fine. Hey, can we play with your room's touch table when you're done?"

"Sure. Once I'm done." I take my helmet from Emmaline, and then send her back toward our parents. Walking on, I pass the hangar and head toward the boat dock. A flock of terns flies overhead, fighting the wind. Najma, Anna, Tomoki, and our mentors have gotten ahead of Rahim and me, and we hurry to catch up. But before we do, Esteban intercepts us.

"Miranda!" He shoves his tablet at me. "It's Mr. Burnett!"

I blink. "What?"

Esteban's glowing tablet screen is covered in lines of code.

"My program finally finished. I wanted to find you earlier, but Lizzie said I couldn't go to your rooms when you were changing. But it's Mr. Burnett! He's the one that was sending you messages!"

"Mr. Burnett?" I repeat.

"Of course." Rahim nods in comprehension. "Dr. Schuber didn't make your quiz. Mr. Burnett's his grad student. I bet he did."

"He must've had to switch methods to talk to you when you weren't getting the Wirldwindo messages," Esteban says. Wind blasts past us, stinging my raw cheeks. I glance back at the security team following us, but the howling wind makes me doubt they heard any of what Esteban said. Meanwhile, thoughts crash over each other like overlapping waves inside my head.

This changes everything.

It hasn't been Dr. Schuber warning me at all. It's been Mr. Burnett since day one. He's the only one who's been trying to help me, while also having to deal with the paranoia of knowing what's going on and keeping his knowledge secret. Which means Dr. Schuber never knew anything about any of this. Either that, or . . .

"Guys." I shudder, remembering the conversation I overheard between Mr. Burnett and Lizzie in the kitchen all those weeks ago. *Why didn't I see this before?* "What if Mr. Burnett knows because he's close to Dr. Schuber?"

Esteban frowns. "But if he knows who Dr. Schuber told about your replacement, why wouldn't he go to the ISECG when he found out they were trying to hurt you?"

I shake my head. "No, I don't mean Mr. Burnett knows who Dr. Schuber *told*. I mean he knows *Dr. Schuber*."

The boys both look at me. There's a motive there—a motive

that makes me feel like I'm going to throw up.

I swallow, trying to steady my stomach. "Dr. Schuber wasn't warning me about the attacks. He wasn't trying to look out for me. Mr. Burnett was." The queasy feeling gets worse. "Maybe everyone's been right all along. The United States probably *did* force Dr. Schuber and the ISECG to pick me. And maybe this is their way of trying to get rid of me."

Rahim's eyes widen.

"Everything okay back here?" a voice asks, and I nearly jump out of my flight suit.

It's Dr. Schuber.

I grip my helmet and stare up at him. My response is a dead giveaway that we've been talking about something secret, but I can't help myself.

"Everything's great!" Esteban gushes. From anyone else, it would've seemed suspicious, but from Esteban, it's totally believable. "Ready for our practical!"

"Glad to hear it," Dr. Schuber says. "Better catch up to everyone else. They're already at the launchpad."

The three of us follow the professor. Esteban keeps shooting me looks, but if I acknowledge him, I know he'll end up saying something revealing. We can't afford that right now. I think back to Mr. Burnett's reaction to my suit earlier. *What exactly is going on? What is Dr. Schuber planning?*

"Here's where you'd usually get briefed by Mission Control," Lizzie says, interrupting my thoughts as we arrive at the helicopters. She's clearly already begun talking to the other three cadets.

"But we'll save that part of practice for a later exam. Today, just concentrate on launch procedures."

Kreshkov nods by her side. "After the countdown is complete, Mission Control will talk to you as if you've lifted off. We expect you to act like you have, and go through all procedures until you've reached the thermosphere."

If the ISECG is behind all this stuff, maybe Kreshkov is innocent. And that makes Sasha innocent! But that still doesn't explain why Sasha's dropped off the face of the planet. . . .

"At that point, you proceed with Miranda and Tomoki's quick change," Kreshkov continues. "And then we'll end the simulation, and you six will be allowed to leave the spaceplane to meet with us and get your grades."

"But don't let the grading part of this get to you," Lizzie interjects. "Seriously, use this as practice. The grades will only reflect which areas require more training and go toward determining if we've made the right decision regarding your individual job assignments."

I grip my helmet with my right hand. Even with everything else going on, I can't help but worry about my place in the group. *Please don't take flight engineer away from me.*

"Speaking of." Lizzie looks at me as if she's read my mind. "We really should all give a big thanks to Miranda. She's stayed late every night working to get your spaceplane as operational as possible."

I can tell my face is red, and not just from the windburn.

"Indeed," Dr. Schuber says from behind me. "Kudos to Miranda."

I turn, and he smiles at me, but it's a fake smile and alarm bells go off in my head.

"And to all of you," the professor continues. "Though when we're done with this practical exam, perhaps one of you could enlighten me as to why you've been trying to break into my email?" Dr. Schuber holds up his tablet. A flashing red X flickers in the left-hand corner. "Got this notice last night." His eyes fall on Najma, and she starts to tremble in her flight suit.

Oh god. He knows. Keep it together, Najma! I will my thoughts at my friend. We all remain silent.

"Anyhow, it's time to go." Dr. Schuber gestures to the helicopters, which are lined up next to the heli-jets that brought our families here.

If only there was a way I could tell the others about my new suspicions without Dr. Schuber noticing. *I wish Mr. Burnett was here.* I look around for my newly unmasked secret messenger. *Where is he, anyway?*

"Do your best. We'll talk about this breach in trust later," our professor finishes, rolling up his tablet and tucking it behind his back.

"Good luck!" Lizzie says brightly—a complete contrast to the head of the ISECG.

"I have every confidence you will do well," Kreshkov adds. Maybe his words are meant to be reassuring, but his dark eyes aren't even looking at us. They're fixed on Dr. Schuber's tablet, and I can't decide what that means.

Esteban jumps in front of me to high-five both of our mentors. Not to be outdone, Tomoki high-fives them as well, and soon, each of us are getting high fives from Kreshkov and Lizzie. I give Esteban a grateful smile for breaking the tension. He gives me a giant thumbs-up in return.

When it's my turn for a Lizzie high five, she clasps my hand and holds on to it for an extra moment, squeezing it. A smile wrinkles the corners of her mouth. "You'll do great. Remember to have some fun."

"Thanks," I say. And then we're whisked away. Lizzie and Kreshkov wave as all six of us get shuttled onto helicopters for the trip to our launchpad. Before we depart, Dr. Schuber calls all of our attention back to where he stands on the helipad under a set of extremely bright lights.

"Headsets on," he instructs, miming the motion.

We do as we're told and flick on our headsets. Mine has a brief burst of static as it pops on, and I flinch. Dr. Schuber looks my way, and I gesture weakly to my earpiece. "Static," I explain. He nods.

"Best of luck to all of you," he says. "We'll be watching from Mission Control."

CHAPTER 14

It's like the speed of my thoughts is somehow influencing the speed of reality. The helicopter ride goes *way* faster than I remember from the first time. What feels like just moments after we've departed, we're already at the launchpad.

"Miranda," a voice calls as I go to leave the helicopter. I barely hear it over the roar of the rotor blades.

I turn. Wearing the pilot's headset is Mr. Burnett. I forgot that all our professors were flight certified. That must be why he wasn't there to see us off.

I step farther in for a moment to hear him better. "Yeah?"

Do I have time to ask him about Dr. Schuber? I hesitate. Behind me, Najma waits. We're on a schedule, and I'll lose exam points for any delays. But if there's another attack planned, maybe he'll give me a clue.

"You're going to do great," he says, taking off his headset. "Just don't let yourself get distracted. You are incredibly talented, even though I know you don't always feel like it. You can do this."

I nod, sighing. It's just awkward motivation. Par for the course from Mr. Burnett. "Thanks." I fiddle with the straps on my suit. "Would you mind if we talked after the practical? You once said I could come to you with questions. I . . . well, I have some."

Mr. Burnett's eyebrows pinch together. "Y-yeah. Yeah. Of course."

"Thanks," I say again. I wish that promise made me feel better, but I can't shake the undercurrent of worry. Regardless, I climb out of the helicopter and join Najma, repositioning Ruby to a more comfortable pose on my suit.

We head into the building across from the safety bunkers. I try to force my mind to relax as we ride the elevator to the gangplank. *Now isn't the time to be panicking. You can solve this mystery later. You've got an exam to complete. Settle down, concentrate, and prove to Dr. Schuber that you're not going to let him bully you out of the program!*

The elevator door opens and I wrestle my fears into my brain's file folders as we march across the gangplank. Just like before, each footstep lands with a metallic *clang* and the freezing wind threatens to blow us right off the walkway. We persevere, though, and soon enough we're at the door to *Ambassador*. Once we file inside, I climb the ladder to my seat, unhook Ruby from my back, and rehook her to the edge of my vertically tilted chair.

"Is this your mess?" Anna gestures to several scattered tools against the far wall.

"Oh, yeah, sorry," I say, scrambling over to clean up. I pile the tools into their box, including the new handheld 3D printer that Dr. Bouvier lent me. Hopefully he won't take points off my score for forgetting to give it back.

"*Ambassador, can you hear us?*" a voice calls over the speakers.

"Mission Control, we can hear you," Anna replies. I climb into my tilted seat just as the large metal door shuts behind us. The cabin door closes next.

"Commencing MCLC," the voice says. Then, moments later, "MCLC complete; commencing preflight alignment."

Tomoki sits in the pilot chair, tapping away at the keyboard. "Pressurization complete," he states, moving forward with our practical exam. "Cabin air is seventy-eight percent nitrogen, twenty-one percent oxygen, one percent water vapor."

"Confirmed," Esteban says from his seat to my left.

Rahim, on my right, nods. "Life support systems online."

"Najma, how many computers are running?" Anna asks.

"Eighteen of the twenty-six main drives are up," Najma replies. "Full power in seven minutes."

"Good," Anna says. "Miranda, begin diagnostics in eight minutes." Anna is our mission commander for this practical, but that's a job that will switch for each exam we do. Her official role is planetary geologist and copilot. Tomoki is pilot and secondary flight engineer. The two of them sit directly in front of me.

Rahim is our medic and also an engineer in his own right, specializing in life-support tech. He sits to my right. Najma is lead programmer, and she sits all the way to the left, just to the side of the pilot seats. Esteban is both secondary programmer and our communications officer. He sits in a seat directly behind Najma.

"Copy that," I reply, bringing up my console. The screen flickers to life, extending in a curve around my seat where nothing but air had been moments ago. The glow of the letters is brighter than ideal, and I make a mental note to ask Najma or Mr. Burnett to recode the brightness when we're done today.

Beside me, Rahim brings up his own display. He's running backup to my lead to catch anything I miss.

"All computers online," Najma reports, seven minutes and five seconds later.

"Miranda?" Anna says.

"I'm on it," I cut her off. With a tap of my finger, the diagnostic tests begin. I train my eyes on the flow of data as it rushes past me. Unlike last time, the tank systems and open/close mechanisms are all as they should be. To my surprise, we're operating at full fuel levels.

"They're really going for realism here," I say. "We're at one hundred percent fuel capacity."

"Awesome," Esteban replies. "Who's ready to go to Mars?"

Our laughter is cut off by a call from Mission Control. "Engineer Regent, repeat fuel assessment?" they request.

"One hundred percent capacity," I say.

"Are you certain?" Mission Control responds.

I review the data on the screen I've paused on. "Yes . . . ?" I answer slowly, glancing around at my crew. *They won't abort our practical because of another data discrepancy, will they?* I wonder to myself. *I mean, it wouldn't be my fault! If the numbers don't match, then the numbers don't match! Please don't make me responsible for another practice exam cut short . . .*

Mission Control is silent for a few moments. My breath is held. I don't dare go past this data screen. "Carry on," Mission Control eventually says.

I let out a huge sigh, which apparently everyone hears in their headsets because there's a lot of nervous giggling after it. I flush and go back to my data reading. The diagnostic tests have continued without me, and I have some catching up to do.

As I scroll through what I've missed, I'm amazed at how far we've come in five and a half short months—both our spaceplane and us as cadets. We're beginning to operate as a real astronaut team, and *Ambassador* is practically space ready, if not Mars ready. I scrutinize every detail passing in front of me on the screen. I won't be the weak link. I'll be just as ready as everyone else. I won't be distracted.

I spend the next two hours making sure of it.

"T minus ten minutes and counting," Esteban says as our preflight procedures wrap up. "Final safety check."

We all shuffle about in our seats, double-checking our safety belts and making sure our helmets are secured next to us. We've gotten permission not to actually wear our helmets during this practical exam, since they restrict head movement. I suspect Lizzie might've talked our professors into that decision.

"Confirm safety check," Anna commands.

"Safe for launch," Najma reports.

"Safe for launch," Esteban chimes in behind her.

"Safe for launch," Rahim says from my side.

"Safe for launch, yo," Tomoki pumps one fist into the air from his seat next to Anna.

I finalize the closing of our orbital vent valves with Mission Control. "Safe for launch," I confirm, once the vents are shut.

"T minus nine minutes and holding," Esteban says.

Even through the noise-reducing headset, I can hear our auxiliary engines begin to rumble. I hadn't realized they were going to actually fire them up. I was almost certain we'd just be getting cheesy commands like, "engines on," from Mission Control. But as I flick through my console, I confirm to myself that yes, in fact, our auxiliary engines are firing, even though we're "holding."

"Go, no-go, Mission Control?" Esteban asks during our designated prelaunch pause.

"You are go for launch," Mission Control says, and any worries I had about our engines fade away. Mr. Burnett did say they were trying to make this realistic for us, after all. I've gotten too paranoid for my own good. There's no way Dr. Schuber would risk danger to his spaceplane just to scare me off the mission. I need to settle down.

"T minus nine minutes and counting," Esteban says next.

I run the wing flaps, coating them with a fire retardant fluid that will soak into their insulating bricks as double protection for our "flight" through the atmosphere. Rahim checks their coverage next to me and gives them the green light when all is well.

"T minus eight minutes and counting."

"Booting up the secondary engines," Najma says. I hear another noise humming from our spaceplane. My stomach tingles with pride. I worked on those myself.

"*Ambassador,* this is Mission Control," a communication comes through. "*Abort mission,* repeat, *abort mission.*"

The stomach tingles stop. I freeze in the middle of retracting the tower arm. The tower arm, however, doesn't stop moving.

"T minus—" Esteban cuts off. "Abort mission?" he asks, obviously thrown. "Why?"

"Abort mission," the voice through the headset insists even louder. "Explanations later, abort now."

Is this part of the test? Or something else? I try to recapture control of the tower arm.

"Is there danger?" Rahim asks.

"Keep calm," Mission Control says. "Just abort *now.*"

"Wait," Esteban says. "Why can't you abort for us? Don't you have control?"

Good question. I certainly don't. The tower arm continues to leave us, and without any command from me, devices continue to become launch ready. *What's going on?*

"We've been locked out," the voice says. "Abort control is in your hands only."

Locked out. My breaths come in short, small bursts. This is . . . this is . . .

"Is this a drill?" Anna asks. "We're T minus five minutes and counting."

"This is not a drill."

And there it is. This isn't a drill. It's a real problem. And no one out there can help us.

"Then you heard them," Anna says, her tone back to commanding. "Abort."

All six of us immediately go to work. My brain fires at superspeeds. *Aborting from inside the spaceplane . . .* I try to recall the exact procedure, but everyone else is mumbling to themselves and I can't concentrate through the headset chatter. *Shutting down the main engine means first I need to override the—*

My screen freezes up the moment I finish entering the codes. "Najma, have you locked us from the override codes?" I ask.

"That's not me! I've been locked out of the entire spaceplane!" she responds in a panic, her fingers typing furiously. I can see that her screen is frozen just like mine.

"I can't get in, either," Rahim's usual calm voice quavers beside me.

"The whole plane's locked us out!" Esteban exclaims, slamming a hand hard against the side of his console.

I shake. *No. Dr. Schuber wouldn't. He loves this program too much to . . .* The thoughts loop on horrific repeat.

"Pilot controls still operational," Tomoki says. "But I can't shut down from here."

"What *can* you do?" I ask him, powering up Ruby and bringing my head back into the game.

Tomoki puts shaking hands on the flight controls. I swallow.

"T minus three minutes and counting," Anna whispers. We're all silent then, except for the panicked chatter of Mission Control over our communicators. Something has taken over our spaceplane. And whatever—or *whoever*—that something is, it's going to force us to blast off.

For real.

Ruby climbs onto my stomach, reaching for my screen controls. She's booted into mimic mode.

"I've got one last idea," I say. Ruby's head swivels to stare back at me. "If the computer controls are dead, maybe we can shut down manually."

"How?" Tomoki rapidly pushes a series of flight-related buttons at the console.

"My mechbot," I answer. "She can get into the wiring. Short-circuit it and cut our fuel."

"Won't that run the risk of us, oh, I don't know, *exploding?*" Tomoki asks, still slamming his hands around the cockpit controls.

"Only a small risk," Najma says. "As long as your mechbot is as good as you say she is."

"She is," I promise.

"T minus two minutes and counting," Anna says. "Do it. Send the robot in."

"Mission Control," Esteban says into his communicator.

"We're going to try and cut the fuel lines."

"Ruby," I say, blocking out Esteban and Mission Control's conversation.

She bobs her head.

:WAITING FOR INSTRUCTION:

I take a deep breath, typing in commands on her datapad as I blabber. "Get to the fuel center. You know where that is. Unhinge the blast door and disable the launch system. Then eject our fuel by cutting the lines and *get out of there*."

She retracts her datapad and skitters off, using her clawed legs to hook along the vertical flooring.

"Aren't you worried she'll be hurt?" Najma asks.

Yes. Terrified. "She should be fine. Twenty seconds to the blast door, eight to break through, thirteen to disable the launch system, thirty-five to cut the lines and eject the fuel, and twenty-two seconds to get back."

"What if it doesn't work?" Rahim asks.

I look over at him. "I don't want to think about that."

"Well, we have to," Anna says firmly. "We have less than a minute and a half to figure out what we do if we end up heading to space."

"Guys, I'm good, but I'm not that good," Tomoki says. I can hear the grimace that must be on his face. "With the controls locked this bad, I won't be able to turn us around. Right now I'm just focusing on getting us safely out of the atmosphere from this latitude."

Oh god, I'd forgotten all about the latitude. We're nowhere

near optimal launching point. Not to mention the winds.

"Najma, you have to break us back into our computer systems," Anna orders. "It's our only chance."

"What do you think I'm trying to do over here?" Najma asks. Her voice sounds strained, and I realize she has tears in her eyes.

My droidlet pings, and I look down at my communicator. "Ruby's stuck." The words come out shaky, but I can't help it. "The blast door has been reinforced."

Tomoki kicks the main console.

"Get her through!" Anna commands.

"Her welding equipment will take at least a minute to break through, and that won't be enough time to do a manual stop," I say. "I'm bringing her back." I go to push the return button on my communicator, but Anna growls first.

"Have her try anyway!" she yells. "She has to try!"

"She is!" I yell back. Now I have tears in my eyes. "She's doing her best, but she's not magic! I'm bringing her back before the heat from liftoff melts her!"

Anna fiddles with her belt, and I realize she's going to try to come back and physically stop me. The others must realize it, too. Tomoki throws a hand out. "Anna, no!"

"T minus one minute!" Najma shouts. "You'll be loose in flight!"

"T minus fifty seconds," Rahim says gravely. "Bring her back, Miranda. We're going to need that mechbot for whatever comes next."

I nod and press the recall button.

"Oh, great!" Anna throws her hands in the air. *"Du hast uns alle verdammt!"*

I don't know what that means, but I get the gist. "Ruby will do more good helping turn this ship around in space than melting before we get there!" I snap back.

"T minus forty seconds," Najma says.

Come on, Ruby. Get out of there.

Esteban has been speaking nonstop into his headset to Mission Control. "No, we can't get that—no, that won't work—we've tried—you're going to have to get past it on your end!"

Tomoki has the console in front of him torn open, fiddling with the wires underneath. "Does anyone have wire cutters?!"

"T minus thirty seconds," Najma says, her fingers still flying across her keyboard.

Anna growls, swinging her chair to Tomoki's side and yanking at the wires with him.

"How about these?" Rahim pulls out a pair of surgical scissors from his med kit. He tosses them up to Tomoki, who catches them by the handle.

"No good!" Tomoki shakes the metal scissors in frustration, dropping them back to Rahim. "No insulation! I'll get fried!"

Just then, Ruby's *clitter-clatter clitter-clatter* of legs sounds from the cabin behind ours.

"Ruby has wire cutters! She's on her way!" I exclaim. *"Faster, Ruby!"*

"T minus twenty seconds." Anna slams the metal grate she's

been holding for Tomoki down on the pilot console. "Get that robot over here!"

I thought you wanted her down in the fuel cells? I want to shout back, but there's no time for that sort of thing. "Ruby, get up front!" I order.

Clitter-clatter clitter-clatter. Ruby skitters up the flooring of our spaceplane toward Tomoki and Anna, her red casing glowing orange with the darkened lights around us.

"T minus fifteen," Najma says softly.

My droidlet pings.

:TASK COMPLETE. WAITING FOR INSTRUCTION:

"Ruby, wire cutters!"

Ruby's right and front-most leg flips around, twirling out a selection of specialized tools.

"She won't be able to cut it herself unless I'm up there to program it in her!" I yell. "Just grab her arm, slide the silver switch, and you can operate her manually!"

"T minus ten seconds," Najma says.

Tomoki grabs Ruby. I flinch as she dangles from his grip.

"Careful!" I shout before I can stop myself. He throws me a glare, and I shut up.

"We've lost contact with Mission Control," Esteban reports, his face pale. "I can't connect."

"We won't need to, as soon as I—" Tomoki jerks Ruby and her wire cutters toward the open dashboard, but gets shaken back by a rumble from our spaceplane. The main engines roar to life with near-deafening power.

"T minus five seconds!" Najma shrieks. "This is it!"

My fingers are in a death grip on my armrests. I watch the digital numbers in front of us tick down.

Five.

Four.

Tomoki lunges forward again, Ruby dangling from his hand.

Three.

He tugs out the wires. Something clicks over in my brain.

Two.

"WAIT!" I realize, finally registering which wires Tomoki's working on. "Don't cut those!"

Tomoki looks back at me, nearly dropping Ruby, startled by my command. And that's all the moment it takes.

One.

With an ungodly loud roar, we're thrown back in our seats. My face feels like it's melting backward and my ears hurt so badly I scream. Smoke billows up over the front windows.

And we're lifting off to outer space.

CHAPTER 15

"What the hell?!" Anna screams. How she's managed to get her voice louder than the engines, I don't know, but I *do* know her question is directed at me.

"Cutting those wires would've destroyed our chances of manually piloting this thing in space and wouldn't have stopped the fuel lines from firing anyway! We would've exploded!" I shout back. My eyes feel like they're being sucked to the back of my head.

"What?" Anna shouts. The roar of the engines engulfs everything.

"Cutting those wires would've—oh, never mind!" I yell. "I'll explain later!"

"WHAT?" Anna shouts again.

"I'LL EXPLAIN LATER!" I yank up my console, fighting

the extreme force pulling it back, and ignoring Anna's continued yelling. We have to break through the atmosphere, or we'll be toast. But no one's ever done it from this latitude before.

"The linear velocity, Tomoki—" Rahim begins.

"I know!" Tomoki screams back. "I'm working on it! Someone open up a third fuel cell. We're going to need it. This thing's trying to take us to a fifty-degree orbit." He twists the steering system. I can feel the spaceplane wrestling with his direction.

"Ruby!" I shout. Even above the engine noise, Ruby hears me and swivels her head to face me. She clings to Tomoki's seat as we rip through the atmosphere. "Come!"

Ruby swings from the back of Tomoki's chair and flings herself toward the flooring, which is still nearly at a ninety-degree angle to where flooring usually is. She scampers down it toward me. When she reaches my feet, she releases and falls into my arms.

"Ruby, datapad."

She turns on my chest and extends out multiple rows of buttons. I type quickly, programming in instructions that would take way too long to explain verbally. Escaping the atmosphere from this latitude—much less moving into position for a fifty-degree orbit at our speed—will need at least 70 percent more fuel than what we're giving it now. "We're going to need two more cells open!" I yell into my headset. I can feel my teeth rattle in my jaw.

"That's going to use up more fuel than we can spare!" Anna yells back.

"It's either that, or crash and burn."

Anna doesn't say anything in return, and once Ruby's orders are entered, I send her off.

"I'm sorry," Najma says through her tears. "I'm trying to break us back into the controls, but this lockdown is like nothing I've ever seen."

"Don't worry, Ruby's got it," I reassure her.

"We're losing pressure," Rahim warns.

"I'm on it," Esteban says.

My mind flies, trying to figure out how to repressurize our cabin, but then Ruby's signal bounces back to my console and I have to let the boys handle it on their own. It's time to remote control my robot. After tapping several buttons, Ruby's video feed starts up. I direct her through the cabins to the fuel cells.

"Hurry, Miranda," Tomoki says.

"Working on it," I say.

"Twelve PSI and dropping," Rahim says.

"I got it, I got it!" Esteban says. "I need someone to catch the nitrogen leak, though!"

"I'll take care of that," Rahim says.

"We're approaching the mesosphere," Anna says.

"I know, but I can't do anything about it!" Tomoki growls.

"I'm not talking to you," Anna retorts. "Just making sure everyone knows that we need this ship space ready, *now*."

"What do you think we're trying to do?" Rahim asks tersely. "We, who are actually working to make sure we're safe, while you just sit there shouting orders?"

"Someone has to take charge," Anna replies.

"And that someone is you? Why?" Rahim asks. "Because you've scored highest on our exams? Because they made you Mission Commander for this one practical?"

"Because I'm the only one who's noticed that our thrusters are stuck!" Anna says. I look up at that, just having finished finagling two more fuel cells open via Ruby.

"I'll get those," I say.

I direct Ruby away from the fuel cells out toward the thruster control panels. Her vidcam immediately shows me the problem. The metal plating isn't locked down. The engineers hadn't gotten to that yet.

"Ruby, we're pinning those down *now*," I say urgently. "We'll be reaching the thermosphere soon."

Without the plating pinned, the thruster trigger mechanisms won't fire. I know, because we installed those with that safety feature in mind.

But now we need them to fire. We need them, or we won't be able to aim ourselves as we escape the atmosphere, and we'll crash back onto the planet.

As Ruby sets to work, I ignore the words floating around my mind. *Fixing this only ensures you won't crash right now. Instead, you'll fly through space toward a different death.* I grip my right hand with my left to stop it trembling and finish the project. It doesn't take long, thankfully. Sweat pours backward over my ears down my head. We're beginning to curve up now, straightening our position so we're not lying on our backs anymore. My sweat stops dripping down, but not because it's not there. It's just that gravity isn't what it used to be.

"Thrusters clear!" I shout.

Tomoki wastes no time kicking them into gear. We burst forward at a mad speed, tearing through the mesosphere straight into the thermosphere. Our boosters fall away from us with another massive shudder as we enter the second phase of the launch. Technically, we're now in space.

We're in *space*.

"PSI rising again!" Esteban shouts in success.

"Gas levels stabilized," Rahim reports.

"Still no contact from Mission Control, though." Esteban tabs through his display.

"We have bigger problems," Najma warns, her hands moving across her own console screen, sliding programs back and forth. "Tomoki, tell me this isn't happening."

"What's not happening?" I ask. I shut off Ruby's vidcam and call her back.

"It's happening," Tomoki says. "No control up here, anymore. Sorry, guys." He spins around, showing us his gloved hands. The spaceplane continues to fly, moving on its own.

"Pilot controls have now been locked out as well as everything else," Najma explains.

"Well, get them *un*locked," Anna orders.

"Right. We'll just snap our fingers and do that," Tomoki says. Clearly being in space has not changed his sarcasm levels. "I don't know what or who we're dealing with, but they've got full control now. I don't even know where we're flying to."

We sit in silence, jerking up and down as the spaceplane pulls us into orbit. Ruby floats into the main cabin, and I grab her and pull her to me. She latches onto my chair. Esteban's helmet floats past next. *Maybe we should actually put our helmets on now . . .*

I watch a wrench drift past me and blink, registering what's happening. Things are *floating.* My body bobs in my seat, pushing gently against the straps. It's like the Vomit Comet, but instead of diving back to Earth, we're moving around it.

I undo the straps holding my helmet to my suit, just to watch it float next to me. Somehow, this is all actually happening. Outside the front window, the blues, greens, and whites of Earth are visible, and I lean forward to get the best view possible. "Guys. Look."

We all pause, going silent. It's beautiful.

I knew someday I'd get to see our planet from this vantage point. Seeing it *today* has been a complete surprise, but as I watch, I realize I never would've been fully prepared for this view. All the pictures and recordings from other space missions don't do it justice at all. There's no way to even begin describing it. It's just . . . *home.* And it's beautiful.

Our silence has become almost reverent. Even Najma has temporarily stopped her work.

"Wow," Esteban says.

I nod. Wow, indeed.

The spaceplane jerks, and Tomoki grabs for the controls. "Sorry to bust up this moment," he says, "But I think whoever's controlling this thing has plans on where they want us to go."

"Look!" Esteban points. Ahead of us, a small dot is approaching. Or rather, we're approaching it.

"A satellite?" Najma asks.

Anna shakes her head. "Not just any satellite." She crosses her arms. "That's a fuel station."

She's right, I realize. It's one of the old refueling points for AEM—from back when NASA thought they would be doing multiple asteroid missions. "Just where is this ship programmed to eventually go?" I ask.

We watch the fuel station get closer. Then we sail right on past it.

There's one last moment of relative stillness on the spaceplane, then Najma bursts into a flurry of typing. Tomoki begins smacking at the control console again.

"This is our chance!" Anna orders. "We weren't aligned yet, we still have time. We need to get back to Earth before we finish enough orbits to connect with that station!"

Rahim shows me some numbers on his console. "Two more orbits, and we'll meet up."

The ISS 2 orbits every hour and a half, but we're not orbiting at ISS 2 speed. We're orbiting at asteroid freighter speed. Which means we're being flung around this planet three times as fast. Which means we've got less than an hour to break free before we dock with that fuel station and head off to wherever this ship has us programmed to go.

I've never had an hour fly by so fast in my entire life. Screaming, crying, reading numbers after numbers after numbers, reprogramming Ruby's orders over and over . . . nothing is working. Earth continues to turn underneath us, and we continue to zoom around it. Light, dark. Light, dark. It's beautiful. It's surreal. And it's happening too fast.

The ship shudders, but we're still on track with the fuel station, this time on our final approach.

"You know this ship best, is there anything else we can do?" Esteban asks me, his bright eyes desperate. In our final moments before docking, I scan through the systems, trying to pinpoint which ones are firing. I feel dizzy from reading so fast, but I can't stop. We have to get free. If only the numbers would stop fuzzing out in front of me.

"Her?" Anna snorts from her copilot seat. "We have only minutes to change our fate, and you turn to *her*? She's not even supposed to be here."

My hands freeze over the console board. "Really? That's what you're going to bring up right now?"

Anna doesn't even look back at me. "I'm just looking out for our safety."

"Yeah. I'm sure." I undo my seatbelts. I tell myself it's so I can get up to examine some of the spaceplane hardware, but I also can't help but clench my hand into a fist as I begin to float.

"Um, Miranda?" Rahim asks.

"You've messed up enough already," Anna says. "Don't make it worse."

"I've *what*? No. You know what? No one else seems to care whether or not I'm meant to be here. Why do *you*? Are you threatened by me? Is that it?" The ship jolts as we dock with the fuel station, and my shoulder slams into the wall, but I'm too angry to pay it any attention.

"Threatened? Hardly." Anna climbs out of her own seat, pushing her way toward me. "I'm just looking out for my crew. A crew that you aren't even supposed to be a part of!"

"Anna, just shut up already!" Tomoki demands.

"We have to get this ship back under control! We don't have time to fight!" Esteban insists. I can hear the fuel lines pumping, and part of me realizes this really is a moronic time to argue, but Anna's smug expression doesn't let me quit.

I pull on some piping so I can float over and stare Anna square in the face. "Right. So if you're so convinced I'm an idiot, how did I manage to tie with you at the Advancing Astronomy Competition?"

"Rigged to get you the right credentials for the Mars program," Anna says, holding her chin up. "You shouldn't have even placed."

My mouth drops open.

"It's all been rigged right from the start. And now, thanks to the ISECG forcing *your* stupidity on us, we could all *die*."

I glance around, desperate for some assistance in my defense, but everyone has completely tuned us out by now. Esteban floats through the cabin, flailing to catch his arms on something and stop himself. "Come on, Rahim!" he says. Normally, I'd laugh at the sight of Esteban floating aimlessly, bumping into things left and right, but laughing is the last thing I feel like doing right now.

"You're the one who told your replacement we were onto them," Anna's biting words continue. "*You did this, Miranda.* Now they have to get rid of all of us, because we *know.* So you'd better just sit down and let us real cadets fix your mess."

Rage courses through me like sparks from a loose cable.

"You think I'm not supposed to be here?" I sputter. The ship is refueling, and the others are doing what we *should* be doing—working to get us free from this preprogrammed track so we can regain control. "Well, news flash, Anna—*none of us* are supposed to be here right now! I'm the only one of us who's spent any serious amount of time working on this spaceplane, so it's you who needs to shut up and listen!"

I spin at Rahim and Esteban, who are both out of their seats working at the side console that handles fuel input and output.

"Quit trying to stop the refueling!" I order. "You two know programming, go help Najma crack this autopilot!" My peripheral vision is fuzzy, so I have to turn to fully face Tomoki. "Tomoki, hold us steady, because if they break through, we'll need you to keep us from spiraling out of control. Who knows what this ship is meant to do if we manage to wrangle it back under our power."

Esteban and Rahim look at one another, uncertainty crossing their faces, and Anna's eyes fly open. "Don't listen to her! Stop the refueling! We can't let whoever is behind this do whatever they want to us!"

"Yeah, because if we regain control, having fuel at one hundred percent capacity won't be any use to us at *all.*" I let the sarcasm drip as heavily as I can.

"I'm Mission Commander!" Anna barks back at me. "Stop giving orders!"

"Then stop giving *stupid* orders!" I retort.

The ship shudders again.

"I think I might be onto something," Najma says. "But it would really help if you two would shut up so I can *concentrate*!"

I grin in triumph as Esteban and Rahim leave their console to go help Najma. With the fuel tanks now full, the station's pipelines automatically separate from our ship, and the autopilot fires our thrusters to maneuver us away. Anna is about to keep up our argument, but then Najma speaks again, cutting her off.

"Oh no."

"Did you do it?" Anna floats over to hold onto the back of Najma's chair and peer at her console.

"No," Najma says quietly.

Tomoki lets out a curse from the pilot's chair, then swivels to face us. His eyes are wide, and his whole body trembles.

Najma looks at him. "You see it, don't you?" she asks softly.

Tomoki nods. I've never seen him so shaken. Ruby grips onto the side of my chair, and I put one hand on her for the reassuring feel of her cold shell.

"What?" Esteban floats up to Tomoki and grabs him by the shoulders. "What do you see? What did you two figure out?"

Tomoki cricks his neck back and forth, regaining composure. "Oh. Well, you know. Just sorted out where this autopilot is taking us."

Our spaceplane finishes its slight turn, and we begin rocketing away from the fuel station. I press my fingers into Ruby's red plating.

"Where?" Anna demands.

Tomoki shrugs. "I suggest we all get comfortable, and you two stop fighting." He gives Anna and me a nod. "Because this is going to be a long flight."

A terrible hypothesis begins to form in my brain, as I look at the pattern of constellations outside our viewing window. *Oh no. No, that can't be. It just can't be.*

Tomoki leans back in his chair. "Yep. I think you've all got it figured out now. We're going to Mars, kids."

CHAPTER 16

"Mars," Esteban whispers.

Tomoki nods. "Eight and a half years too early, but that's where we're going."

"We'll never make it," Rahim says.

Everything has crawled to a stop. It's hard to tell if the floating feeling in my internal organs is from terror, lack of gravity, or both.

Mars. We're going to Mars.

I think through everything we have on this spaceplane. *There's rudimentary food-lab equipment and a water recycler, but with only my small 3D printer there'd be nothing to build proper shelter or greenhouse equipment . . .*

"Even if we did make it," I rub my temple, ignoring the queasy feeling in my stomach, "we'd have next to nothing to work with once there."

"We need to call for help," Rahim says. "Esteban, are the communications systems working yet?"

Esteban shakes his head. "No. I'll keep trying, though."

The spaceplane flips over gracefully. Some part of me registers the sound of Najma crying at her console and Tomoki swearing at his controls. Mostly, though, my mind fluctuates between two thoughts: *We're flying to Mars. I need to get this spaceplane prepared. We're flying to Mars. I need to get this spaceplane prepared.* It's like the rest of me is in suspended animation. *We're flying to Mars.*

And I have no idea how to stop us.

Esteban lets out a wail of frustration from his computer. I unhook Ruby and have her clasp onto my flight suit. Then I let go, and we float together. "It'll be okay," I whisper, keeping one hand on her. She mimics the gesture and places one of her arms on me. "We won't actually go to Mars. We'll get home somehow."

"Well, I don't see how," Anna says. I blink at her. She looks blurry. Everyone looks blurry.

"Shut up!" Tomoki snaps at her. "We'll get home. We'll figure this out."

"Najma will get us in control of the spaceplane!" Esteban insists.

"Does anyone else feel dizzy?" Najma asks meekly.

I slowly turn my gaze toward my arguing crewmates. Esteban is wiping tears from his eyes. His hair pokes out of his headset.

I find that I have to look at each of my peers carefully in turn, because the edges of my vision are going darker and darker.

"Rahim," I murmur. "How's our oxygen?"

"Fine," he replies. Then I feel his hands on my shoulders. "Maybe you should sit down."

I waver in the air. *Do I look that bad?*

I must, because both Rahim and Esteban push me into my chair and buckle me in. I don't even resist. Ruby's with me. That's all that matters.

"Great." Anna snorts. "Our flight engineer's about to faint, and our programmers can't stop crying. Really sounds like we're going to get this spaceplane turned around soon."

"Just stop it already! *Please!*" Najma yells, shaking where she sits. "We can't keep fighting. It's going to take all of us to figure this out and get home."

"No, it's going to take *you* to break us back into the system." Anna spins at her. "Stop bawling and get working, or we're going to be stuck in this metal coffin forever."

A new gush of tears floods Najma's eyes, and she has to scrub at them to clear them, since the surface tension of water won't let a single drop out.

"Way to go, Anna," Tomoki says. "How's she supposed to work now?"

"Najma—" I start to say.

"No, she's right," Najma says, still wiping her face. "I need to get back to work."

Esteban puts a hand on her shoulder, using his other to secure himself from floating away. "Let us know what we can do to help."

Tomoki nods. "If you want us to bind and gag Anna, that can be arranged."

Anna's nostrils flare, and for the first time, *her* eyes finally look damp. "Whatever." She floats out of the main cabin to a side chamber. The door slams behind her, and I cringe. The doors aren't meant to slam.

Rahim sighs. "At least she picked a pressurized chamber."

"I'd better inspect that door." I fight the dizziness and unbuckle my belts, scanning the hatchway. Ruby follows. "Maybe we can figure out a way to pressurize more sections, if we really are going to be here a while," I say to her.

:GOING TO BE HERE A WHILE:

She repeats my last words, miming my hunched shoulders and drifting along. She's got the right idea. I really do feel like I could just slip into sleep . . .

But I *shouldn't* feel that way. I straighten up, narrowing my eyes. Calculations start going through my head—how much nitrogen and oxygen our tanks contain, how many cubic meters of space there are on this craft—and soon I find myself back at my console, running simulations.

"Oh, for crying out loud." I slam my hand down. "There's a nitrogen leak, Rahim! Oxygen levels are normal, but only averaged over the entire spacecraft. In here, they're *way* off."

"Really?" Rahim asks, floating over. He's got his hand on his head, and I know he's feeling it, too.

"Yes!" I push away from my console, frustrated. "I thought you fixed that earlier! How did you miss that it's still leaking?"

Rahim winces. "I'm sorry."

"Ugh!" I hold on to Ruby and push out of the main chamber. "Come on, Ruby, let's get this fixed."

"Can I help?" I hear Rahim call from behind me.

"Help Najma," I tell him. "Keep Esteban working on fixing communications. You and Najma need to get us back in control." Then I shut the door and float through the tunnel toward the cryo dock.

It's been several hours of small fixes, starting with getting oxygen levels normalized. Ruby and I haven't had more than five minutes to rest. But it can't be helped. We've got to keep this spaceplane working. It's all I can contribute as Najma does everything she can to regain control for us.

Anna has finally slunk back into the cockpit, sitting next to Tomoki and quietly working with him to get the steering system back online. We still haven't been able to send or receive any communications, though Esteban hasn't given up. And Rahim's been avoiding me ever since I snapped at him, which I do feel bad about, but have chalked it up to my deoxygenated brain at that moment. He's been assisting Najma, like I suggested.

My droidlet pings.

:TASK COMPLETE. WAITING FOR INSTRUCTION:

"Thanks, Ruby," I say. She's wrapped up fixing the wiring in our food lab, so we can rehydrate some packets of space food that we thankfully found stored onboard. "Let's tackle the water filtration next, okay?"

"I've got it!" I hear Najma exclaim from the cockpit.

I spin, dropping my screwdriver, which would've clanked on the metal floor if we weren't out in space. It only takes half a second before we're all hovering near Najma's console, desperately staring at a screen of code that's way over any of our heads.

"Don't get too excited," she cautions. "It's a hypnotivirus."

Esteban groans.

"What does that mean exactly?" Anna asks carefully. I'm glad she does, because I have no idea what a hypnotivirus is, either.

"It means that I can't delete it, for one thing," Najma replies. "It's like a parasite. It gets in and doesn't leave. Hypnotiviruses evolve to fight whatever you throw at them. They are placed in a system and given a task, and they will find a way to complete that task. This one's task is to take us to Mars."

"So, let me get this straight," Tomoki says. "This thing will do everything in its power to take us to Mars, and there's no way of stopping it?"

"I didn't say that," Najma says. We all perk back up. "I can try to isolate it. Quarantine it on a different system. Our spaceplane has two main computer systems that would be able to house such a complicated virus; if I put it on the backup system rather than our main system, we should regain control of most of the spaceplane's functions."

"Najma, that's fantastic!" I gasp. "You're a genius!"

Najma smiles at me. "Thanks."

Esteban gives her a huge hug. "Thank *you*," he says as her cheeks darken. "You've just saved us all! See?" He lets go of her and looks at all of us, grinning. "I knew we'd be okay!"

"Good," Anna says, nodding in approval. "How long will this take?"

Najma shrugs. "Once I create the code, it'll probably need a while to run. Maybe . . . ten to twelve hours?"

Tomoki whistles. "That's a while."

"Better than a nine-month trip to Mars, though," Rahim says.

We all laugh. Even Anna.

There's hope yet.

I've never had to strap myself into a sleeping bag mounted on a wall before, but that's basically what I did last "night." Of course, on the spaceplane, there is no real day or night, but we all agreed that we should try to sleep as Najma's programming runs. With any luck, now that we're awake, we should be only minutes away from regaining access to the ship's controls.

Not that that really means anything.

In the back of my brain, I've done some rather terrifying calculations that I'm not sure I'm ready to share with everyone yet. Even if we regain control of our spaceplane, it's not just a matter of pulling a U-turn. Stopping this thing and turning it around is next to impossible with the remaining fuel we have, even if Tomoki and I literally got out in our EMUs and pushed.

I shrink back in my flight suit. *No. We'll think of something.* For now, our best bet is to keep the survival basics working.

My droidlet pings.

:TASK COMPLETE. WAITING FOR INSTRUCTION:

I turn to my robot. We're in the back chamber, securing the spaceplane air cyclers. Ruby's finished soldering the piping in place, and I've just finished installing the filter. A few screws float loose around me. I snatch at them, missing the first couple times. Maybe I'll build an electromagnet later if I get a chance. For now, that's just one more item we don't have with us that would be useful.

"Come on, Ruby," I say. Ruby swivels her head to me, and I snap her back into place on my flight suit. "Let's go check and see if Najma's code is done running yet."

Heading back through the various doors to the main cabin, I pass Anna, who's coming in from the side. She hasn't talked to me since everything went down yesterday, but she does follow me to the cockpit, and I can only assume it's because she wants to see Najma's progress, too. When we reach the main cabin, all three boys are already there.

"Good, you're here," Najma says, catching sight of Anna and me. "I'm ready to test and see if this worked."

"Fire it up," Tomoki says. He's casually leaning up against the wall, which is a serious feat in zero gravity. I have to hand it to him. He really does know how to look cool in any given situation.

"Ready?" Najma asks.

"As ready as we'll ever be." I find myself crossing my fingers, even though it's an absurdly pointless gesture.

Through the windows in front of us, space is dark. Najma

boots up the computers, and the effect is almost blinding. Every screen on the ship flickers to life with a flash of light.

"Yes!" Tomoki pumps his fist in the air.

"You did it!" Esteban exclaims. "This is fantastic!"

My heart beats so fast, I'm worried it might just burst from some sort of weird microvacuum up here in space. Ruby bounces up and down next to me, and I choke out a relieved laugh.

We're back. The spaceplane is ours.

"Just a warning," Najma says, cutting off Esteban's string of high fives to everyone around him. "Remember, the virus isn't gone. Only quarantined on the back drive. That means some systems still won't work, and it's going to keep trying to pursue its directive of getting us to Mars. But hopefully this will at least allow us to get back flight controls and control over fuel output."

"Thanks, Najma," I say in a rush. "We can work with this." I quickly head back to my seat and grab my console. I don't think I've ever been this happy in my entire life to have a computer boot up in front of me.

"We need to call home," Rahim says.

"I'm on it!" Esteban straps himself into his chair and flips on the main screen. "Let me just . . . oh, wait, that's incoming, not outgoing—"

The screen beeps at us. There are over three hundred messages.

"Wow," Najma whispers. "They've really been trying to get ahold of us, haven't they?"

"Hmm, yeah." Esteban fiddles with his console. "I can't seem to get a call started. Najma, is this one of those backup drive things you'd mentioned?"

"It shouldn't be." Najma frowns. "Try to get the messages, maybe it's just overloaded."

Esteban clicks a few more buttons. Nothing happens.

"So communications are still down," Anna says.

"It would seem so." Najma sighs. "Sorry. I'll work on those. Might just be a glitch."

"Or another layer of encryption to keep us from communicating," Anna replies. "Whoever did this must know we could reveal them and likely doesn't want us tattling. Remember, Miranda let it slip to Kreshkov's nephew—"

"Oh, don't even bring Kreshkov into this," Tomoki says before I can protest about Sasha. "I'm so sick of you all pinning this on him!"

"I don't think it's Kreshkov," Najma says carefully. "Not with this level of programming. This is something only someone like Dr. Schuber could have managed."

Esteban and I exchange glances. I nod at him.

"So, about that . . ." Esteban begins. Then he reveals to the rest of the group what he learned about Mr. Burnett being the secret message sender, and I explain my suspicions about Dr. Schuber and the ISECG. I'm careful not to make it sound like I'm excusing Sasha of anything, though, since I already know how the group would react to that.

"Why didn't you tell us this *earlier*?" Tomoki demands when we're done.

I wince. "Well, this all happened just before the start of our practical. I guess we got sidetracked. I mean, it's not like it matters *now*."

Anna just shakes her head at me.

"Though I really did think it was just me he was after," I say, apologetically. "Why he did this to all of us, I don't know."

"Here," Esteban says, clicking quickly on his keyboard. "Looks like we can access video streams. This will have more information for us." He pulls up a news stream and a woman's face appears on the main screen in the front of the cabin. "It'll be a few minutes delayed, but we can at least find out what's been going on since we left." Esteban presses another button, and the reporting woman now has a voice.

"—in ruins, as yet another tragedy strikes. We go now to live coverage with Jack, who is on-site in Houston."

The screen flashes to a horrific sight of billowing dark smoke. It takes me a moment, but then I gasp. "That's the Johnson Space Center!"

Our entire previous conversation comes to a screeching halt. Questions about Dr. Schuber will just have to wait. All our eyes are glued to the screen, too nervous to even blink.

"Thanks, McKayla," a man replies. "As you can see, the drones decimated this world-renowned Mission Control center in mere minutes. We're reporting fourteen casualties and another eighty-seven hospitalized, over a third of whom are in critical condition."

Najma throws a hand over her mouth. My brain tries to make

sense of it all while my heart skips several beats. *More people dead? Don't tell me it's because of—*

The reporter continues to speak, as the smoke flows behind him. "The center was running at full capacity, trying desperately to establish contact with the lost *Ambassador*, when the bombs hit."

It's like my chest has just been rammed into by an asteroid freighter. Just like with the helicopter attack, people have died because of me.

Again.

"No!" Esteban shouts. Tomoki punches the wall he was leaning against. I want to crumble into a corner, but I know it's physically impossible with the weightless environment.

"Investigations are underway, but it seems likely this is, in fact, the latest in a series of attacks on worldwide space programs."

"The latest?" Tomoki watches the screen intently.

"Do they mean us?" I manage to ask. Somehow, I don't think so.

"Thanks, Jack." We're back with the female reporter. "No organization is taking credit for these attacks yet, and speculation continues. The order does suggest that at least the latter attacks may be retaliatory, but no nation is willing to go so far as to point fingers—years of war has left us all more than a little cautious in laying blame. However, Secretary of State Erwich has urged the United States to temporarily close its borders, as Russia has already done. Other countries around the world are following suit."

"We must remember that Russia has been hit as well," a third voice chimes in. The camera refocuses on another reporter sitting at the news desk. "Multiple countries have been struck today to varying degrees, with over a dozen space centers currently in ruins. The death toll, now including the Houston attack, has reached one hundred and twelve."

"Why?" Najma asks, her hand still clamped over her mouth.

"Possibly one hundred and eighteen," the reporter named McKayla cuts in gently. Her eyes look genuinely pained. "We still have heard nothing from the Mars cadets."

"We have to contact them." Esteban's voice is hoarse. "My family . . . they need to know we're okay."

Oh god, *my family.*

"As for now, it looks like all rescue operations have been officially suspended," the other reporter says. "Now, the only major space center still intact is the Destined for Mars training base itself. Perhaps this final blow to Houston will quiet those who've insisted the attacks over the past few months have all been an American conspiracy."

"And on the note of conspiracies and explosions, we are joined now by Sandra at Cape Canaveral."

"Thanks, McKayla," Sandra says. The screen changes to the Canaveral base, which thankfully looks free of smoke and debris. "Everyone here is devastated by the disasters that have befallen all of us in these past twenty-four hours. However, the number one emotion running here isn't sorrow, but guilt."

The screen switches to a prerecorded interview with several

NASA employees at some sort of press conference.

"We should have caught it," one employee says. "I don't know how we missed the fuel leak. We haven't missed something like that in decades."

"We must not lose sight of the fact that the real culprit is yet to be found," Sandra's voice-over says, "as our president asserted earlier today."

The news feed changes to a message from President Nelson. I can't stop shaking.

"It is understandable—even easy—to be suspicious when your country experiences a devastating attack just after refusing to lend aid to a US operation," President Nelson says against a backdrop of blue curtains. "But we cannot stress this enough: *we are not behind these attacks.* While we search for answers, we continue to deeply mourn the loss of space center employees and innocent bystanders from all corners of the globe who have lost their lives this past day—especially the brave astronauts who threw caution to the wind to try to recover our missing Mars cadets."

I grab Najma. "Did she say astronauts?" I demand.

And then a recorded video clip plays. A spaceplane launching . . . and exploding.

Five headshots hover around it moments later, with a scripted "Rest in Peace" above them all. Three I don't recognize, but two . . .

"Lizzie!" I shriek. "No!"

"No!" Esteban floats up and grabs the screen. "No, no, no, no, no!"

Tomoki curses over and over. "Kreshkov! *Why?!*"

Rahim's eyelashes are damp. Najma buries her head in her knees, pulling them to her chest. A single, stunned tear fills one of Anna's gray eyes.

I cover my face with my hands. "Lizzie . . ." I let go of everything and float freely through the cabin. Curling up as tight as I can, I sob.

CHAPTER 17

"With all the devastation seen in the past twenty-four hours, space programs worldwide have been decimated to an extent we likely don't yet fully understand," a newscaster says. "One thing is clear, though: it will be decades before they'll be rebuilt to previous levels. The short-lived World Peace Treaty has come to a tragic end."

"Turn it off," Tomoki says to Esteban.

Esteban looks at him through teary eyes. "But—"

"TURN IT OFF!" he demands. "I don't want to hear any more!"

Esteban jumps, startled, but does as he says. The screens flicker to black, and not one of us moves. My eyes continue to well up and part of me remembers that we're low on water and should be conserving it. Somehow, though, I don't feel like my tears are a waste.

"Now what?" Rahim asks.

No one answers. I grab hold of Ruby. She gives me a hug as my breathing comes in uneven spurts. *One hundred and twelve dead. Plus the two from the helicopter attack. One hundred and fourteen. Could we have done anything to stop this?*

"We go to Mars."

My eyes snap open. Everyone is staring at Anna.

"What?" Tomoki asks.

Anna takes a deep breath, her shoulders straightening. "I said, we go to Mars."

"But how?" Esteban wipes tears out of his eyes.

"And why?" Najma asks. The spaceplane's dim lighting casts shadows on all our faces, but even without it, I think we'd look exhausted.

"This is our only chance," Anna says. "You heard them. Space programs are destroyed. By the time they rebuild, we might be too old. Or too frightened to try again. But if we go now, we can still do what we're meant to do. We can prove that they haven't scared us away from our dreams."

I find my eyes drifting out the dark windows at the front of the spaceplane. We're on a trajectory to Mars, but Mars is nowhere nearby yet. That's another nine months away.

"We'll never make it," I say. "For one thing, we don't have proper landing equipment."

"Actually," Tomoki says slowly. "We could land, possibly. If we get our reentry runners aligned and use that 3D printer of yours to build the final components. We have nine months to get the math right."

"What about water?" Najma asks. "And food?"

"The recycler's almost repaired," Rahim says. "And we have the basics to get our food laboratory up and running."

"We do . . ." Esteban reluctantly agrees.

"But what about when we land?" I say. "Will we have enough oxygen?"

"If we get a few instruments fixed, we might be able to produce enough to last a while, especially if we tap into the ice on Mars." Rahim sighs. "I just don't like it."

"Neither do I," Najma says. "Have you all forgotten that if we managed to land on Mars, we'd have absolutely no way to get home again?"

I haven't forgotten.

"What home do we have left?" Anna asks, crossing her arms. "Our lives were supposed to be dedicated to the world's space programs, and those are gone. Unless we act now."

I narrow my eyes at her. "So you're okay with going to Mars, just to die there?"

"I think we owe that much to our mentors," Anna says quietly, and any further tirade I have is cut short.

She's right. Isn't she? Lizzie and Kreshkov died for us. They *died* for us. I use a hand to steady myself on the wall.

"I don't want anyone to think we're too scared to finish our mission," Tomoki says, after a moment's pause. "But this is . . ."

"Why don't we take a few hours to think about it," Anna says. "And mourn."

I nod. That, at least, sounds reasonable.

I float down the hall, aimless. I pass Tomoki, who is channeling his anger into building a second water recycler. Then Esteban, who is doing nothing.

I pause, watching him. I've never seen Esteban's face so devoid of emotion. He stares at a gray wall—his only movement the occasional blink. After a few moments, I can't bear the sight of him like that, and continue on my way.

Eventually, I find myself in the meditation cabin, staring blankly like Esteban. But instead of facing a wall, I look out the windows at the stars.

It's not really a cabin for meditation. Or maybe it is, if you're into that sort of thing. All I know is that we were building it in to give us cadets a private area for contemplation during our long trip to Mars. I installed the ventilation a few weeks ago, staring out these very windows into the hangar back on our island.

While I've thought it before, I think that right now, for the first *real* time, I'm consciously experiencing how time is relative. Then again, it could just be a trick of the darkness. Moving through space doesn't feel much like moving at all, because nothing around us seems to move. Yet I know with every second, we draw closer to Mars.

Does Anna actually have a point for once? We are Destined

for Mars, after all. At least, *they* are. If we go home, who's to say we'll ever get this chance again? Will we ever fulfill the mission that Lizzie and Kreshkov trained us for?

I cling tightly to my flight suit, with Ruby attached to my side. We float together, and I use my legs to push against the wall and keep myself relatively upright.

When the door hisses behind me, I startle.

"Sorry," Rahim apologizes. "I didn't know you were in here."

"It's okay," I say. "We can share."

He nods and shuts the door, rubbing his arms. The insulation isn't the best in here.

"I didn't realize anyone else knew about this room," I say.

Rahim floats to my side, hooking his foot on the floor loops to steady himself. "Medical team wanted it in, right?"

Rahim's our medical officer. Of course he knew.

"How are you doing?" he asks.

I shrug, going back to looking out the big paneled window in front of us. "Okay, I guess. You?"

"Okay," he replies.

We're quiet again. After a few moments, Ruby pokes me in the side from the lack of activity. I wave at her to settle, and she gives me a slow wave in return.

"I hope Sasha's okay," Rahim says.

"Me too," I say. I haven't let myself think about it, but the fear hasn't left me for a moment since I heard about all the attacks. "And I really wish the others weren't so suspicious of him. But now that his uncle is dead—"

"Maybe they won't think he's involved," Rahim finishes for me.

I nod. *Please be okay, Sasha. Please don't be dead.* But I don't know who I'm kidding. He mysteriously vanished just before a giant plot unfolded to cause terror and murder worldwide. Probability says . . .

I still can't let myself think about it.

"Do you miss it?" Rahim asks after another moment.

"Miss what?" I ask, turning. "Our training base?"

"Earth," he replies. "Home."

Oh. "No. Well, yes. I mean, I haven't let myself think about it much." I grimace. "There's a lot I can't let myself think too much about."

"I guess that makes sense." Then he's back to gazing out the window, so I do the same.

This is one of the longest, non-group-based conversations I've ever held with Rahim. He's always so quiet, and we've just never had much time to talk before, one on one. Plus, he's . . . well, he's a *he*. And not like Esteban, who anyone can talk to. Or Tomoki, who no one can talk to. Rahim is in-between. I never know how to approach him.

But here we are. Grieving together.

"I miss my home," he says, startling me again out of my silence. "My real home. Not our base. I miss my family."

I blink. Rahim's never talked much about his home. I did see his family briefly the day we lifted off—*was that really just yesterday? It feels like a lifetime ago.*

"My parents, they saw a lot of stuff when they were younger,"

225

Rahim continues. "Back when the world was at war. A lot of bombs. Explosions. That sort of thing. They saw people die."

He goes silent again, and the question I'd never had the chance to ask finally surfaces. "Rahim, did anyone die when you were attacked on the way to the training island?"

Rahim doesn't respond right away, and I immediately wish I'd just kept quiet. Eventually, though, he turns to face me, holding on to a gray pipe by the side of the cabin to keep steady.

"I've put a lot of thought into it," Rahim begins. "This whole situation, that is. The attacks. They've only really ever gone after you and me. Not the others. There has to be a reason." He looks back out toward space.

I watch him. *That's true. It wasn't just me who was targeted. Not at first. So when did that change? And why did I never think to talk to Rahim about any of this before now?*

"You know what my parents always said?" he asks. I shake my head, and he continues. "They said that the best way to honor the dead is to live."

I try to reply, but can't find the words. Rahim's advice echoes around the empty cabin like a penny dropped into a deep, deep well.

The stars are steady points of light out here in space. There's no twinkle effect, like on Earth with our atmosphere. Yet, even so, my thoughts drift back to warm summer evenings in Ohio. Smacking at mosquitoes, looking through Mom's telescope in the backyard. She bounces baby Emmaline on her knee, and I adjust the focus so that Mars comes into view. It's just a big red dot.

"Aww, I wanted to see the rovers!"

My mom laughs. "Oh, honey, you can't see that much detail through this scope. Maybe when you grow up, you can go to Mars and see the rovers in person."

"Really? You think so?"

"I don't see why not."

"Mars!" my sister chimes in, leaning to grab at the telescope with chubby, toddler hands.

"You have a brother, right? And two sisters?" I ask, still watching space out the window.

Rahim nods. "Two baby sisters."

"I have a baby sister, too." I hold onto Ruby. "Though she's not really a baby anymore. She just turned six."

Rahim smiles. "My littlest sister is two. She's talking now, but back before I left for training in January, she was still just . . ."

"Babbling?" I supply.

"Yes," he says. "Babbling."

"I remember when Emmaline babbled. She's growing up so fast." I think back to the day I left Ohio and the sniffling hug my sister gave me in the airport.

"You're coming back, right?"

I pinch my arms tighter across my chest.

"We can't go to Mars." My voice is barely louder than a whisper. "It's a one-way trip. Even to avenge Lizzie and Kreshkov, we can't just go there to die. You have your brother and your baby sisters. I have Emmaline. We both have our parents. They're all waiting for us to come home again."

227

I keep my eyes focused on the blackness in front of me, waiting for his reaction.

"I agree," Rahim says. "We have to go back. Mars isn't home. It's a dream. A nice one that we don't have to give up. But home is where we have people to return to."

"Exactly," I say.

"We should go find the others."

"Yeah," I agree. I turn, and we head out the door back into the main cabin. Along the way, we run into Esteban. I'm relieved to see he's back to moving around, but my shoulders fall slightly when I notice his eyes are just as dead as before.

"Hey, guys."

"Hey, Esteban," I say gently, shuffling Ruby on my side as she continues to float forward once I'm stopped. "We, uh . . . we did some thinking."

"We decided we need to go home," Rahim says. "We want to see our families again."

"Oh, good," Najma says, coming out of another side cabin and floating over to us. "I was hoping someone else would be voting for that. Besides, this isn't our only chance to go to Mars. If we can pilot this spaceplane back home and land it, then that's one piece of equipment they *haven't* blown up. We can use *Ambassador* to rebuild and prepare for a future mission!"

"Yes!" I say. "Brilliant, Najma! I hadn't even thought of that."

"What do you think, Esteban?" Rahim asks.

We all study him carefully. Najma inches closer to him, her eyebrows pinching in concern.

"Okay," Esteban says.

"Okay?" I ask. "That's it?"

"Yeah," he answers. His eyes drift away. "How do we do it, though?"

"We find everyone and put our minds together." I offer Esteban a smile. "We're six geniuses. We should be able to figure this out."

He just nods once more. I meet Najma's helpless stare, grimacing in sympathy.

"It's a plan, then," Rahim says. "Now to find Tomoki and see what he thinks about landing *Ambassador* on Earth."

"On Earth?" Anna floats in behind us. "So we don't want to go to Mars?"

We all fall silent, slowly turning to face her. Anna's expression is stone cold, as usual, but her skin is much grayer. Or maybe that's my imagination.

"Well," Rahim begins cautiously. "If we put our minds to it, we could find a way home to—"

"And give up on going to Mars?" Anna crosses her arms.

"No," Najma says. "We can rebuild *Ambassador* once we land her. Tomoki could—"

"I could what?" Tomoki asks, joining the group.

"Land us on Earth," Rahim says. "You're the superstar pilot, aren't you?"

"Wait, so we're going home now?" Tomoki pulls himself toward us. "I thought we were going to Mars."

"We decided we'd like to get home to our families," I say. "Rather than die on Mars."

To my great relief, Tomoki nods. "Well, good. Were we ever seriously considering Mars anyway?"

Anna spins toward him, and I can see her eyes glisten. "So you don't care, either? No one here cares about finishing our mission?" She looks around at each of us.

"What mission, Anna?" I ask. "This wasn't supposed to be a mission. This was a training exercise. Our mission isn't for nearly another decade!"

"No, it isn't," she bites back. "You know that. We all know that!" She continues to spin around, glaring at each of us. "This is it. The space program is over for a long, long time. But we can prove to them that they can't take everything away from us! We still have Mars. If we all work together, we can get there." For once, her glare isn't menacing, but desperate.

"Anna . . ." I say slowly. "I'm sorry. But we don't want to die." Ruby's head turns back and forth as I shake mine.

"Don't you want to see your family again?" Najma asks.

"I only have one person in my family." Anna's face darkens. "My father. And he won't want to see me again if I fail at this."

She floats in place, and a long silence falls on us all. *She can't mean that, can she?*

"Anna," Najma begins tentatively. "I'm sure that isn't true."

"What do you know?" Anna snaps. "None of you have your priorities straight! You think your families are going to be proud when you come home? When you mess up your one chance to go to Mars? When you *fail*?"

"It's better than being dead." Tomoki shrugs. "I don't know,

230

Anna. I think you've got Space Madness or something. You aren't making sense."

"You have no idea, do you?" Anna glowers at Tomoki. "No idea what it's like to be under pressure, all day, every day. You, with your carefree, solar-car-racing lifestyle!"

"Are you *joking*?" Tomoki floats up to stare down at her. "Pressure? You're talking to *me* about pressure? Who's the celebrity, here? So you've got your father's expectations to live up to. I've got an entire country's expectations on me, and you don't see me ready to die for that!"

"Fine!" Anna's eyes fill rapidly. "You all think I'm crazy, then do what you want! But don't expect any help from me."

With that, Anna pulls herself out of the main cabin via the piping, muttering in German. I stare after her. I can't imagine my parents wanting me to go to Mars and die rather than try to come home. Does her dad really feel that way? I just can't believe it.

I shake my head. "Listen, if we're going to go home, we need to figure out how."

Tomoki doesn't take his eyes off the door that Anna disappeared through. It's a moment before he speaks up, and when he does, his tone is flat. "The good news is that we've pretty much been traveling alongside Earth so far." He turns back to us. "Our flight path matches fairly closely. If we cease our outward momentum, we can get to the point where we match exactly. Then we just boost a new vector."

I've already done the math hours ago, but I imagine the vectors in my head once again, trying to convince myself it's possible with the fuel we have. Like before, though, as I crunch the numbers, I'm just not seeing it. "Tomoki, we'll need almost all our fuel just to *stop*."

"We don't want to stop, Miranda," Tomoki begins. "We—"

"You know what I mean," I cut him off. "We need to stop moving away from Earth. That vector has to stop. The other one can keep going." I grab a console, roll up its screen, and use my fingers to trace out what I'm talking about. I draw a circle for Earth, a dot for us, and two arrows leaving the dot. One arrow is pointed in the direction that Earth is traveling. That's the bigger arrow. The other, shorter, arrow is pointing perpendicular away from Earth. Then I trace a third arrow, this one also leaving our dot, but between the two arrows already there. I point at the third one. "So here's our actual path."

Everyone nods. Well, everyone except Esteban. Najma grabs him by the arm and gently guides him into our makeshift circle.

"What we need to do is stop this arrow." I point at the second arrow, the short one taking us away from Earth. "But the vector taking us along with Earth," I point at the first arrow, "is fine. We don't have to do anything to that one. What we *do* need to do is start up again in the opposite direction. And that's what worries me. I don't think we have enough fuel for that."

"It's going to be close," Tomoki agrees. "But remember, we have solar panels. We can use those if we need an extra dose of energy."

"Right." I scribble on the screen, recrunching my numbers. I'd forgotten about the solar panels. They just might be our ticket home. I let out a deep breath before allowing myself to get too excited. "So that's one kilowatt per meter squared . . ." I drag myself over to my seat and strap myself in. "I'm going to need a few minutes. Tomoki, give me anything you can on what our solar panels can do for the ion engines."

"No problem."

"Rahim, you need to make sure whatever we do won't kill us. How fast is too fast to stop for our bodies to handle? And for the life-support systems?"

Rahim nods. "I have some preliminary data on that already. I'll get that ready for you."

"And Najma, you and Esteban keep trying to get into the full system. We need to contact Earth. We have to tell them we're okay, and if we have time, try to run our plan by actual engineers. We're only going to have one shot at this," I say.

"Right." Najma goes back to her console, tugging Esteban along with her. He doesn't object.

"I'll figure out what we physically need to do to get our rockets turned and those solar panels unfurled." I think of the origami-style folded panels on the side of our spaceplane. They aren't meant to be used yet. Nothing is. But we don't have a choice. "And Ruby can take inventory of the smaller cryo tanks."

I send my mechbot away, and everyone sets to work. The sooner we figure this out, the easier and faster it will be to get home. Numbers fly past my face as I fling them from console to console. It's not looking good. "Tomoki, you got anything for me yet?"

"Working on it," Tomoki says from his seat.

"Okay," I reply. "Just know—it's what I thought. We have enough fuel to stop, which will eat up the vast majority of our supply. Then we'll have enough for about eighty-two percent of the energy required to start up again in the opposite direction. We're eighteen percent short."

"I'll see what I can do," Tomoki says. "But no promises."

Over at her console, Najma encourages Esteban in his work. I notice a couple of lines of code get executed, and he does appear to brighten up temporarily.

"Great job, Esteban!" I call over. "See? Things will be okay."

At that, Esteban freezes. Then he slowly turns to look at me. "How can you say that?"

I flinch. "What?"

"How can you say that?" Esteban asks again. "How?" The words are spilling out now, like the oxygen leak on Apollo 13. "How can any of this be okay? How are *you* okay? How have you been okay ever since that helicopter exploded? HOW?!"

"Esteban . . ." Najma puts an arm out.

"No!" He twirls, his usually bright eyes manic. "People are *dead*! People *died*! Because of *us*! How can we just keep pushing on when that kind of thing can happen? Why are we trying to return to a *place* where that kind of thing can happen?!"

With that, Esteban shatters in front of us.

Najma offers him a hand, and after a moment's pause, he grabs back for her, pulling her close and letting her hold him as he lets out huge, wracking sobs.

Tomoki gestures. I tear my eyes away, and he, Rahim, and I all leave the cockpit. There's still work to be done on the life-support systems, so at least for a few moments, we quietly decide to switch gears and let Esteban finish his breakdown in peace.

Najma sends us an all clear message about forty-five minutes later. The three of us rejoin her and Esteban in the cockpit, and I'm immediately relieved to find Esteban wearing a toned-down version his familiar smile.

"Hey, guys," he says, a little sheepishly. "I'm sorry if I freaked you out. Najma and I talked, and I'm doing a lot better now. It's just . . . it's upsetting. The whole thing."

"It is," Rahim agrees.

"I usually try to see the good in things," Esteban says, with an encouraging nod from Najma. "But that's not always easy."

"We're all dealing with it in our own way," Najma says. "You don't have to put on a brave face for us."

Esteban nods. Then he turns to me. "I don't know how you've managed to hold up so well all this time, Miranda. I'm seriously impressed. Knowing people died because of . . ."

"Yeah, it sucks," I say, sharing a glance with Rahim. He gives me a faint smile. I'm glad we had a chance to talk.

"It does!" Esteban agrees. "Anyway, I'm sorry for yelling earlier. I don't like to yell."

"Hey, yelling can help," Tomoki says.

"Being cheerful all the time is truly a superpower only you seem to wield," Rahim adds.

"Thanks, everyone." He smiles at each of us. "And especially you." He looks at Najma, who flushes deeply. "I owe you."

There's a mutual silence for a moment in the main cabin, until Tomoki coughs.

"So . . . back to work?" Tomoki asks.

"Back to work!" Esteban agrees, mustering a grin and fist-bumping Tomoki.

All of us head to our stations, diving once again into our efforts to prepare this ship for turning around and heading home. Esteban throws himself into his work, with the single-minded purpose of getting our communications back as quickly as possible. He's got his console ripped open on one side, yanking wires and rerouting systems. The other side flashes code that's completely incomprehensible to me, but must make sense to him because he keeps updating it.

Rahim, Tomoki, and Najma are all engrossed at their own stations, and I spend my time running the numbers over and over to make sure the calculations for what fuel we need to stop are correct.

I've given up on waiting for Anna to join us, which hurts more than I thought it would. She's a part of this team. She should be in here, with us, but she's chosen not to be, and I shouldn't waste time wondering why.

But I am.

After a couple of hours of mind-melting work, Ruby skitters back into the cockpit, her fuel assessments in hand—or rather, in pinching mechanical appendage. She clips herself to my flight suit and feeds me the numbers. As I'm entering them, Najma pipes up.

"Guys." Her voice sounds as thin as graphene. "Come here."

"What is it?" I ask, unbuckling my belt and floating over to her console with Ruby.

Her face is pale. "This coding style . . ."

"We're in!" Esteban exclaims, pulling up the main screen again and startling all of us. "Communications are back! We can call home, guys!"

"Really?" I spin.

Tomoki pushes off from his chair, doing a backflip and cheering loudly. "Yeah! I knew you could do it, Esteban!" He zooms over for a high five.

Esteban laughs, then begins typing rapidly. "Time to call Earth."

"Najma?" Rahim asks, ignoring Esteban's news. "What's wrong?"

I turn back. I'd nearly forgotten.

Najma shuts her eyes. "It's not Dr. Schuber," she croaks. "This is the same style of code from your quiz, Miranda. That weird language I'd never seen before. And Dr. Schuber didn't make your quiz."

By the time Najma's words truly register, Esteban's already sent a call to our training base.

"No." I stare at Najma. She just shakes her head, sad and slow. "No, it can't be . . ."

The call gets answered. Mr. Burnett's face appears on our main screen. His eyes are wide in shock, and huge dark circles run under them. He looks like he might be in his office.

"Yes!" Esteban turns to Najma. "See? Totally works!" He turns back to Mr. Burnett. "Hey, Mr. Burnett! You have no idea how happy we are to see you!"

I can feel myself begin to tremble, and it takes all of my will-power to look at the man on the screen.

"Kids!" Mr. Burnett says. "Oh wow. Wow. This is a surprise. I didn't think . . ."

"Don't underestimate our awesomeness." Tomoki smirks. "We're still alive!"

"Oh, no, I don't," Mr. Burnett says, running a hand through his messy hair and glancing over his shoulder. "I counted on it."

Najma glares up at him, her eyes glistening. "You *bastard*."

"Whoa, whoa, *whoa*!" Tomoki spins at Najma. "Wow! I never knew you could swear, Najma."

"What's going on?" Esteban asks.

"It's *his* code," Najma says. "*He* programmed this ship."

CHAPTER 18

The betrayal stings like ten thousand volts. I don't want to believe it, but the man on the screen isn't denying anything.

"Mr. Burnett, why would you do this to us?" I ask.

Rahim's eyes have steeled over, and I can see his knuckles going white gripping the side of his chair. I reach for Ruby, trying to make sense of this.

:WHY WOULD YOU DO THIS TO US?:

Ruby repeats on my droidlet, hugging me back.

"So you know, huh?" Mr. Burnett sighs, crumpling a little where he sits. "Well, then you should know that I didn't *want* to do any of it. Not really."

"What's that supposed to mean?" Tomoki asks. "Did someone force you into this? Was it Dr. Schuber?"

"Dr. Schuber?" Mr. Burnett asks. "No! Oh no, he would never!"

He's not . . . ? And then it hits me. Horrified, I feel like the biggest idiot to have ever lived. It's so *obvious.*

"Mr. Burnett worked for Valorheart Industries." The pieces fall together in my mind. "They're a weapons manufacturer. And they lost tons of money when the war ended."

"Except now war is probably starting again," Esteban says miserably.

"Exactly. You were never *really* fired, were you?" I look at Mr. Burnett.

He grimaces. Then his eyes track up toward the cockpit door and go a bit wide. "Oh, hello, Anna. Uh . . . enjoying your role as Mission Commander?"

I look back. I hadn't realized she'd come in. I wonder how much of this she's heard.

Anna crosses her arms. "Shove it."

Clearly, she's heard enough.

"You're trying to get a war started again," Rahim accuses.

"You have to understand," Mr. Burnett starts. "All I wanted in life was to be Dr. Schuber's student. That's all! I thought if I could work under the head of the ISECG, I would have really made something of myself. But I was rejected. Until Valorheart offered me a way in."

"They needed someone on the inside," I realize.

"Yes." Mr. Burnett's eyes are pained. "They did. But it wasn't supposed to be like this! All I was supposed to do was set up a few Mars nominees. But then Valorheart kept asking for more and more—"

"Miranda being a target . . . it's all your fault." Tomoki gapes.

"Is that why I haven't actually been killed yet in any of the attacks?" I ask, shaking. "Because you've needed me alive as your puppet to make the Americans and Russians fight like they did during the AEM War?"

"We had to get people angry, Miranda," Mr. Burnett explains, using the same tone of voice he'd use when he'd help us with our programming homework. "Valorheart had to give the world a reason to buy their weapons again."

"But people are *dying.*" Esteban's eyes are wide. "Why would you let that—?"

"If this was a plot for Miranda, why target me first?" Rahim interrupts Esteban, leaning forward. It's an intensity I'm not used to from Rahim, but I can't really blame him.

Mr. Burnett runs his hands over his face. "So much of the war played out on the fringes of Russia and China, and then the India-Pakistan conflict got roped into it all. We weren't sure who'd be the bigger international spark—you and Professor Singh's cousin, Deepa Kaur—"

"Dr. Singh is related to Deepa Kaur? I know her!" Najma exclaims.

"—or Miranda and Vladimir Kreshkov's nephew, Sasha Oskev," Mr. Burnett finishes. "We had to test the waters. Miranda definitely won."

Rahim recoils. We catch each other's eyes, and in that moment, an alternate version of the past few months races through my head:

Rahim as the focus of the attacks.

Rahim getting the threatening messages.

Rahim as the ostracized cadet.

My stomach churns. Everything would have been different. Except that we'd probably still be here, floating to our deaths in the end.

"You're a sick human being," Anna hisses.

Mr. Burnett shakes his head violently. "I swear, I didn't want any of this!"

"If you don't like this, you should turn yourself in!" Esteban glances desperately around at all of us. "Tell everyone what's been happening. Stop Valorheart Industries. You can do it, Mr. Burnett. You can save us all!"

Mr. Burnett looks down. "I can't. Valorheart can't know that I've said anything. They will kill me. And right now, that means killing everyone here—including your families. The heli-jets that brought your families are all Valorheart made. One of them is filled with explosives. Enough to take out the whole island."

My chest freezes.

"We're on lockdown." Mr. Burnett exhales, closing his eyes. "No one can leave. That unfortunately includes me. No one knows about the bombs, and if I say anything, they blow." Beads of sweat glisten from under his matted hair. "They also blow if you send any communications outside of this channel. Valorheart asked me to program your comm systems to go through their headquarters, but I programmed them to go through me instead. So don't try anything sneaky. If you mess with the systems, Valorheart will be alerted and will find out what I did. They won't like that."

"So you're just going to *sit there?*" Anna asks.

Mr. Burnett grimaces. "It's my only option. I'm in too deep now. You have to believe me; I did what I could! At least I made sure you'd be able to survive your launch, and I even programmed your ship so you could get to Mars. I thought . . . well, I thought even if everything else was getting destroyed, it might be at least an okay consolation prize."

No one says anything, and Mr. Burnett looks at me, dabbing the sweat off his brow.

"I tried to warn you, Miranda," he says. "I did as much as I dared. You were supposed to figure it out and leave before Valorheart could use you. But I guess that didn't happen." Mr. Burnett looks over his shoulder again. "I'd better go before anyone finds me talking to you. I'm sorry. To all of you, I'm so, so sorry. Try to enjoy Mars for me, okay?"

With a trembling hand and tears in his eyes, he ends the call.

"So it wasn't the fault of any country at all," Tomoki says, sitting down in his pilot's seat and strapping himself in. "The attacks were coordinated by an international corporation of greedy jerkfaces. Why am I not surprised?"

My brain spins like a loose bolt. *Mr. Burnett sent us away to die. He could have saved us, but he didn't. He tried to warn me . . . but there's no way he could have expected me to figure this all out from his messages. No way. He sent us away to die.*

"We have to go back and set things straight," Najma says.

He sent us away to die.

"You know, if we go home, land secretly, and tell people in person, then it won't be a transmission," Rahim muses. "We can find a way to get those bombs deactivated without Valorheart knowing. Then the bad guys get caught, and our families stay safe."

"Way ahead of you." Tomoki sits at his console, tapping away. "Miranda, you have those figures finalized?"

I pull my brain back from the edge of shock and sit down at my station. Time to set this right. "I will momentarily."

"So I guess this makes going home official?" Anna clarifies.

I just give her a look.

My finger hovers over my keyboard. This is it. "And . . . fire engines," I say.

"Firing engines," Tomoki replies.

I hold my breath. The engines roar, rattling us inside the spaceplane. I grip my armrests.

Please work.

For a terrifying eleven minutes, our spaceplane slows down amidst a headache-inducing level of noise. When it's finally over, my ears continue to buzz, but I can't help but accept Tomoki's fist bump. We've stopped along the vector that matters. Now to actually turn the spaceplane.

"Nice work, everyone," I say. All of us let out sighs of relief, except for Anna, who opted to stay out of the main cabin during this phase. "Tomoki, how are the solar panels looking? We'll need them for the last eighteen percent of our energy reserves, remember."

Tomoki grimaces. "Not so hot. They're stuck."

"Stuck?" Rahim asks.

Tomoki nods. "Stuck. They won't unroll. It's an electrical short, I think. Outside the ship."

"Outside?" I shudder. That doesn't sound good. In fact, that sounds horrible. Fixing something outside would require . . . "Wait. Could Ruby fix it?"

"They're *huge*. She won't be able to maneuver them and adapt for when one inevitably gets jammed up, unless you've installed some serious programming in her that we're unaware of."

I rest a hand on the robot attached to my chair. "No."

"Right then. That means someone has to go out there." Tomoki stares at me, his eyes sparkling in a way mine are definitely not.

"And we're the only two with space-ready spacesuits," I say.

"Which may or may not actually function properly," Tomoki finishes, grinning at the prospect. I shake my head at him.

Everyone else is silent, and then the back door swooshes open.

"So we've stopped, I see." Anna pulls herself in. "And I trust that now you all have a master plan for taking us home?"

"Working on one," Rahim clarifies. "There's a small glitch."

"Great." Anna rolls her eyes. "Whose fault is it?"

"No one's," Najma says. "It's just that the solar panels won't unfurl."

"And someone has to go out to fix them," Esteban adds. "But that's either Tomoki or Miranda."

Anna shrugs. "Obviously it should be Miranda."

I cross my arms. "What? Why?"

Esteban puts a hand on my shoulder. "Tomoki has way more experience with solar—"

"Tomoki is our pilot," Anna interrupts. "He can't be risked. Miranda can."

"You can't just say that!" Najma gasps. "No one can be risked!"

"Then what do you propose we do?" Anna asks. "If you're serious about going home, obviously someone needs to go out there and fix this thing."

"Yeah, *me*. You know, solar-car guy—?" Tomoki begins.

"No," Anna cuts him off. "If we're not going to Mars, I'm not dying because one of us screws up piloting our way back. I'm still technically Mission Commander, no matter how many decisions you're all making without me, and I say we need you in here. Miranda is the only option."

I lock eyes with Anna.

"Aww, come *on*!" Tomoki pouts. "I want to do the spacewalk!"

"It's okay," I say. "I'll do it. Tomoki, you just need to walk me through it."

"This is totally unfair," Tomoki says. "Why do I have to be stuck in here when—oh! Wait! Hah!" He slams a fist into his hand in triumph. "You're going to need a partner with solar panels this size! It's going to take two sets of hands out there to even them out."

Anna shrugs. "She's got that robot."

"Human hands," Tomoki clarifies. He beams as Anna fails to come up with a response. "So it's settled. I'm going, too."

"Wait," Najma says. "Anna has a point. Tomoki, we need you in here flying this thing."

"But then who's going to—"

"Anna," Najma answers before Tomoki can even finish his question. "Anna's about the same size as you. She can wear your EMU. She can be Miranda's assistant."

Anna's eyes fly open, and mine do the same. "Oh, no way—"

"That's completely unnecessary—"

"Totally out of the question—"

"Not going to happen—"

"Oh, stop it! Both of you!" Najma says. Anna and I fall silent. "We need this spaceplane operational, and if that means two people out there fixing it, then that means two people out there fixing it! Whether or not you like each other. And you." She spins at Tomoki. "This isn't about being cool. Grow up and do your job."

Everyone's quiet now.

"There," Najma says. "Now let's get this spaceplane fixed."

As I snap my gloves in place, I have to admit, I'm actually excited to try this whole spacewalk thing. Terrified, but excited. And also pretty pumped that I'll get to test out Ruby's rocket thrusters. But of course, I can't say any of that out loud. Tomoki's the one putting my helmet on for me, and his bottom lip pouts worse than Emmaline's when she's not allowed to play with my robotics equipment.

"Lucky," he says, attaching the front of my helmet to my EMU. "Lucky, lucky, lucky." He repeats the word for each clasp he closes. His voice sounds mildly electronic as it comes through my helmet's speakers.

I shiver as the air-conditioning system kicks on. "Yeah, unless we get pummeled by space debris, or have our EMUs malfunction."

Anna taps a console unit on her right arm. "That's why I have this. Nothing will come near us that I won't detect ahead of time so we can get out of the way."

Now that Anna's resigned herself to going out into space, she's made it clear that she's not going to just take orders from me. She made Tomoki walk both of us through the entire process of opening the solar-panel sails, and she's bringing her own Tool Carrier Assembly, though it doesn't have a handy-sized 3D printer like mine.

For the next forty minutes, we sit in silence until our suits have transitioned to one hundred percent oxygen. We need to get all the nitrogen out of our lungs before going into space. It makes my body feel a little giddy, but not in a good way.

"Ready?" I ask Anna, once we've made the transition to oxygen-only air.

"Are you?" she counters.

I don't bother responding. Instead, I turn and head to the exit hatch. There's a series of two doors awaiting us. The first leads to the crew lock, and the second actually leads into space.

Tomoki floats along with us. "Now, remember, solar panels are delicate!" he says. "You need to coax, not coerce. Too much force and they won't operate at full-functioning levels. That's why their accompanying shields are going to be so critical."

"Yes, yes, we got it," Anna says. "You told us all this already."

I smile. I've never heard Tomoki talk this way before. It's like the solar panels are his children or something.

"What are you grinning about?" Tomoki yanks on my arm. "Come on! Are you trying to rub it in my face that I'm going to be stuck in here while you two are out doing cool space stuff and working with the most advanced solar materials ever developed?"

I shake my head, smiling even more. "Nope. Not at all."

"You two be careful, okay?" Najma asks, floating by the first set of doors. "Don't take any unnecessary risks. Your suits are operating purely on internal battery power now, so technically, your spacewalk has already started."

"And remember to have fun," Esteban says. "I can't believe you get to actually go out *into space*. That's so completely awesome!"

"Oh, shut up." Tomoki punches him in the shoulder, sending him sailing backward in the zero gravity of our ship.

I laugh. It helps dispel some of my nervous energy.

"All right," I say, getting myself back under control. My breath feels warm on my face, trapped inside the helmet with me. "Let's get those panels working."

"I'll be in here if you need anything," Tomoki says. "Or, you know, if you want to swap out—"

Anna responds by hitting the open button on the door. Both she and I maneuver our bulky suits into the crew lock. Tomoki crosses his arms on the other side of the door as it closes behind us. We struggle to fit in the tight space together, and I end up with one arm over my head and Anna's knees in my face.

"Test, test, test," Esteban says into our earpieces. "Can you still hear us?"

"Yep," I reply.

"Yes," Anna says. "Ready for EVA procedures."

I look outward. There's only one more set of doors between us and the cold vacuum of space. Normally there would be a second chamber, an unpressurized payload bay, but it hasn't been built yet. Which means we've had to modify the entire Extra-Vehicular procedure process. I can only hope our calculations were right, and that this all works.

The air gets sucked out of our chamber in preparation for the final door to open. I move my right arm to buckle myself to a tether that will keep us connected to the spaceplane. Even with zero gravity, moving my arms in this suit feels like trying to swim in sand.

Something to correct in the future, my brain notes. *If we're going to live in these on Mars, we'll need to*—I cut off my train of thought, watching the stars outside the window.

Right. The space programs have been demolished back home. We're not going to Mars. I glance at Anna, who's watching the stars, too. I wonder if she's thinking the same thing.

So far, the noise has been incredible in this crew lock. There's whooshing, whirring, and chugging, but as the pressure drops lower and lower, the sound fades.

Esteban's voice sounds in my communications earpiece about twenty minutes into the procedure. "Pressure at five PSI. Holding."

Our suits are at 4.3 PSI. Anna and I report in and do a final mobility check, and then Esteban resumes the pressure drop. Usually this would be where we would maneuver into the second chamber, but we're winging it here and instead taking the first chamber to full vacuum. If our suits aren't working, this is when we're going to find out. Oxygen will rush from any small gap in our EMUs out into the crew lock once its PSI is lower than ours. As for what that will mean for us . . .

"Approaching vacuum. Everything okay in there?" Esteban asks.

"Yes," Anna confirms for us.

"Miranda?"

"Yeah," I say, steadying myself. So far, so good. The pressure remains steady in our EMUs.

"Okay, time to go full vacuum. Depress valve opening in three, two, one . . ."

I hold my breath.

The hatch swings open, completely silently. I don't know what I expect, but my entire body is tensed, bracing against the exposure. However, I quickly discover that it doesn't feel any different than inside the ship. There's no gravity, so Anna and I just slowly drift out . . . into nothing.

Oh wow. Okay. Yeah. Nothing. We're in nothing. And this nothing goes on. And on. And *on.*

"Depress valve open," Esteban says.

My heart speeds up to an absurd rate. I grab for Ruby, clinging to her even though I know she's latched on to me—and even if she wasn't, could use her thrusters to fly back to me. Next to me, Anna grips the railing outside our spaceplane. I can hear her breath quicken through our communicators. It's nice to know I'm not alone in my sudden panic.

I reach for the railing with my free hand. Knowing I have a tether holding me to the ship is of next to no comfort. Out here, the darkness stretches on forever. It's a thin, silky blackness that is everywhere and nowhere all at once. Impossibly dark shadows make everything that's not in direct sunlight disappear like it never existed. Our spaceplane looks chopped in half. My brain almost forgets to direct my lungs to breathe out here in the inky depths, and when I finally do, it's a shallow, shuddering breath. It's as if I'm inhaling the very last shred of air that the vastness of space holds for us.

"Hatch opened and stowed. Everything okay out there?" I hear Esteban ask.

I swallow. "Uh-huh," I manage.

Anna and I exchange glances. It's hard to see her through the reflection of her helmet's shielding, but I imagine she's in just as much terror as I am, given the tight grip she has on the gray railing and the fact that she isn't taunting me for my own obvious nerves.

I take several more deep breaths. Slowly, the reassuring feeling of my lungs filling with oxygen steadies me. A new sensation kicks in. It takes a moment for me to recognize it, but my nerves fire along, creating a tingling inside me. Before I know it, I'm smiling.

"Guys," I say into my mic. "I'm in *space*."

"Hey, you said you weren't going to rub it in!" Tomoki moans.

I laugh. Even Anna laughs, though I can hear her nerves chitter through.

"All right," I say. "Anna, you set?"

"Yes," she replies, though her grip on the rail doesn't loosen.

I tap Ruby, waking her up. "Tomoki, run us through this."

Ruby waves at me from her mounted position next to the third panel base.

:TASK COMPLETE. WAITING FOR INSTRUCTION:

"Thanks," I tell her through my helmet radio connection to her receiver. "Next panel, please."

Ruby floats up, then uses her thrusters to direct herself to the fourth solar panel and sets to work replacing the wiring. Anna and I work together to straighten out the second solar panel sail, aiming it toward the sun, which itself is probably the weirdest thing out here. First of all, it looks smaller than it does from Earth, even though we're not significantly farther away than our planet's orbit. Second, the sun's surrounded by black, not blue. I have to be careful not to be hypnotized by it.

"Incoming dust," Anna says, reading from her scanner. "Zero

decimal seven meters per second. Safe range."

I quickly finish tugging the shielding we've been pulling out to protect the solar cells. Tiny grains of space dust sail past us, silently washing over our spacesuits, our spaceplane, and Ruby, who hunkered down in preparation when I gave her the order to do so. Pulling asteroids into position for mining created a lot of small junk to watch out for here in space.

After the dust passes, I unhook my pistol-grip tool, and we go back to work. Everything is going relatively smoothly, and Ruby in particular is making it all possible. I smile in pride as I watch her rocket to the next panel. *My little mechbot is growing up.*

"At least that robot is one thing you got right," Anna says on our private channel.

I sigh. Again, with the insults. *Why?* "Anna, listen. We're alone out here. Any chance you'll finally explain what your problem is with me? Because I'm getting really tired of it. We're supposed to be a team."

Anna doesn't respond for a long moment. She finishes straightening the panel she's working on, and after she's done I hear her radio click. "Fine. You want to know? I'll tell you my problem."

"Good. Finally."

Anna turns. "If it wasn't for you—"

"We wouldn't be in this mess, I know that one already!" I finish for her. "And maybe I should have listened to the warnings and left so none of this would've—"

"That's not what I was going to say," Anna interrupts.

I pause what I'm doing, slowly lowering my wrench. "Then what were you going to say?"

Anna is still. Space is like that—if you don't move, there's nothing to move you. "If it wasn't for you, *I* wouldn't be here. At all. I wouldn't have applied to the program."

"What?" I stare at her. "Wait, why? *What?*"

Anna remains motionless by the side of our spaceplane. "When we tied at the Advancing Astronomy Competition, we didn't really tie. You won. I lost."

"Anna, do you need me to explain to you what the word *tied* means?"

"Shut up," she barks. "Listen. You're a year younger than me. If we tied, that means you're better. That's it. And I couldn't stand that. I've worked too hard to make sure I'm the best of the best, and I'd lost my chance to prove it."

"Anna—"

"My father suggested I apply to the Destined for Mars program when they announced it. It was another chance to prove myself. Another way to be the best. But then you had to go and win that, too."

"What about Najma and Esteban? They're younger than you, too!"

"Yeah, but they're competent! You're a buffoon!"

"Thanks." I'm shaking my head at her, but I don't think she can tell because our helmets are set in fixed positions.

"But what does that make me, then?" Anna's voice is barely loud enough to register over the radio channel. "I don't . . . I can't be worse than *you*. I can't. But everyone likes you. And they don't like me. Everyone listens to you. I'm supposed to be Mission Commander, but who am I fooling? You're the one leading this team. I'm just the girl no one likes."

"Anna, no, you're . . ." I honestly don't know how to finish my sentence without lying, so I shut myself up.

She turns from me. She knows. And for some reason, that makes me feel sad instead of smug. "Come on," she says. "We've got a job to complete."

I watch her pull herself to the next solar panel, stunned. I had no idea Anna had all these secret feelings bottled up. No idea. Guilt twists through me, along with flares of residual anger.

Ruby uses her thrusters to float over and poke me after ninety seconds of inactivity.

"Thanks," I say.

:YOU'RE WELCOME, ASTRONAUT REGENT:

I smile at my mechbot as she gets back to work. Priorities: get the panels ready and get home. I can sort out Anna later.

I propel myself after Anna, and the two of us move through the next several panels in a silent rhythm. Our Primary Life-Support System backpacks have newly designed rotor systems in addition to thrusters, which help us stay steady so we don't topple over our feet when we move. An hour ticks by, and we're nearly done.

"Last one," I say, as we swing around to the other side of the spaceplane for the final time. I flip my radio channel to the team channel to reach Esteban. "How're our energy levels now?"

Esteban doesn't answer. "Anna, did you hear a reply?" I ask, before calling in again.

"No," Anna says. "Esteban? Come in, Esteban."

Still no reply. We finish pulling out the last solar panel, and I try to stay calm. "Maybe they're just busy?"

"Hey," Esteban finally says. "Hey, yeah, sorry, we were busy. We, uh . . . well, maybe Najma can explain."

We pause our work as Najma starts talking. "So, there's a problem," she says. "A major one."

"Let's hear it." Anna's voice is grim.

:TASK COMPLETE. WAITING FOR INSTRUCTION:

"Hold steady, Ruby," I tell her. My mechbot holds on where she is, patiently waiting. "Go ahead, Najma," I say. "Is it something we can fix while we're out here?"

"That's just it," she says. "I don't know if there's any way to fix it."

We're both silent for a moment, and all I hear is the sound of our breathing. Finally, Anna says, "And this problem is what, exactly?"

"Remember the hypnotivirus?" Najma asks. Before we reply, she continues. "Remember how I quarantined it on the back drive? Well, it turns out the back drive is responsible for supplying our power from the solar sails."

My brain clicks through what this means.

"We can't use the solar energy," Najma says. "It's locked up. We won't have enough power to get back to Earth. This . . . this is it."

257

My insides go cold, and not because we're in space.

"No," Anna says. "No, there's got to be another way."

"There isn't," Najma crackles over the helmet's speaker.

"Then you're not trying hard enough!" Anna barks. "Find us a way!"

"There isn't one," Najma repeats herself. "What do you think we've been doing in here?"

"Apparently nothing useful!"

"Unless you can build us a new supercomputer capable of holding a virus of this size, then I'm sorry, but that's it," Najma says. I can hear the tears in her voice. "We're stranded. There *is* no other way."

"Ridiculous!" Anna says. "I'm coming back in. I'll find a way."

"Oh, like you'll be able to, if Najma can't," Tomoki chimes in. "Trust me, she's done everything anyone could do."

"She really has," Esteban says. "I just don't think there's anything more to do."

"So we've been out here, risking our lives to fix these solar panels for *nothing*?" Anna demands to know. "We're just going to die anyway?"

"I suppose so," Esteban says. I shut my eyes.

We're stranded. Doomed to a slow death in space, unless we find another supercomputer to quarantine the virus on. I shake. It's not the prospect of a slow space death that's gotten to me . . . it's . . .

No. I can't. I look at Ruby, who has her optical sensors trained on me, awaiting instruction.

"Guess we're not going home after all," Rahim says quietly.

I remember our conversation from the meditation cabin. Sunlight gleams off our hull, and I feel like it's searing into my soul.

"No," I say out loud. "No, we have to go home."

"But we—" Anna starts.

"We do have another supercomputer," I say, each breath harder to take than the last. I blink, wet tears fogging my view of my mechbot.

I finally manage to finish my thought. *I'm so sorry.* "We have Ruby."

CHAPTER 19

No one speaks for a moment.

"Ruby?" Anna eventually asks. I still can't see her face clearly, but she's definitely watching me. Closely.

"Y-yes," I reply, taking a deep breath. "We can put the virus on her. She's separate from the ship."

"But won't she just direct the ship to Mars herself, then?" Tomoki asks.

"No," I say. "If I understand things right, the virus tries to get the thing it's housed on to Mars. So, we just need to put it on Ruby . . ."

"And then release her into space," Najma says softly.

"Yeah." My voice is barely above a whisper.

Anna speaks again. "And you're okay with this?"

I turn to her, using the rotors on the back of my bulky suit to steady myself. "I don't think we have any other choice. It's like what you said before. Lizzie and Kreshkov died trying to save us. We wouldn't be honoring their memory much if we just let ourselves die out here for nothing."

"But you *love* that ugly metal spider," Anna says.

"Yeah, you don't have to remind me," I say, probably in a gruffer tone than necessary. She goes silent. "Najma, what do we need to do?" I ask. I can't bring myself to look at Ruby, who is still waiting for me to tell her what to do next.

"You'll need to plug Ruby into the output port in the control panel," Najma says. "It'll take probably thirty or forty minutes to transfer the virus. Then you'll need to release her *immediately*. Get her away from the spaceplane."

I nod in my helmet. "Okay," I say. "Got it." Logically, I know this is the only way. People come first. Ruby's just a robot.

She's just a robot.

But the moment I reach up to collect Ruby, everything in me breaks again.

Competitions and trophies suddenly seem utterly pointless. All I can think about are late nights back in Ohio, working on Ruby under my covers when I was supposed to be asleep. Years of exchanging challenges with Sasha as we tried to outdo each other with new upgrades. The hug Ruby gave me the day I fell out of the training ropes.

A hiccup escapes me, and I crumple, my EMU folding around me. "I can't, I can't, I just *can't*."

"Do you want me to do it?" Anna asks.

"No." My protective instincts rear up. "I'll do it. But we're not sending her away until she's got a parachute." I float over, pick up Ruby, and then pull myself toward the exterior control panel. My backpack rotors steady me as I go, which is helpful since I'm a shaking mess.

"A what?" I hear Tomoki ask over my headset.

"A parachute," I repeat myself, plugging Ruby into the output port through the insulation blocks on the outside of our space-plane. "I'm making her a parachute. And she's going to use it to land on Mars."

"Miranda . . ." Najma says gently.

"She's going to use it to land on Mars!" I yank my 3D printer from my Tool Carrier Assembly and switch it on. "Now, start transferring that virus so we can get home."

Anna stays back as I program in commands to the printer, forming a cloth-thin material out of the strongest polyplex that it can create. I know it's absurd. I know that all odds are against her survival, but if this parachute gives her even a 0.000001 percent chance of making it there in one piece, then it's worth it.

Tears spill out. "Oh, Ruby . . ." I go to rub my eyes, but my helmet blocks me.

Ruby, hearing her name, looks up at me, rubbing her optical sensors with her front arms.

:WAITING FOR INSTRUCTION:

It takes all my willpower not to completely break down. "Ruby, listen," I say. "You're going to get some orders soon from a new code. And it's going to direct you to Mars."

:GOING TO DIRECT US TO MARS:

"No," I clarify, wondering if she misheard me or if I misspoke. "Just you, Ruby. I'm not going there right now."

There's a pause before my robot's usual acknowledgement. After a five-second delay, her familiar message appears on my console.

:INSTRUCTION NOTED:

"Initiating virus transfer," Najma says.

I cradle Ruby in my arms as the transfer commences. Anna—thankfully—stays away and says nothing.

After the parachute prints, I hook it into Ruby's back chamber, and then have her bolt it into herself. "You can use this to help you land," I say, as she folds it rapidly and tucks it into a compartment. "Save your fuel for your descent," I advise. "That's your best bet."

:THAT'S YOUR BEST BET:

I flinch at her repetition. I know it's irrational, but I swear I can detect a hint of betrayal in that reply. Ruby doesn't look at me the entire time the virus transfers.

Then she starts shuddering. Pulling. Her thrusters swivel, and I have to hold her out in front of me to keep them from hitting me. It gets so bad that I can't control her myself. To stop her from snapping her transfer cable, I unbuckle my tether and use it to lash her to the spaceplane, wrapping my feet around a ladder rung to hold myself in place in the meantime. I can hardly believe it's already been thirty minutes when Najma's voice is in my ear again.

"Transfer completed, Miranda. It's time to let her go."

Ruby's full-on shaking by now, and so am I.

"I copy." My voice comes out as a whisper.

As gently as I can, I unhook Ruby's transfer cable from the output port. She's still too violent to undo her tether just yet. I wince as she slams herself over and over into the side of the spaceplane, fighting to break free of her bonds.

"Ruby, thrusters at low power," I say, hoping that will keep her from wasting her fuel.

:TASK COMPLETE. WAITING FOR INSTRUCTION:

This is it. No more putting it off. I need to send her away before she finds a way to login to our spaceplane and doom us all once again.

I exhale and tip my head down, bumping my helmet against Ruby's optical sensors. She finally pauses her intense struggles and turns to face me, tilting her optical unit against my helmet to mimic my posture one final time.

My breath catches in my throat. I can't even kiss her goodbye.

"Ruby, I know it doesn't look like it right now, but I love you. So much. It . . . it might be a little while, but someday I will find you," I promise. Trembling, I keep my eyes locked on her, capturing this last moment in my mind. "Wait for me on Mars, okay?"

Her final message appears on my arm console.

:INSTRUCTION NOTED:

Before my resolve completely crumbles, I unhook her tether, pull my clunky gloves away from her, and let her go with a small shove. Immediately, we move away from her, flying onward. She floats back in space, booting up her thrusters. All I can do now is hope.

I set my shoulders. "It's done," I report. My voice crackles over the communication system. Holding on to a rung with my right hand, I allow my boot to disentangle itself. My leg hurts from being tensed against the ladder for so long. I wrinkle up my toes, trying to get rid of the soreness running through my foot and up my calf, even if I can't get rid of the same feeling in my heart.

"Miranda . . ." Anna says, her voice softer than I've ever heard it before. She's right behind me, which I hadn't realized. I turn to face her. "That was—"

Then she jerks her arm toward her helmet, reading her scanner.

"Miranda! *Incoming debris!*" She looks back at Ruby, who's drifting away. A cluster of dark space rocks, the biggest not even the size of a golf ball, hurdles toward my mechbot.

"NO!" I scream.

The rocks might be small, but at the speed they're traveling, they'd be enough to do serious damage. I let go of the spaceplane and kick off the side to dive after Ruby.

"RUBY, LOOK OUT!"

"MIRANDA!" Anna shrieks.

Something slams into my back. My backpack rotors misfire, and my personal thrusters shoot me forward nearly faster than my skeleton can keep up. But then I'm whiplashed backward with almost the same amount of intense force.

"*Aaaarrh!*" Anna screams out—a *horrendous* screech of pain. Her hand grips my EMU, and my body clunks against the spaceplane.

Out of my desperate reach, one of the rocks sails straight into Ruby, silently crunching her red plating, and sending her spiraling into the dark depths of space.

"NO!" I cry again, struggling as my backpack thrusters push me forward and Anna holds me back. "NO, NO, NO!" I hit my hands on the hull of the spaceplane.

"What's happening? Are you guys okay?!" I hear Najma ask over our headsets.

"You idiot!" Anna screams at me, clinging to my spacesuit with one hand and the spaceplane with the other. "Hold still!"

"What's going on out there?!" Najma asks again.

"RUBY!" I scream. I watch her disappear, spinning out of control behind us.

"*Miranda*, your thrusters are broken! The debris . . . !" Anna yells. "ARGH!" Her second cry of pain actually makes me look back at her. Her right hand is still clenched on my spacesuit, and I realize that she's just *saved my life*.

"Anna!" I gape at her. I never hooked my tether back on. My backpack thrusters are still misfiring after getting hit by one of the space rocks. The only thing keeping me in place is . . . "You—"

"Yeah, I'm hurt, I know!" she says.

"Right, that, too!" I say, still in shock. I'm caught in an intense tug-of-war between her hand and my spacesuit. "But you saved me! Thank you!"

266

"Thank me later."

"Right, yes." I quickly grab on to the railing, so she can let go. But she doesn't.

It takes all my strength to fight the force of my thrusters smashing me into the hull long enough to punch in the override code on my sleeve. With the last number pressed, the power shuts off to my propulsion system, calming my spacesuit. I feel like a human sack of jelly once the last shudder's gone through me. I shut my eyes. *Ruby . . .*

No. No time for that. I'm finally steady, and I need to address the next problem. I grip the ladder rung with one hand and use my other to peel Anna's fingers off the padding of my EMU. She makes a small noise each time I pull one of her fingers away. God, I can't even imagine what must be wrong with her arm after pulling me back like that.

"Come on." I loop a padded spacesuit arm around her, and she cries out again in pain.

"Careful!" she says.

"Yeah, sorry," I say. "It's not easy to move in these things with the rotors busted." I pull her with me toward the door, holding back the overwhelming urge to look out into space for Ruby. My mind is in too many places at once, and I need to concentrate on what's happening *now*. I maneuver Anna carefully around the spaceplane. I have to get her inside.

It's easier said than done.

"Miranda! Anna!" Esteban says through our headsets. "Please tell us what's happening! Are you okay?"

"Anna's hurt," I say. We reach the door, but I can't take my hand off the safety rung to operate it. "I can't let go of her, someone else needs to open the door for us."

"Did you get the solar panels open?" Tomoki asks.

"Tomoki, that's not important right now!" Najma berates.

"Really? Pretty sure that's critically important," he says back.

"We got the panels open." Anna growls. "Just open the damn hatch!"

The outer door swings open, and I pull the two of us inside in reverse. "Hold still," I tell Anna. "Don't move too much. We'll get you taken care of."

"Yeah, yeah," Anna says.

The hatch closes silently behind us, and I have to shove away the feeling that I'm forgetting something as it locks into place, trapping the emptiness of space outside once more. It's like my brain is trying to remind me that I've left some vital piece of my spacesuit outside—something critical for survival.

Stop it, Miranda, I tell myself, fighting another wave of tears. *Ruby is gone.* I carefully unhook Anna's tether, doing my best not to move her arm. I don't know what's wrong with it, but if it's got Anna admitting to pain, it must be bad. It takes all my muscle control not to shake as I move Anna farther into the tiny crew lock, positioning her so she's in the least awkward orientation I can manage. Of course, this leaves me sprawled against the hatch, with my arms and legs contorted uncomfortably.

We've got to repressurize and convert our air back to a mix of nitrogen and oxygen before we can leave this space. Until then,

I'll just have to deal with being shoved up against the door, and Anna . . . well, she'll just have to deal with the pain.

Nearly thirty long minutes later, I hear, "Pressurization complete. Oxygen to nitrogen ratio normalized."

The door slides open. I lean back instinctively, like I'm expecting to topple forward into a room where gravity actually affects us like it would back home. Instead, Anna and I slowly float into the port cabin, where artificial lights, gray metal, and the arms of our fellow cadets await us.

"Thank goodness!" Najma exclaims, pulling me in and hugging me tight. "You're both safe."

Esteban and Rahim take Anna from me, and she protests in pain. Najma unlatches my helmet for me, as the boys do the same for Anna. Tomoki isn't nearby, and I realize he must still be up at the pilot controls in the main cabin.

"What happened?" Esteban asks, as soon as both of us are free of our helmets.

Anna's face is far paler than normal, almost as gray as our spaceplane's metal interior. Our helmets float past us, forgotten, as I explain what Anna did.

"Wow!" Esteban says. "You're a hero, Anna!"

"Shut up," she says.

He and Rahim continue to get her out of her EMU, and Najma and I work on mine. "Anna, I'm so sorry," I say each time she whimpers in pain.

She doesn't say anything back, which I guess is a better reaction than what I expected from her. When they finally get Anna

269

out of her EMU and the sleeve of her flight suit, I actually gag and have to throw my recently freed hands in front of my mouth.

Anna's right arm dangles by her side. Her shoulder does *not* look like a shoulder. A large bump protrudes out the front of it, pushing against her skin.

"Dislocated," Rahim says.

"Anna dislocated her shoulder?" Tomoki asks over our headsets.

"What angle did you pull her at?" Rahim asks Anna, ignoring Tomoki.

"I grabbed her in front of me," Anna says. "But the momentum of the spaceplane pulled me backward as she went forward, so my arm twisted out and . . ." she trails off, taking several hissing breaths through clenched teeth.

I move over by her side, wishing I could do something to help.

"A dislocated shoulder means she'll be okay long term, right?" Tomoki asks.

"Yes," Rahim replies.

"Good! Then hold up, Rahim," Tomoki says. "Wait for me until you pop it back in. I've always wanted to see someone do that!"

Anna's eyes go noticeably wide.

Rahim shakes his head. "I'm not going to pop it back in, Tomoki," he says. "Well, not unless this has happened before. Have you ever done this before?"

"What? Yank an idiot back from flying off into space after they jumped in front of a meteoroid?" Anna asks.

I smile. That sounds more like Anna.

"Dislocated your arm," Rahim clarifies, calmly moving her toward the wall where there's a padded bedframe she can be buckled into.

"No," she says.

"Then I won't push it back together." He pulls out some cloth and wraps it around Anna, forming a makeshift sling. "I could just hurt you worse."

"So what do we do?" Esteban asks, hovering.

I want to know as well, but then Najma pulls me aside. "Is everything all set out there?" she asks me. I miss whatever Rahim's response is about Anna's treatment.

I nod at Najma. "We should be good to go."

She puts a hand on my arm. "I'm sorry about Ruby."

I nod again, my brain replaying the image of Ruby floating away and getting hit by that space rock. Something starts to sizzle inside me, like water dripping onto a laboratory hot plate. First Lizzie and Kreshkov. Now Ruby.

"You know what?" I ask. I clench my fists, looking at everyone around me. At Anna, with her dangling arm. *Sizzle.* "Yeah. That's it. I'm done with this. I've lost too many people, hurt too many people, all because of Valorheart Industries. We *have* to stop them."

Najma squeezes my arm where her hand rests. "We will. Tomoki is using the solar panels to reenergize our ion engines right now."

"No." I float up and grab on to some piping. "That's not good enough. What if we don't make it back?" I ask, gripping the piping tighter and tighter. "We're the only ones who know about their plot. We have to contact someone else, before they hurt more people."

"But if we do that, our families get blown up," Rahim says.

I turn away from everyone and pull myself toward the main cabin. I need to get to my console. "If we can just find a way to get in touch with people through some other means—"

"We can't," Esteban says behind me. "I'm sorry. I've tried. I really have."

"But—" I look back desperately.

"Miranda," Esteban says. His big brown eyes are pained. "You know I would do something if I could. You know. There's no way. We could've maybe sent word with your mechbot, but now she's heading the wrong way—"

Najma shoves him, glancing pointedly at me.

I just turn back around. *"It's okay,"* I want to say. *"You can talk about her in front of me,"* I try next. But the words won't come, so instead I drift into the cockpit and settle into my seat.

"About time you got in here, Flight Engineer," Tomoki says. "Panels charging to max capacity. It'll be another eight hours before we have enough energy stored to add the right boost to our fuel supply and rocket us back home. You'll need to help me get the engines ready."

I nod, pulling my console toward me.

"And cheer up!" Tomoki says. "We're saved now. I'll get us all back to Earth, no problem."

I begin my programming, holding back from saying the words in my head: *we aren't all going back to Earth.*

A few hours later, it's practically pitch black in here. And not just because we're in space.

The whole spaceplane has gone dark, except for a few emergency lights. We're using all our energy to get our engines firing on a trajectory back to Earth. With our journey home just beginning, the unanimous vote was to try to get some sleep during the flight.

But I couldn't sleep. So I'm up, sitting at my console and fiddling with my 3D printer, working out larger models of parachutes for each of us. Not that I don't trust Tomoki's piloting skills, but he's never actually landed a spaceplane on a planet before, and I'm not taking any chances.

As I do the final calculations for our parachute surface areas, a comforting thought strikes me. *It's been a little while now. Maybe someone else back home has figured out who's behind the attacks.*

Or maybe the training base has already exploded, and all our families are dead

I don't like that thought nearly as much. And even though I don't want to hear about anyone else dying, I find myself waking my console out of hibernation to get the news stream running again. Now that the thought is in my head, I can't shake it.

A woman talks on the screen from the same American news channel that we watched before, and I unmute the volume so I can hear her in my headset. "All eyes remain focused on the skies tonight, as people continue to wonder: Where are the Mars cadets now? Are they still alive? And just how long will the astronauts in the ISS 2 last without any reliable spacecraft left to bring a repair crew for their leak?"

Oh no. I'd completely forgotten about the leak on the International Space Station. Lizzie was going to let a new crew go fix it, but now . . .

"Meanwhile," a man cuts in. "The United States continues to move naval vessels into a blockade along the Pacific coast."

Wait, go back! I will the broadcast. But they've already moved on to a different story.

As I watch, it becomes quickly apparent that there have been no attacks on the Destined for Mars training center. Our families are still safe, and I settle my breathing, refocusing on making parachutes. Then comes a story that I was not prepared for.

"With the shocking reveal that the six Mars cadets each had a secret replacement selected for them, and that Miranda Regent's was none other than the Russian candidate, Sasha Oskev, grandstanding has given way to both Russia and the United States dusting off their remaining weapons stocks from the AEM War. Cyber attacks have already begun, leaving millions without access to internet and cities scrambling to keep their infrastructure functioning. It is only a matter of time before more violence is unleashed."

I watch, horrified, for another forty-five minutes before they revisit the ISS 2 story. Valorheart Industries is getting exactly what they want. The world really is going back to war.

One parachute finishes printing, and I pull it toward myself, hugging it as I listen in on the state of the ISS 2.

"Three astronauts—Canadian Patricia Glower, Ming Chen of China, and Jean Pilotte of France—remain stranded in space tonight, as each nation argues over how to best bring them home before the station leak becomes fatal. Their lifeboat pod has malfunctioned, and preliminary reports say they may only have enough oxygen to last three weeks, at the most. But with the six-month timeline for building either a rescue or repair ship, these astronauts may unfortunately be added to the ever-growing casualty list."

"Sad news, indeed. But now, for a special report on the heroic actions of one first responder and how he saved NASA employee Kiernan Song—"

I turn the news feed back off and stare at the blinking lights on the plane's dashboard, my eyes drifting to the stars outside. This is all so much bigger than I'd thought at the beginning. So much more was going on—so many other pieces in play. And yet, I feel responsible. If I hadn't been so distracted about what it meant for *me* to not really be a Mars cadet, maybe I could've seen through the bigger illusion and figured out what that would end up meaning for so many others.

I tighten my grip on my computer, concentrating on the one thing I can change. Three astronauts are stranded on the International Space Station. Narrowing my eyes at the starry field glinting outside, I reach my decision: *No one else is going to die because of me.*

I begin number crunching. I need to determine the exact angle at which we'll be approaching Earth. I need to determine the change in payload. I need to determine the change in velocity and calculate the orbital position of the ISS 2.

And then I need to wake everyone up.

CHAPTER 20

"It'll be tight, but it is possible." Tomoki taps his chin thoughtfully. We're all in the main cabin. Outside in the far distance we can see Earth, lit up like a crescent moon. We're slowly drawing closer.

"You really think you can pilot us to connect with the International Space Station?" Anna raises an eyebrow.

Tomoki waves a hand at her. "Don't you worry about that. If Miranda's numbers are correct, I could dock us with my eyes closed."

"Please don't," Najma says.

I smile. So far, everyone's in with my plan. Even Anna, which is baffling but welcome. "Thanks," I say to my fellow crewmates. "You guys are the best."

"It'll be a nice change to save some lives, instead of the opposite," Rahim says.

"And you?" Anna asks Esteban. "You've been oddly quiet this whole time." She instinctively goes to cross her arms, but quickly finds she can't because her right arm is in a sling.

"I've just been thinking," he says slowly.

"Uh-oh, watch out," Tomoki jokes. He punches Esteban in the side, and Esteban punches back at him.

"Hey, wait to hear my idea first!" he protests. "It's a really good one!"

"Okay, what is it?" I ask.

Esteban floats up near the pilot's chair, one hand on the wall, his eyes growing wide with excitement. "All right, so, you know how Mr. Burnett said our families will blow up if we use our comm systems to try and contact anyone?"

"Yeah, funny enough, I hadn't forgotten that little tidbit," I say.

He puts up one finger to shush me as Anna snorts. "And remember Dr. Mayworth giving us that calculus problem? The one without any answer?" he rambles. "And saying that sometimes problems don't have answers, and the best solution is to change the problem?"

"Just tell us your idea already!" Anna orders.

"Okay, okay!" Esteban puts his hands up. "So I was thinking—we need to change the problem. Instead of communicating to Earth through our comm systems here, let's use the ones on the ISS 2."

Anna's glare dissipates. "Esteban, that's brilliant."

"Thanks." He beams at her.

My mind is already racing with the idea. We were planning on docking with them long enough to get the astronauts onboard our spaceplane, but we could spare another few moments so that we can send a communication. The numbers start running through my head again. "Yeah. Yeah, this could work. We could do this, guys! We could actually call Earth and warn them! That way if we . . ." I trail off.

No one finishes my sentence for me. Instead, we all look at each other, then slowly at Tomoki, who spins around away from us, making a grunt of annoyance.

That way, if we crash and die, people will still know who was behind it all.

"So I guess the last question is, how do we make sure we connect successfully with the space station?" Rahim asks. "Our doors aren't compatible. We can't risk any gaps between us and them, or someone could get lost to space."

I find Anna's eyes in the back of the cabin. She looks deep in thought. "Anna, what do you think we should do?" I ask.

Everyone gapes at me like I just asked if the universe revolves around Earth. Anna, however, has her mouth dropped open the widest. "You're asking me?"

"You're Mission Commander, right?" I ask.

There's a long period of silence. Our fellow cadets stare back and forth between us, gawking, none of them daring to speak.

Slowly, a smile breaks across Anna's face. "Yes. Yes, I am." She pulls up her comp screen and gathers us around. "I have a plan. But it will take all of us to make it work."

My fingers move over the datapad of my console, tapping away instructions to our engines to prepare for our next move. We've been traveling for hours and are finally within spitting distance of Earth. In fact, the moon pulls larger and larger into view by the moment.

And we're about to slingshot around it.

This is the only way that we could build up enough speed to knock us into orbit and match with the ISS 2. By doing this one last—admittedly, risky—stunt, we'll have an actual chance of saving the ISS astronauts with the limited power we have left in reserve.

"Let's *do* this," Tomoki says once we're in range. He tilts the controls, and we go into our dive toward Earth's giant, rocky, natural satellite.

It's exhilarating. We're so close to the moon's surface, I feel like I could reach out the window and touch it. Instead of faint splotches, like they appear through Earth-bound telescopes, the craters are fully realized. Valleys, mountains, crevasses . . . the moon is beautiful. If we can't get to Mars in the future, getting to the moon would definitely be a great second choice.

"Yeah!" Esteban high-fives everyone he can reach. "Look at us go! Take that, moon! We got this!"

"We're not back yet," Anna cautions. "Don't get too excited."

"Boy, are the people on the ISS 2 going to be surprised when they see us pulling up," Esteban says, ignoring Anna and continuing to jabber. "Maybe they'll even be able to pilot us back to Earth."

"Hey, no way, that's my job!" Tomoki protests. "I haven't gotten to do anything awesome yet on this trip, so you'd better at least let me land this thing."

I decide not to tell Tomoki about the nine parachutes I've printed.

It's been a relatively restful past forty hours, and this moon side-trip is peaceful in its own special way, too. The only disturbance has been my stomach nausea, likely from a continuing spell of nerves and hunger. I don't want to say anything out loud and jinx us, but so far our trip home has gone really *well*.

It actually worries me. Nothing has gone smoothly so far in any of this. Why should it start now?

But as we pass the far side of the moon and Earth pulls back into view, I can't help but cheer along with everyone else. Our rockets fire, shooting us at superspeeds toward home. *Maybe there really isn't anything left to worry about*, I think, as Esteban doles out another round of high fives. *Maybe we've finally got the advantage.*

It takes a few more hours, but eventually we get near enough to start easing into orbit around our planet. During our entire approach, my eyes have eagerly scanned Earth's surface, waiting to get a glimpse of the United States. I allow myself a small smile when it finally comes into view. It's dawn there. As Earth turns, daylight begins spreading over the Midwest. It's cloudy, but I can make out the Great Lakes and know that just south of those is my home.

"Moving into orbital position," Rahim announces from my side.

I can actually hear each of us suck in air and hold our breath as we finally drop into orbit around planet Earth.

"Hah!" Esteban shouts. "Yeah! Here we come, International Space Station!"

"Thrusters at forty percent power," I say. "Main engines coasting."

"Orbiting Earth at nine thousand two hundred and four meters per second," Anna reports. "Crossing paths with the ISS 2 in twenty-one minutes. Three more orbits until we're aligned."

I watch outside our windshield. *This is for you, Lizzie. And for you, too, Kreshkov.*

The minutes tick by as we loop around planet Earth several times, and those minutes soon turn into hours. None of us say much during that time. It's like we're all just drinking in the view below. Earth. *Home.* We're here. We've made it back.

Once we're on our final orbit, Tomoki slows our spaceplane to a crawl in preparation for what we need to do next. The quick turnovers from the dark side to the sunlit side of Earth slow down, keeping us in the light for this final task.

"There it is!" Najma gasps.

I tear my eyes away from the greens and blues below. The space station is in view. Its elaborate, multisectional body is something I've seen countless times in broadcasts, online videos, and toy models. But in person—even after everything we've been through—it doesn't seem real.

I shake off that feeling quickly, knowing that there's still a *very* good chance that we won't dock with it properly. "Okay, Tomoki, this is all you," I say.

"Don't miss," Anna adds.

I smile in spite of myself. Maybe it's some sort of Space Madness talking, but Anna definitely seems way more hilarious lately.

"Will you all relax? I got this," Tomoki reassures us.

Relax. Right. I fold my hands together and squeeze them tight.

"Easy . . . easy . . ." Rahim mutters under his breath as we draw closer to the space station.

Tomoki jerks us downward.

"What are you doing?" Najma hisses.

"Trust me," Tomoki says. A moment later, we're moving back up. "And don't talk anymore. I need to concentrate."

We jostle up, then down, then to the side, and back up. I feel like Tomoki's taking us in every direction except toward the ISS 2, but nevertheless we continue to be on course with it.

"He's like a twenty-first century Buzz Aldrin!" Esteban says. "We should call him Dr. Rendezvous!"

"What did I say about talking?" Tomoki growls.

"Right, sorry," Esteban says. But I smile. It's true. Docking manually with an object in orbit is one of the trickiest things an astronaut ever needs to do. From what Lizzie had explained, it's entirely counterintuitive. You have to move down before up, move far to one side to swoop back on path, and essentially spirograph yourself toward your target. I'm really glad I'm not in the pilot's seat.

"Call coming in," Esteban says. "I think it's the ISS 2 crew."

"NO TALKING, Esteban!" Tomoki barks.

"Don't answer," Anna warns. "Remember what Mr. Burnett said."

"Right, I know," Esteban says.

"Is no one listening to me? Can't you all just shut up?" Tomoki tilts us down once again.

I watch the incoming call light turn on and off by Esteban's console. *I bet the ISS crew is beyond surprised right now!* I grin a little, helping to relax some of my nerves as Tomoki continues to bounce us around.

"Got it, got it, just a little more . . ." Tomoki mutters, slipping into Japanese for a moment. "Okay, Flight Engineer," he goes back to English, "Get that hatch ready!"

We must be close. I hop up, floating back through the main cabin to the port door to ready the airlock seal. Anna's plan was much simpler than mine would have been. Instead of building a complex connecting pod, we'll lock on to the ISS 2 mirror door and cut into their outer plating, pinning us to them. Then we'll plaster it with suction material to block any cracks, and open it to bring the astronauts inside.

"Esteban, come on!" I call. "You're going to need to get into the ISS, remember?"

"Right!" he calls back. "Sorry. Just distracted up here. This caller keeps calling."

"Headsets on, you two," Anna orders. Esteban and I both do as she says.

Our ship shudders to a halt, and I pull open the control box, getting to work on hotwiring the door. It's not meant for this exact purpose, but if I can just get the outer latches to move in, then the ISS 2 should be able to grip on, just like it would to a resupply spacecraft.

"Got it!" I shout, as it clicks into place with a solid *thunk*. "We're connected."

"Whooo!" Esteban cheers, floating into the cabin behind me and wrapping me in a giant hug. "We are so *awesome*!"

Tomoki exhales loudly. "Yeah. Super easy. No problem. Go team." I can see him collapse in his chair from through the cabin door. Next to him, Najma sends signals to the ISS 2 to unlock their hatch. Anna sets the cutters to dig in for a full grip, while Rahim finishes printing out a tubular version of flex-cast material to stick to the inside of the tunnel.

I pull myself out of Esteban's grip. "Yeah, now we just need to open up the hatch and—"

All the vidscreens through the entire spaceplane flash on at once, drawing our attention upward. When I see who's on the screens, my blood freezes straight through me.

Mr. Burnett.

"You!" Najma gasps.

"What do you want?" Tomoki demands.

My own mind topples over itself, running through all the possible reasons he might be contacting us, but then he starts talking, and my multiple trains of thought come crashing to a halt.

"What do you think you're *doing?*" Mr. Burnett glares at us through the vidscreen.

"What are you talking about—?" Anna starts to ask.

"You know, for the smartest kids in the world, you're all being pretty stupid right about now," Mr. Burnett says. "The ISS crew just called Earth to report that they've spotted your ship heading toward them. Did none of you think of what Valorheart would do once they heard that news?"

No one answers him. Some new *kathunking* on the other side of the port door tells me that the ISS 2 crew is working on getting into our spaceplane. I edge my way toward the control panel. If I can just get the door open . . .

"If you hadn't stopped to pick up the ISS astronauts, you actually might have made it back without anyone noticing," Mr. Burnett continues. His hair is plastered against his forehead with sweat. "But you had to be all noble. Why couldn't you just be happy with going to Mars? Don't you think Valorheart has a plan for if you try to return home? They're going to kill you!"

"Their stupid rigged spaceplane couldn't kill us," Tomoki says. "What makes you think anything they're going to do now will?"

Mr. Burnett's eyes turn, presumably to glare at Tomoki on his own vidscreen. It's just a moment, but it's enough.

I slam my hand into the control panel, opening the door to the ISS 2. Esteban releases the tunnel of suction material, which gets sucked to the sides immediately. Three astronauts pull their way in, a flurry of limbs that grab at anything and everything to yank themselves through the tunnel into our spaceplane.

"Oh my gosh, kids! You aren't dead!" Ming Chen gasps.

"Esteban, go!" I hiss, shoving him through the door under the cover of the other astronauts.

"You're okay!" Patricia Glower says, fawning over me. "You're all okay!"

"Hey, where's—?" Jean Pilotte begins to ask, motioning to point at Esteban, who's flying through the tunnel to the ISS.

I elbow him sharply and give him a warning look to say nothing. He seems to understand and shuts up immediately.

"This is pointless. Those astronauts are just going to die anyway!" Mr. Burnett says. The edges of his eyes crinkle in distress, reading something from his droidlet, which just beeped at him a moment earlier. "Valorheart is messaging me. They know where you are. They're blaming me. Oh god."

My hand flinches. Now I'm *really* thankful I've been keeping Esteban's mission secret. Luckily, Mr. Burnett hasn't seemed to notice Esteban slipping off, and I purposefully avoid looking through the tunnel into the ISS 2 so as to not raise his suspicions.

"None of you get how serious this is! Do you have any idea what Valorheart is aiming at you as we speak?" Mr. Burnett asks.

"No," Anna says. "And we don't particularly care."

"Well, you should!" he responds.

I bring the three astronauts up into the cockpit to keep Mr. Burnett's eyes away from any video feeds near the port door. The astronauts position themselves around my fellow crewmates, staring up at the large vidscreen.

"What's going on here?" asks Ming Chen.

"Valorheart just aimed four missile-launching satellites at your space station," Mr. Burnett says, reading from his droidlet. "And they want me to . . ." He pales on-screen. "They want me to fire the missiles if you make any move to come home. If I don't do as they say, they'll blow up the island. As punishment."

Missiles. That's a new development. I edge backward, heading back to the port door, just to check to see if Esteban needs any help. It sounds like this is probably it. Our end. But the only thing my brain can focus on right now is the worry that we won't get the message through in time.

"Tomoki, get us moving," Rahim says softly. "Get us moving, and they won't hit us."

The ISS astronauts start scrambling, getting systems ready for departure.

"You'd like to think that, wouldn't you?" Mr. Burnett says, the sweat glistening on his face now. "Miranda—I see you back there. Where do you think you're going?"

I freeze.

"Guys, please." He's *begging*. "If you stop what you're doing, and just stay up in space where you're supposed to be, I'll tell you everything! Miranda, I'll tell you what happened to your friend Sasha. Don't you want to know if he's safe?"

Sasha. I look up at Mr. Burnett, anger bubbling through me like boiling water. "What did they do to him?" I growl.

"Don't rise to his bait, Miranda," Rahim says. "It's what he wants."

I take a shaky breath. "No. Never mind."

"No? Well, then why don't I tell you about how you ended up as a Mars cadet?" Mr. Burnett changes tacks, desperation coloring his voice. "I know the truth. I can tell you, once and for all, if you were meant for this program."

I grip the side of the cabin door. I want to ignore him. I want to block out his words.

"You *do* want to know whether you were just chosen as a pawn or if you got in for real, don't you? That's important to you, right?"

I'm about to finally snap, when instead, Anna slams her good hand down on the dashboard.

"That's it!" she yells. "You listen here, you *worthless* human being! Do you know what Miranda has been through? What she's done for us? For this mission? For our lives? *Do you?* I don't know if she was picked for your greedy game or not, but I do know that it doesn't matter. She's a part of our team! So you can just shut your face, you horrible, horrible, *coward!*"

I gape through the doorway at the back of Anna's head in her copilot chair.

Anna continues to shout, brushing away Patricia Glower as she tries to calm her down. "We're coming back to Earth, and you can't stop us!"

"They. Will. *Blow. This. Island!*" Mr. Burnett shouts in return. "They're going to—! Oh, wait." He stares at his droidlet. "Oh god. Oh no. Oh god no."

"What?" Rahim asks.

"What is it?" Ming asks.

"It's too late," Mr. Burnett whispers. His voice is hoarse, and I can barely hear him. "They've signaled the rigged heli-jet. They're giving me one final chance to redeem myself. If I fire the missiles at you, I get the Valorheart heli-jet override code to unlock one for my escape." He looks up. "If I don't fire . . . I die with everyone else. Five minutes until detonation."

No. My heart clenches. *Mom . . . Dad . . . Emmaline!*

"NO!" Tomoki screams. Behind him, Anna looks like she's been shot in the stomach, and Rahim's eyes are instantly filled with tears.

"Mr. Burnett," Najma says, tears pinching in her eyes as well. "Please."

I clutch at my suit, as if I can shield my heart from the terror of knowing my family has five minutes to live.

"I'm sorry," he says. "Anna's right. I am a coward. I've been one all along."

"Mr. Burnett . . ." I say, reaching desperately. "Remember what you told me? How circumstances can make you feel like a failure, but it's not always that simple? I don't think it's that simple with you!"

"That's right!" Najma exclaims. "You're an amazing programmer! You can stop the detonation sequence, I know you can!"

Mr. Burnett lets out a humorless laugh. "I'm not an amazing anything. I only got where I am because of Valorheart, and now I've failed even them."

"All you failed at doing for them was murdering us!" I exclaim. "And I, for one, think that's a perfectly acceptable thing to fail at."

He hangs his head in response.

"Mr. Burnett, please trust me," I beg. "I get it! Sometimes you can feel like the worst, like your success is all a big lie, but that's only true if you let it be! Look at all you've done. Your programming fooled everyone! All you need to do is do it one more time. *Please*."

Something in Mr. Burnett's face changes. A small twitch. A widening around his eyes. Our entire cabin is silent, waiting for his response.

"You know what?" he asks. "Maybe you're right. There is always the chance I could reprogram the heli-jet's detonator. I . . . I could still save people." He reads his droidlet once again, and his shoulders shrink. "But I'd need all the time I could get. I can't waste minutes hacking past the jet's security system. Not when Valorheart could just hand me the access code."

Mr. Burnett shuts his eyes, grimacing. Then he presses a button and lets out a shaky breath. Too late, I realize what he means.

"I'm so, so sorry. The missiles are launched. You've made it this far. Whatever miracles you've been pulling off, please pull off one more for me."

Oh god. I tear myself away from watching the now darkened

291

vidscreen and push off with my legs toward the port door. "Esteban!" I shout. "Get back in here! Now!"

"What's that boy doing in there?!" Jean Pilotte demands.

"Tomoki, move this thing!" Rahim says.

Tomoki lets out a scream that says everything my heart is feeling.

"We can't leave him!" I hear Najma cry out.

"I'll get Esteban, you get us going!" I shout back, pulling myself through the hatch into the ISS 2. Time moves in flashes and bursts. I have to go through several doors in the space station before I find him.

Esteban is talking into their communicator, "That's right, none of it's real! It's all just a plot by Valorheart Industries. They've been behind every attack, framing countries and trying to get the world to fight again!"

I kick off a metallic wall, sailing toward Esteban and reaching out to him. I can't even take a moment to glance around the ISS 2 and appreciate the brilliance of this international collaboration, seven years in the building.

"Esteban!" I yank at him. "Come on!"

"What? What's going on?" Esteban asks, still holding the communicator.

"This thing's about to blow!"

"What?!" Esteban exclaims.

"They're still in there, we can't leave!" Najma is crying over the headset.

"Listen, the missiles are incoming, we have to pull away

now!" Tomoki says, his voice strained. "Miranda, Esteban, hurry up, will you?!"

"*Come on!*" I tug on Esteban even harder. We move back toward the door, and he finally drops the communicator. We start our weightless race back to the spaceplane, past chambers and corridors I'll never get the chance to explore.

A tearing sound begins, metal shredding against metal, and I realize that it's happening. They're physically ripping our spaceplane away from the ISS.

But we're not back inside yet.

"Come on!" We pull ourselves along the piping. One arm over the other. One arm over the other.

"Go!" Esteban shouts. "Faster!"

The metal screeches even louder as we reach the door. I dive through, Esteban right behind me, pushing me into the spaceplane.

And then it tears.

"ESTEBAN!" I scream, spinning.

The small crack in the tunnel pulls our air out immediately and yanks Esteban back. Space sucks at my skin, and I can feel blood vessels bursting on my forehead.

"No!" I yell, though the word falls silent as our air scatters into the darkness of space.

CHAPTER 21

Esteban crunches against the slim crack in the tunnel, and it starts to widen. Using my last bit of adrenaline, I grab Esteban from the abyss, and then I'm tugged backward into our spaceplane.

The airlock closes. My arms are wrapped around Esteban, and Jean Pilotte's arms are wrapped around me.

"Are you *trying* to kill them?!" Anna shouts at Tomoki over our headsets.

"I thought they'd make it back faster!" Tomoki replies. I can hear the distress in his voice just as clearly as I can hear Esteban's labored breathing next to my ear.

"They're back now!" Jean calls. "They're in. Go, go, go!"

"Esteban!" I hold him tight. "Esteban, say something!"

He lets out a slow, raspy moan.

"His lungs!" Jean says. "Get him oxygen!"

"Rahim!" I scream, pulling Esteban with me into the main cabin. Esteban floats like a discarded plastic bag in the ocean, and his eyes roll back in his head.

"Got it!" Rahim unbuckles and flings himself toward the medical storage wall, clicking a switch and yanking out a yellow mask. He shoves the mask over Esteban's face as our spaceplane twists around.

"We're going in too shallow!" Tomoki shouts. "We're going to have to do a skip entry. Hold on!" He yanks at the controls, and we fling upward from the atmosphere, like a rock skidding over water.

BOOM!

A silent explosion ripples through each of us—and through our entire spaceplane. Esteban's eyes bug out and he coughs. Rahim pushes the mask tighter onto Esteban's face, and Jean Pilotte grabs hold of them both, steadying them. Behind us, fiery debris sails by.

The space station is no more.

BANG!

"We're hit!" Tomoki yells.

BANG! BANG! BANG! BANG!

"That's it!" Ming exclaims, as debris pounds against us in a shower of flames. "Take us in *now*!"

"No!" Tomoki shouts. "No, one more minute—we have to—"

Fire surrounds us, and it doesn't look like Tomoki's got a choice anymore.

"ARGH!" he screams, fighting with the controls. Patricia

Glower grabs onto the copilot controls, straining to keep things steady.

"Landing gear is shredded!" Najma reports.

"The pitch angle's too steep! We need more RCS fuel!" Patricia orders. "Then we drop."

"We're still hypersonic!" Tomoki yells. "No way!"

Everyone begins shouting at once. We spiral down toward Earth, our blue ocean flipping around the black sky as we punch through the atmosphere. The entire spaceplane rattles, and then orange flames cover the windows, blocking the view.

"We're passing into supersonic, it's got to hold for longer!"

"Keep this at trim until fifteen thousand feet! Then we're going to have to jump!"

"No!" Tomoki yells, slamming his fist. "I got this; I can get us home! I can land this!"

"Don't be an idiot!" Anna screams at him. "We don't even have usable landing gear. We're going to crash!"

My eyes fly open, and I jump toward the side cabinet, hitting my shoulder blade against the wall as the ship turns. Gravity is back, and the metallic sides of this spaceplane aren't forgiving. "Parachutes!" I yell. "I've got parachutes!"

I throw open the cabinet, gripping on to its handle as we spin violently. I pull out the nine parachutes and start thrusting them at anyone and everyone I can reach, covering my head every other moment as we crash around inside.

"So much for saving one working spaceplane," Najma says as I hand her a chute.

"Let's just concentrate on saving ourselves." I latch my own parachute on to my belt loops. *Now to find out if these will actually do what I designed them to do . . .*

"Everyone got theirs?" Ming yells, as Patricia wrestles Tomoki out of his chair and forces a parachute into his hands.

We all shout confirmations, except for Esteban, who is still in Jean Pilotte's arms wearing an oxygen mask. I wince, looking at him. "Esteban—"

"I'll hold him!" Jean says. "Don't worry!"

I nod, then punch in a code at the port door control panel, grasping the side to steady myself as we plummet. We're below 15,000 feet. Jumping range. It's now or never.

The hatch blasts open, and wind rips through the cabins. Rahim and Najma line up on either side of me. Tomoki grabs Anna by her good arm, linking his around hers. The ship is going to be torn apart; I can feel it. I put one last hand on her metal interior, thinking about all the hours I spent working on her . . .

Good-bye, Ambassador. *It's been quite the ride.*

We line up and jump from the crashing spaceplane, holding hands as best we can for most of the way down.

My parachute opens, jerking me upward moments before I splash into the ocean below.

I flail, the parachute material washing around me in the saltwater, temporarily trapping my arms before I can push through it and tear it off myself. Waves roll, and I tread water with more force than I've ever had to use at any beach or swimming pool in my entire life.

But I am alive.

I'm in the ocean, and I'm alive.

I blink the salt from my eyes and breathe deep breaths, keeping my head above water as I sob. I'm home. I'm back on Earth. But where is everyone else?

I begin to swim, shouting at the top of my lungs. "NAJMA! ANNA!" I bob up and down, pausing to look around again. "ESTEBAN! RAHIM! TOMOKI!"

"HEY!" a voice shouts. I turn. About fifty yards from me, several people are clustered in the water. "MIRANDA!" one of them shouts back at me. Rahim, I think.

My shoulder throbs, but I swim on, desperately trying to count heads as I come up for air after each stroke. *One. Two. Three.*

Breathe in. Breathe out.

Four. Five.

Breathe in. Breathe out.

Five. That's it. Only five. Who's missing?

I reach the others, scanning. Jean Pilotte, true to his word, holds Esteban in his arms, somehow still treading water with his legs. *Okay, that's six.* Esteban, I notice, is still breathing. Next to them, Najma and Rahim swim near Ming and Patricia.

But Tomoki and Anna are nowhere to be seen.

A horrible thought hits me: "Anna—her arm is in a sling. *She can't swim!*" I scream, flailing in the water. "ANNA! TOMOKI!"

I spin, surveying each section of the ocean, mapping it in my mind's eye and looking for any sign of my friends.

"ANNA! TOMOKI!"

Then—there. A splash. Not ten yards away, Tomoki surfaces, Anna clutched in his arms. I swim over to them as fast as I can, with whatever strength I have left. Tomoki wipes his hair back with his free hand, his communication cap long gone. Anna spits up water next to him, shaking her head and coughing.

"You okay?" Tomoki asks her.

She nods, and I fall backward, letting out a laugh of relief. Salt water splashes up around me, stinging cuts on my face.

Tomoki grins, then winks at Anna, who's still gasping for breath, her gray eyes widening with each exhale. "Hey, I wasn't going to let you drown," he says.

Anna coughs some more, and I just know she's trying to get her voice back so she can give a proper scathing reply. Before she can, Tomoki turns to me and toward all the others who have just reached us, swimming over. By their shouts, I can tell they're just as relieved as I am.

"Hey, did everyone see that amazing rescue job?" Tomoki's grin turns sly. "I finally got to do something awesome!"

The three astronauts had emergency lights and GPS signals on their flight suits, and not long after activating those, we were airlifted by helicopters out of the ocean.

Now I'm in a hospital bed, wearing one of those ridiculously revealing hospital gowns and clutching my mom, my dad, and my sister. They're all alive. Mr. Burnett did it. He got the bomb deactivated in time.

And his reward was getting arrested.

"You're safe!" my mom repeats over and over, her curly hair tickling my nose.

My dad says nothing, holding us all together. They've just arrived in Florida, at the hospital near Cape Canaveral where we're all being treated. Somehow after everything, we managed to crash just a few miles north of the Caribbean. Not a bad place to recover.

And we are recovering. From what I've heard, Anna's shoulder surgery went well, and Esteban is due to be off his breathing tube later today. As for me, they just removed my IV drip this morning. I only have one more night for observation to make sure nothing else other than bumps, bruises, and dehydration is seriously wrong with me. My face and hands are still all splotchy from when I was exposed to space, but the doctors said that should heal in time.

"They said you were dead!" Emmaline grips me tighter. "The people on the news said you were dead!"

I look up at my mom, who grimaces. I doubt Emmaline watching the news was intentional on my parents' part.

"Well, I'm not dead," I say, pulling back to smile at my sister.

"I know!" Emmaline sits upright on the bed next to me and bounces. "I *told* them you weren't! I told *everyone*. I knew you'd come back. You're a genius and an astronaut, and I knew you'd come back, no matter what they said!"

I laugh a little, trying to shake away the memory of each moment we very nearly *didn't* return. "Thanks for the confidence. I promised you I'd come home, didn't I?"

My dad ruffles my hair on top of my head. "That you did." His eyes are still damp, and the corners of them crinkle as he smiles down at me. I lean over and put my arms around him.

My door opens and then shuts nearly immediately. "Not now, Mary, they're having family time!" I hear a familiar voice say. I look up to see my PR team outside my hospital room window. Michael looks to have his hand firmly on the doorknob, while Mary actually jumps trying to peek through the glass.

Thanks, Michael, I think to myself, smiling as Emmaline crawls into my lap.

After failing in an attempt to locate Najma's room, I wander through the hospital halls, holding on to the latest bouquet of flowers that's been delivered to me. I accidentally stumbled upon Anna's room earlier, but didn't enter. She was with her dad, and they were both crying and holding each other. I guess she was wrong about him after all.

News channels are on nearly every vidscreen I pass, and I learn that around the world, countries are backing down from what was almost full-scale world war. Instead, Valorheart Industries is being torn to pieces. Various employees of the company, from engineering assistants up to the CEO have been implicated, arrested, and interrogated. Mr. Burnett has become the face of controversy. His picture comes up frequently on the vidscreens, with a lot of talking heads trying to decide whether or not he is a hero or a villain.

He's both and neither all at the same time to me. The

reporters on-screen speculate about his eventual trial, and to my shock and disgust, what role us Mars cadets will play in it. I can't even begin to think how that's going to go.

In fact, I can't think about most of what's being broadcast at the moment. It's too painful. But as I pass one screen, I do pause to watch, because it's a press conference with Dr. Schuber.

"I can't help but feel personally responsible for not discovering the truth about my graduate student," Dr. Schuber says. "I hope to travel soon to meet with our Mars cadets and make sure they each understand how sorry and how grateful I am. They're the true heroes in this. It's because of them that the space program isn't dead. We will heal, and we will find a way to get back out there."

After that, the few people standing in the halls of the hospital start clapping their hands and patting me on the back. I quickly move on.

The news broadcast I'm most interested in seeing is—of course—the one story they put the least focus on: the story of our replacements. Apparently with the international threats that piled up in the last few weeks, the ISECG moved each of our replacements to a safe house, cut off from all communication. I finally have an explanation for Sasha's disappearance, and it has nothing to do with him being dead or evil.

I can't begin to describe how relieved I am.

According to the news, all of our replacements are being allowed out today. I'm hoping that means I'll finally get to talk to

Sasha again. I have so much to tell him.

My thoughts trail off as I round a bend, and find myself face-to-face with a memorial in one of the hospital's side alcoves. I stop walking when I realize what it's for.

The memorial is a large, bronzed cube, with a different space exploration disaster cast on each side. It's clearly been around for a long while, as the edges of the marble platform look worn down, likely from being sat upon.

I'm standing near the Space Shuttle *Columbia* side of the memorial. Seven astronaut faces look back at me through the bronze. I shut my eyes, trying to stop my brain from doing the math as to how many more memorial cubes we'll need to account for the 114 deaths that have just taken place.

Instead, I take my bouquet and begin pulling it apart. I set one flower down by each side of the cube, stopping to pay my respects each time. Then I set one down for the memorials not yet made. Then, I pull out three more.

One for Kreshkov, with his dark eyes and constant determination to help us be the best we could be.

One for Lizzie, who did everything in her power to get me to believe in myself.

And one for Ruby.

Back in my hospital room, my bed's been made. I'm guessing a nurse must've come through to do it, because I know my parents never would've.

My family's all sitting around waiting for me. Mom and Emmaline are playing checkers, and when I walk in, my dad hands me a package.

"Just arrived," he says. He looks amused, and I notice he's ripped the return address completely off.

I raise an eyebrow, taking the box and sinking onto my bed.

"Open it!" Emmaline insists, abandoning her game to jump up on the bed with me.

"And who exactly is this mysterious gift from?" I ask, carefully undoing the brown tape. No one answers, so I'm left to my own deductions.

The package is bigger than a shoebox and covered in "FRAGILE; THIS SIDE UP" stickers. But before I even finish getting the tape off, the box goes ahead and opens *itself*.

"Hey, Regent," a familiar voice says from its depths. Dexterous claws hack the box lid off in front of our eyes.

"Oh, no *way*." I set down the box. A black robot scuttles out of it, bowing flamboyantly on the bed. "Comet!" I gasp.

"This is a prerecorded message, so don't bother trying to talk to me," Sasha's voice says through his robot's speakers. Comet settles down, flashing one optical unit on and off in a wink. "I heard about Ruby and figured you could use a friend while you recover."

My parents are laughing, and Emmaline's hysterical giggles can probably be heard from down the hall.

"No way," I repeat. "No way!"

"Hopefully, we can catch up soon," Sasha's voice continues. Comet locks his front legs together and waves at me. "I want to hear all about your little field trip. And don't think that just because you've sent a robot to Mars means that you've beaten me at astrorobotics. Once I have Comet back, I'll be outfitting him with thrusters of his own."

I laugh, shaking my head at the robot. "Of course you will."

"But feel free to keep him around as long as you'd like. Just know that I expect him back in the *exact same condition* that I sent him to you in. No modifications, Regent!"

With that, the voice message ends and I'm left with the biggest grin I've had on my face since the day I was picked as a cadet.

Three days after our hospitalization, the six of us finally have a moment to ourselves. No adults, no nurses. Just us.

We're on a beach outside our hospital. The waves wash up against the shore, and I close my eyes, listening to them. It's hard to imagine that just days ago we were stranded out in those same waves, waiting to be rescued. That just days ago, we were crashing back to Earth. That just days ago, we were thousands of miles away, heading to a planet where water in these quantities has long ceased to exist.

"You know," Esteban interrupts our reverie. "We landed on the moon back when computers were the size of entire buildings."

I open my eyes, glancing his way. Esteban's voice still sounds rough, but his color has returned. It's just good to see him without any breathing apparatuses.

"We did? Really? Tell us more things we didn't already know about the history of space travel," Anna says. Tomoki smirks at her.

"Yeah, what was that astronaut's name? Neil Buzzstrong?" Tomoki teases, tossing a seashell toward Esteban.

Esteban doesn't miss a beat and catches the shell. "No, come on, guys. I'm just saying. We survived, and we could still go to Mars. I'd say it's our duty, actually. And really, I know a lot of stuff is gone, but it's not the equipment that matters."

Najma lies back in the sand, exhaling. Her fingers are wrapped around Esteban's. "I get it," she says.

"I don't," I say, honestly still baffled.

Esteban sighs. "We're so fixated on the blown-up technology and how our space programs are doomed because of that. But I don't think it's the technology that really gets us to the moon or to Mars."

I blink in the Florida sunshine.

"So, what is it, then?" Anna asks, leaning back.

"Isn't it obvious?" Esteban picks up a fistful of sand with his free hand and lets it trickle through his fingers. Then he looks up into the sky. "It's us."

I look up toward the clouds in the same direction as Esteban. "I suppose you're right," I say. We all sit in silence for another moment.

"Actually," Rahim says, "I'm pretty sure the technology helps, too."

Everyone laughs, and I reach for Comet, who's sitting on a towel next to me. *Technology?* I rest my hand on the robot and look back up at the sky above.

I can build that.

EPILOGUE

Nine months, four days, and fourteen minutes later, my droidlet pings. I set down my soldering iron and remove my goggles. Carefully moving the nanowires to one side of my workbench, I turn my wrist to check my message.

Once upon a time, I would've just assumed the text was from Sasha now there are a few more options. But this message isn't from any of my fellow cadets.

:TASK COMPLETE. WAITING FOR INSTRUCTION:

AUTHOR'S NOTE

"TOUCHDOWN CONFIRMED. WE'RE SAFE ON MARS."

—JET PROPULSION LABORATORY, 1:31AM EDT, AUGUST 6TH, 2012

It had been my birthday for all of an hour and a half. I sat on my couch, anxiously watching a livestream of NASA's Jet Propulsion Laboratory as they waited to hear from Curiosity—a rover the size of a car that they were attempting to land on Mars. It was incredibly nerve-racking. NASA called the moments up to its landing the "Seven Minutes of Terror" because of all of the different things that could go wrong. When the news came in that the landing was a success and the first fuzzy picture of one of Curiosity's wheels on Martian ground appeared, the cheers from JPL were ear-shattering. I admit it, I cried.

The generation before mine had the Apollo moon landings. To me, this was as close as I had ever come to witnessing someone reach another world.

I can't wait until I get to see an actual person land on Mars.

311

Despite this book ending with space programs in shambles, I have no doubt that Miranda, Esteban, Najma, Rahim, Anna, and Tomoki will get to Mars eventually. They have the determination and ingenuity to make it happen.

In real life, space programs are far from in ruins, but there are still many, many obstacles between humans and Mars. Just as with Miranda and her crewmates, however, I'm positive we will overcome these challenges and that someday, we will make Mars happen. We're completely capable of it. After all, as I write this, a team of six people are orbiting our planet, living on the International Space Station. Space travel isn't science fiction—it's reality. As such, it was super important to me that the events in my book be as scientifically accurate as possible.

There was just one small problem: I've never been to space myself.

If you've read this book, then you know that a pretty major part of it takes place in space. Another huge chunk takes place in Antarctica. I haven't been there, either, for the record. I've also never built a robot. I've never docked with the International Space Station. I've never experienced zero gravity. In fact, I only had a couple real-life things going for me when I set out to write this space adventure—one, I run planetarium shows at my day job, where I get to simulate flying through space on a weekly basis. And two, I really love learning new things. It's that second point that made this book possible.

NASA's online resources proved invaluable in my quest for accuracy. Seriously, they put so much of their knowledge online that if you actually tried to read it all, it would take a lifetime. I know, because I've pored through huge amounts of it since 2012 and have barely made a dent in what is actually there. My favorite resource of theirs is NASA TV, which I highly recommend checking out. NASA TV livestreams spacewalks, mission announcements, rocket launches, and many other events, in addition to airing what is essentially nonstop documentary-style programming about what they're up to at the moment.

One thing NASA's online archives couldn't teach me, though, was how to turn a spacecraft around as it barrels through space away from Earth. For that, I knew I'd need to talk to someone with an astrophysics background.

Thankfully, I had a chance to speak with Russell Sargent, who is a legitimate rocket scientist with the Charles Stark Draper Laboratory. Through him, I learned instrumental facts about the challenges of space travel, and most importantly, how one might actually go about turning a ship around in a vacuum. I took those insights, retaught myself some calculus, and came up with the ultimate solution for how Miranda and her crew were going to get home.

That aspect of the novel taken care of, my next challenge was in making sure I could properly describe the sensation of being in space. As luck would have it, in 2013 I got to meet Stephen Bowen—an actual NASA astronaut! I was his "pilot" as he gave a presentation in the Museum of Science Charles Hayden Planetarium (meaning I operated the controls to zoom us around in simulated space). I learned from him how one goes about their day while in space, and what exactly happens to a person's body up there.

I wasn't done learning yet. In 2014, I went to the Kennedy Space Center, where I got to see NASA equipment in person, including the Space Shuttle *Atlantis*. While there, I went on an up-close tour of the launchpads, and also participated in the "Shuttle Launch Experience", which mimics what it feels like to blast off. Armed with these experiences, I returned home and infused my manuscript with them.

The Countdown Conspiracy is a work of fiction, but it's my hope the science behind the events is at least in the ballpark of believability. It's based on a reality where actual adventures take place. If you enjoyed this book, the space programs of our world are a never-ending source of excitement. Follow them online! You won't regret it.

Before I wrap this note up, there is something important that I need to stress: while it's true that Miranda loves science, what she's primarily doing in the book is *engineering*. An engineer is someone who comes up with ideas to solve a problem, tests and models those solutions, makes improvements, builds them for real, makes repairs, and repeats any and all of this until they get it just right. The world needs more engineers. To be one, you just need to be willing to try, fail, and try again.

It took hundreds of hard-working scientists and engineers to get Curiosity to Mars. It will take many more than that to get astronauts there. Maybe someday, you'll be one of those scientists or engineers. Maybe you'll be one of the astronauts.

It is entirely possible that you—yes, *you*—will be the first person to walk on Mars.

Sincerely,

Katie Slivensky

PS: If you do end up on Mars, would you say hello to any robots you find for me?

GLOSSARY

Antares: A red supergiant star in the constellation Scorpius.

Apollo 11: A mission launched by NASA in 1969. This is the mission that first landed humans on the moon.

Apollo 13: A mission launched by NASA in 1970. This was meant to be the third mission to land humans on the moon, but the explosion of an oxygen tank forced the crew to return home before they could complete their mission. Luckily, all crew members survived the journey.

Asteroid: A primarily rocky object in our solar system that is too small to be considered a planet.

Astronaut: A person trained for space travel.

Astrophysics: The study of how the universe works.

Calculus: A field of mathematics focused on change.

CCA: A Communications Carrier Assembly is a fabric cap worn under the helmet of a spacesuit, and contains a microphone and earphones.

Comet: A primarily icy object in our solar system. It can display a fuzzy tail when its temperature rises as it nears the Sun in its orbit.

Communications Officer: A member of the crew who monitors in-flight communications and the instruments related to them.

Copilot: A member of the crew who assists the pilot in navigation and flight.

Cosmonaut: The Russian term for a person trained for space travel.

Cryogenic: At an extremely low temperature.

Dream Chaser: A style of reusable spaceplane being developed by Sierra Nevada Corporation Space Systems.

Electromagnet: A type of magnet in which the magnetic field is produced by moving electric charges.

EMU: The Extravehicular Mobility Unit is NASA's technical name for a spacesuit.

ESA: The European Space Agency.

EVA: Extravehicular Activity is any activity outside of the protection of the spacecraft. Also known as a spacewalk.

Flight Engineer: A member of the crew responsible for all systems during flight, who assists the pilot and manages repairs.

Hypersonic: Traveling at a speed faster than Mach 5—which means at least five times faster than the speed of sound.

ISECG: The International Space Exploration Coordination Group is the global group of over a dozen major space agencies who work together to advance human space exploration.

ISS: The International Space Station is a large satellite that can safely house people, has room to do experiments inside, and is built and staffed by a collaboration of nations. The current ISS is the size of a football field and is home to anywhere from 3–6 astronauts at any given moment, orbiting around Earth 250 miles above the planet's surface. In this novel, the fictional "ISS 2" is meant to be a second version of the ISS, after the original gets retired.

JPL: The Jet Propulsion Laboratory is NASA's center for non-human-powered space exploration. JPL builds spacecraft to fly by or orbit objects in our solar system, and robots to land on objects in our solar system.

Launchpad: The place where a rocket stands to be launched into space. This place usually has a supporting structure to hold up the rocket, and must be in a location where it is easy to keep people away during launch, for safety reasons.

Liquid Hydrogen: The liquid state of the element Hydrogen. Abbreviated as LH2, it can only exist at cryogenic temperatures. It is typically stored at -423 degrees Fahrenheit (-253 degrees Celsius). It is a key component of rocket fuel.

Liquid Oxygen: The liquid state of the element Oxygen. Abbreviated as LOX, it can only exist at cryogenic temperatures. Oxygen condenses from gas into liquid at -297 degrees Fahrenheit (-183 degrees Celsius). It is a key component of rocket fuel.

Mass: A measure of how much matter is in something.

high school English classes. When I first began pursuing publication in the children's book world, I reached out to her for advice. She pointed me in the direction of SCBWI, and told me to find a critique group.

Best. Advice. Ever. Tara Sullivan, Lauren Barrett, Lisa Palin, Julia Maranan, Annie Cardi, and Annie Gaughen—thank you all. You're more than a critique group. You're my writing family.

Thank you a thousand times over to my HarperCollins Children's crew, and especially to my amazing editor, Erica Sussman. Erica, your dedication to this novel took it to a level I never dreamed it could go. To say that it's an honor to work with you would be a dramatic understatement. Thank you for giving Miranda an opportunity to fly.

Boundless thanks also go to my wonderful agent, Ammi-Joan Paquette. You took a chance on a girl and her robot, and helped bring them both to life. I am eternally grateful for your insight, encouragement, and enthusiasm.

To Russell Sargent, thank you for taking the time to walk me through the logistics of space travel. To the outreach teams at NASA—thank you for sharing your knowledge. Every event I've attended where your staff have been present, I've learned so much. To the Museum of Science, Boston—thank you for opening my eyes to the wonders of space, and for trusting me with your telescopes!

Thank you to my friends, old and new. Many of you have been reading my stories since they were chicken scratch on school notebook paper, and others have taken up the mantle of "first readers" with gusto in recent years. Oodles of thanks go to my loudest cheering section: Carolyn Nishon, Kara Dowley, Breanne Cremean, Emily Lockwood, Marie van Staveren, and Karen Powers. You have no idea how much your support has meant.

Mom, Dad, Jeannie—I barely know where to start. Thank you for always being there. I know I wasn't always the easiest daughter or sister to understand, but you put up with my eccentricities like champs and have rooted for me my entire life. Look where we are now!

Finally, thank you to everyone who has dedicated their lives to the pursuit of space travel. From the engineers to the astronauts, you have changed our world for the better in your quest to learn about what lies beyond. You are, in the truest sense of the word, an inspiration.